Japanese Religion:
Unity and Diversity

Third Edition

H. Byron Earhart
Western Michigan University

WADSWORTH PUBLISHING COMPANY
Belmont, California
A Division of Wadsworth, Inc.

Religion Editor: Sheryl Fullerton
Production Editor: Judith McKibben
Managing Designer: Lois Stanfield
Copy Editor: Pat Herbst

BOOKS BY THE SAME AUTHOR

Religion in the Japanese Experience: Sources and Interpretations
(Wadsworth)
The New Religions of Japan: A Bibliography of Western-Language Materials, 2d ed.
(Michigan Papers in Japanese Studies)
A Religious Study of the Mount Haguro Sect of Shugendo
(Sophia University)
Translation from the Japanese: *Japanese Religion in the Modern Century*, Shigeyoshi Murakami
(University of Tokyo Press)

The author is indebted to the following for permission to reprint copyrighted material: Sir George B. Sansom and Stanford University Press, for use of material from *A History of Japan*; Masaharu Anesaki and Charles E. Tuttle Company, for use of material from *History of Japanese Religion*.

Library of Congress Cataloging in Publication Data

Earhart, H. Byron.
    Japanese religion, unity and diversity.
    (Religious life of man)
    Bibliography: p.
    Includes index.
    1. Japan—Religion.   I. Title.   II. Series: Religious life of man (Belmont, Calif.)
BL2202.E17   1982   291'.0952   81-12963
ISBN 0-534-01028-8   AACR2

ISBN 0-534-01028-8

13 14 15 16 17- 01 00 99 98

Contents

Foreword

THE RELIGIOUS LIFE OF MAN series is intended as an introduction to a large, complex field of inquiry—religious experience. It seeks to present the depth and richness of religious concepts, forms of worship, spiritual practices, and social institutions found in the major religious traditions throughout the world.

As a specialist in the languages and cultures in which a religion is found, each author is able to illuminate the meanings of a religious perspective and practice as other human beings have experienced it. To communicate this meaning to readers who have had no special training in these cultures and religions, the authors have attempted to provide clear, nontechnical descriptions and interpretations of religious life.

Different approaches have been used, depending upon the nature of the religious data; some religious expressions, for instance, lend themselves to developmental, others to topical studies. The lack of a single interpretation may itself be instructive, for the experiences and practices regarded as religious in one culture may not be particularly important in another.

THE RELIGIOUS LIFE OF MAN is concerned with, on the one hand, the variety of religious expressions found in different traditions and, on the other, similarities in the structures of religious life. The various forms are interpreted in terms of their cultural context and historical continuity, demonstrating both the diverse expressions and commonalities of religious traditions. Besides individual volumes on different religions, the series offers a core book on the study of religious meaning, which describes different study approaches and examines several modes and structures of religious awareness. In addition, each book presents a list of materials for further reading, including translations of religious texts and detailed examinations of specific topics.

During a decade of use the series has experienced a wide readership. A continuing effort has been made to update the scholarship, simplify the organization of material, and clarify concepts through the publication of revised editions. The authors have been gratified with the response to their efforts to introduce people to various forms of religious life. We hope readers will also find these volumes "introductory" in the most significant sense: an introduction to a new perspective for understanding themselves and others.

Frederick J. Streng
Series Editor

Preface to the Third Edition

I WELCOME THE OPPORTUNITY to bring out a third edition of this book. Since the appearance of the second edition, continued study of Japanese religion (and study and travel in Korea, China, and Japan) have provided me with more information and the insight of other scholars for expanding and improving the previous edition. However, my intention remains unchanged—to present a general introduction to the history and dynamics of Japanese religion. This book is intended for readers interested in Japanese studies or religious studies. It is conceived and written as an introduction to Japanese religion and can be read as a first book in this area. No technical knowledge of Japanese history, Japanese religion, or the Japanese language is required for understanding the material.*

I hope that this book will also be of use to advanced students and teachers who are acquainted with one area of Japanese history and culture and are looking for a comprehensive interpretation of religion in Japan. Whereas general readers may use the book as a steppingstone (through the "Selected Readings" and "Annotated Bibliography") to a deeper understanding of Japanese religion, advanced students and teachers may use it as a unified context in which they can integrate their specialized readings.

The basic format of the previous editions has been preserved—an interpretation of persistent themes through three historical periods and the changing patterns of the various religious traditions (the framing of the third period has been changed somewhat, as indicated by the new title of Part III, "Formalism and Renewal"). However, the third edition incorporates so many changes and additional materials that it is a completely rewritten work. Characterizations and generalizations have been amplified and clarified. Sections on important religious figures and their contribution to Japanese intellectual history have been added. One new chapter has been written to give a closer look at "religious life in contemporary Japan." The suggestion mentioned most frequently by professors who used the second edition was a request for more concrete information on the dynamics of religious life in modern Japan, and it is in direct response to this request that the new chapter was written.

Some friendly critics have pointed out to me privately that the book leaves unmentioned many areas of Japanese religious history — notably the late medieval and early modern periods. Some new material in this area has been included, notably a section on Neo-Confucianism and a section on Motoori Norinaga. But let me be the first to acknowledge that so brief a work as this cannot pretend to be a complete history of Japanese religion. I hope this admission will not prevent critics from registering their complaints with me again. Given the eventuality of a subsequent edition, such critical comments will help me to correct the imperfections and incompleteness of the present edition.

Favorable comments on the usefulness of the annotated bibliography in previous editions have encouraged me to expand the annotated bibliography, especially the section "Histories and Works on Japanese Culture." All sections have been updated, and some older items have been deleted.

Another new feature of this edition is a set of study questions listed at the back of the book. These questions were developed in response to students' requests for me to "program" the text for them, helping them to grasp the significance of each chapter. The questions have a double purpose as a study guide to direct reading and as a kind of self-examiniation for checking the content actually gained from reading. (Students tell me that the questions also are helpful for reviewing.) The questions correlate the text of this book, *Japanese Religion*, with the companion sourcebook, *Religion in the Japanese Experience*. A general note suggesting how to use the questions precedes the list.

From the time of planning the first edition, Frederick J. Streng, Series Editor, and I discussed the advantage of illustrations, and it is only because of space limitation that illustrations were omitted from the first two editions. Now we have the luxury of some space for photographs, and a special word is needed to describe the photographs chosen. They have been selected from my collection of photographs taken during field work in Japan over the past twenty years. Out of thousands of pictures, I have tried to pick those which express the dynamics of religious life: from the New Year's decoration on a Tokyo taxi to a shaman's seance with a client's dead relative. The kinds of illustrations usually found in books about Japanese religion have been omitted. The major temples and shrines, the monumental statues and portraits of famous priests—which make such lovely picture postcards—will not be found here. Such pictures, as important as they may be, are abundant in many Western-language books. But there are rather few illustrations of Japanese religion as actually practiced, and it is photographs of religion being practiced that have been chosen for inclusion. Those wishing to view religion through art and architecture may consult works in the "Annotated Bibliography" (such as Paine and Soper's *The Art and Architecture of Japan* or art works listed in the sections for "Shinto" and "Buddhism"). All photographs were taken by the author, with place and date listed.

Some photographs were taken expressly for this book, during my last extensive stay in Japan, from September 1979 through January 1980. The major purpose of that research trip was a joint study of the new religion Gedatsu-kai with Professor Hitoshi Miyake under a grant sponsored by the Japan Society for the Promotion of Science. Special thanks go to the Japan Society for the Promotion of Science for their research support; to Professor Hitoshi Miyake and Keio University for facilitating this research; to Mr. Kojiro Miyasaka of Rissho Kosei-kai for housing; to Western Michigan University for a grant partially covering film costs; and to the leadership and members of Gedatsu-kai for their generous cooperation.

In addition to those who helped in the writing of the earlier editions, I would like to thank those who made suggestions on style and content for the third edition, especially Frederick J. Streng, editor of THE RELIGIOUS LIFE OF MAN series, and Sheryl Fullerton, Religious Studies Editor, and Jonathan Cobb of Wadsworth Publishing Company. I also would like to thank the reviewers of this edition of *Japanese Religion:* Jeffrey Broughton of California State University, Long Beach, Walter Neevel, Jr. of University of Wisconsin, Milwaukee, Merlin L. Swartz of Boston University, and Richard Alan Williams of University of Texas at Austin.

I would like to thank Mrs. Dolores Condic for typing assistance and my sons David and Paul for help in compiling the bibliography and preparing the manuscript.

For the third time, it is a pleasure to dedicate this work to our Japanese friends and to the continued friendship and mutual cooperation of the United States and Japan.

NOTE

*   All markings for long vowels have been omitted; no publications in Japanese are cited. Reference to Japanese names follows the Japanese convention of giving the family name first.

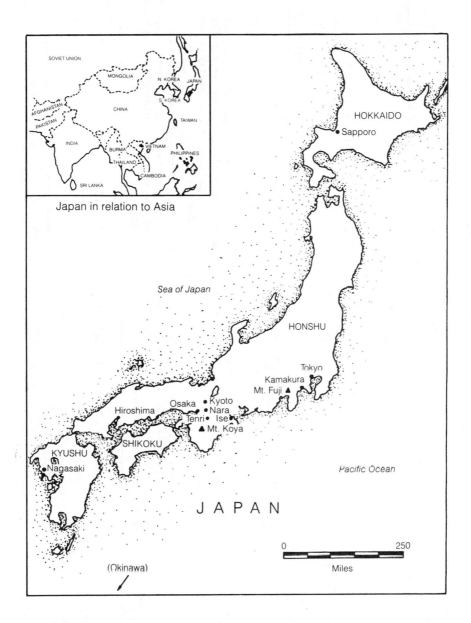

Japan in relation to Asia

For more detailed maps showing the distribution and concentration of various religions in Japan, see Joseph M. Kitagawa, "Shinto" and "Mahayana Buddhism (Japan)," in Historical Atlas of the Religions of the World, *ed. Ismai'il Ragi al Faruqui and David E. Sopher (New York: Macmillan, 1974), pp. 127–32, 195–99.*

Table of Japanese Religious History, with Chronological Periods and Corresponding Cultural Features

For a more complete account, see "A Chronological Table of Religious Affairs in Japan," in Religious Studies in Japan, ed. Japanese Association for Religious Studies (Tokyo: Maruzen, 1959), pp. 467–77.

I. FORMATIVE PERIOD

Chronology in Japanese Historical Periods	Economic, Social, and Political Features	Religious Events and Characteristics
Jomon Yayoi Kofun (Prehistoric and Protohistoric (to sixth century A.D.)	Hunting and gathering culture gives way to rice agriculture and more sedentary, small village organization; increasing centralization around leading families.	Indigenous Japanese tradition: agricultural festivals, reverence for the dead, divine descent of the imperial line, family as the religious unit.
Taika (645–710)	Influx of Chinese culture marks Japan's first contact with a literate and highly organized culture; the first truly centralized government, patterned after Chinese models (such as legal codes).	Importation of foreign traditions: Buddhism, Confucianism, religious Taoism; Shinto organized from the indigenous traditions; earliest interaction of these traditions.
Nara (710–84)	First permanent capital; elaborate life at the imperial court and among the nobility, widely separated from the common farmer; first Japanese writings, including dynastic chronicles and *Manyoshu*.	Six philosophical schools of Buddhism; system of provincial temples with Todai-ji at Nara as the central cathedral; further interaction of the native tradition with Buddhism and Taoism.

II. PERIOD OF DEVELOPMENT AND ELABORATION

Heian (794–1185)	Capital moved to Kyoto; highly developed aesthetic life among court and nobility; *Tale of Genji*, the world's first novel; increasing importance of feudal estates and the warrior class; Mongol invasions of 1274 and 1281.	Buddhist sects of Shingon and Tendai founded, dominate Heian period; Buddhism becomes more closely related to Japanese culture and begins to penetrate the countryside; Shinto becomes more highly organized; *Engishiki* compiled 927.

Period		
Kamakura (1185–1333)	Military dictator controls political power (emperor is secluded at Kyoto): real seat of government moves to Kamakura; attention shifts from the effeminate nobleman to the powerful warrior; rise of the merchant class; growing sense of uncertainty with increased civil strife.	Buddhist sects of Pure Land, Nichiren, and Zen founded, dominate Kamakura period; Buddhism enters the life of the common people and spreads throughout the land; development of highly eclectic medieval Shinto; thorough blending of these traditions.
Muromachi (1333–1568) and Momoyama (1568–1600)	Great civil strife; expansion and development of agricultural lands and techniques; growth of towns and markets; blending of the culture of warriors and noblemen; greater unification of the country under the military ruler, subjugation of religious headquarters to political authority; first major contact with the West.	Kitabatake writes in support of the supremacy of the imperial line (1339); crystallization of sect and denominational lines; Saint Francis Xavier and introduction of Christianity (sixteenth century).

III. PERIOD OF FORMALISM AND RENEWAL

Period		
Tokugawa (1600–1867)	Widespread peace and stability under supreme control of the military dictator; expulsion of Christianity and "closed door" policy limiting foreign access to Japan; dominance of merchant class; cities grow in size and importance; rise of popular arts such as woodblock prints and novels.	Christianity proscribed; Buddhism made a branch of the state; Neo-Confucianism made the rationale of the state; Shinto overshadowed by Buddhism but developing rationale for separation from Buddhism; first appearance of the New Religions; secularism expressed in popular arts.
Meiji (1868–1911) Taisho (1912–25) Showa (1926–) } Modern (1868–1945)	Transition from feudal to modern period; military dictator steps down while emperor is formally made head of state; feudal state is abolished and modern nation-state established with centralized authority at Tokyo; remarkable educational and industrial achievements; three major wars: Sino-Japanese (1894–95), Russo-Japanese (1904–05), World War II (1937–45).	Buddhism disestablished; Shinto established as state religion; ban on Christianity lifted; Catholicism reintroduced and Protestantism introduced for the first time; all traditions become nationalistic; more New Religions appear.
Postwar (since 1945)	Allied occupation (1945–52) marks Japan's first major defeat and occupation of her territory; prewar nationalism and militaristic control give way to greater liberty and tendency toward "democracy" and internationalism; remarkable rebuilding of Japan's cities and industrial facilities; Japan emerges as a major economic and political force in Asia.	Shinto disestablished; complete religious freedom; general demoralization and disorganization among the older religions, with gradual recovery and reorganization; New Religions the most conspicuous religious activity; religious indifference and secularism widespread.

CHAPTER 1

Introduction

From prehistoric times to the present, religion has played an important role in the life of the Japanese people. Religious activities from more than two thousand years ago are reflected in archaeological evidence, and recently many so-called New Religions have arisen in Japan and have become active in other lands such as the United States and South America. However, there has never been a single organized tradition of "Japanese Religion" with its own scriptures, priests, buildings, and rituals. Japanese religion, unlike Roman Catholicism, for example, is not a single institution. The religious heritage of the Japanese includes a number of individual traditions— some native to Japan and some imported, some highly organized and some not formally institutionalized. Through time, these traditions interacted to form a distinctive religious heritage, and it is in this sense that we use the term "Japanese religion."

FIVE RELIGIOUS STRANDS

Japanese religion is a blend of at least five major strands: folk religion, Shinto, Buddhism, religious Taoism, and Confucianism. Christianity, which entered Japan in the sixteenth century, may be considered a sixth strand, but since it did not contribute to the formation of traditional Japanese religion, its history is reserved for Chapter 12.

"Folk religion" generally refers to beliefs and practices that have existed outside highly organized traditions. Some folk practices, such as rituals associated with hunting and rice agriculture, may date back to prehistoric times. Some more recent aspects of folk religion are actually the popular adaptation of formal traditions and might be termed popular religion. Whether called folk religion or popular religion, these beliefs and practices touch people's everyday life in areas such as work, home, and annual celebrations.

Shinto is a formal religion of myths, rituals, shrines, and priests. It emerged from prehistoric Japanese tradition, but in close contact with the religious influences of China and Korea. Central to Shinto is the notion of Japan as the land of the *kami* (gods or spirits), who both embody the national tradition and inhabit the natural surroundings of every locale. ("Shinto" means "the way of the *kami*.") The presence of Shinto shrines in small villages and even on the roofs of city department stores is living testimony to the pervasiveness of Shinto in Japan.

Three strands of the Japanese religious tradition—Buddhism, religious Taoism, and Confucianism—are importations from Korea and China. Buddhism, the most prominent of the three, was founded in India by the Buddha (Prince Gautama) in the fifth century B.C. The Buddha, dissatisfied with the prevailing religious system in India, practiced meditation until he arrived at a realization (or enlightenment) of the true nature of human life. He taught freedom from suffering by avoiding the desire that causes suffering and thereby achieving a peaceful existence. This philosophy of life became the basis for a monastic community that developed commentaries and ritual practices. By the time Buddhism had undergone considerable transformation in China, it was philosophically and institutionally complex. Buddhism entered Japan from China—first by way of Korea and then directly from China—and it was received by the Japanese as part of Chinese civilization. Japanese Buddhists first continued Indian and Chinese practices but later developed distinctively Japanese forms of practice, thought, and organization.

Religious Taoism and Confucianism arose in China. Taoism developed out of the ancient Chinese reverence for nature and notions of the orderly but ever changing pattern of the cosmos. Early texts expressing the Taoist viewpoint, such as the *Tao Te Ching*, have been labeled "philosophical Taoism," for want of a better term. Many Chinese religious practices associated with cosmological notions, the almanac, and divination were loosely related to Taoism and have sometimes been called "religious Taoism." The tradition of religious Taoism was most visible in the Chinese bureau of *yin* and *yang* (div-

Although it never existed as a formal religion, the ideas of religious Taoism heavily influenced Buddhism and Shinto as well as popular religious practices.

Confucianism is the Chinese tradition set in motion in the sixth century B.C. by the teachings of Confucius and thereafter institutionalized by the Chinese state and imitated in other parts of Asia. Confucius, who grew up in a time of great social and political turmoil, insisted on a return to virtue and benevolence. After his death, his teachings became the basis for education and government, serving as the wider rationale for the hierarchical social and political relationships within an agricultural economy. The formal tradition of Confucian teachings and institutions—known in the West as "Confucianism"—provided a comprehensive system for ordering governmental and social harmony, placing great emphasis on family stability and filial piety (loyalty of children to parents). Various aspects of Confucian teachings have been prominent in Japan. At times the state directly supported Confucian teachings and institutions, but the indirect influence of Confucian notions of social and political identity was equally important, if not more important than direct government support.

UNITY AND DIVERSITY

The saying that "the whole is greater than the sum of its parts" is very appropriate to the study of Japanese religion. We must view it as a unified whole because the individual strands did not exist in isolation, either in the course of history or in the dynamics of religious life. Throughout Japanese history each strand was influenced by one or more of the others. Shinto, for example, arose out of ancient Japanese religious practices (such as rituals related to the growing of rice); but it was organized more systematically in reaction to the introduction of highly organized Buddhism, and it assimilated some aspects of Buddhism and religious Taoism. We will trace this process of interaction in later accounts of each religious strand. The important thing to remember here is that any one strand such as Shinto is not just Shinto pure and simple: It is a combination of several influences.

Even more important, people experienced Japanese religion as a unified world-view rather than as separate alternatives or individual traditions. A distinctive feature of Japanese religious history is that individuals usually have not belonged exclusively to one religious tradition but consciously affiliated themselves with or unconsciously participated in several traditions. In the West, people commonly claim to be either Protestant or Catholic or Jewish. In Japan, it has been customary for a person (or family) to participate in both Shinto festivals and Buddhist memorial services and to practice Confucian ethics and follow beliefs of religious Taoism and folk religion. In general, it is better to characterize Japanese religion as "both/and" instead of as "either/or." If we could have asked the traditional Japanese person, "Are you Shinto or Buddhist or Confucian or Taoist?" an appropriate response would have been a simple "yes," meaning that the person was Shinto and Buddhist and Confucian and Taoist. There would be no contradiction in this answer, for the person would have participated in the various traditions at different moments of his or her life. Japanese women and men usually have found religious fulfillment not in one tradition by itself but in the total sacred power embodied in a number of traditions.

How can we make sense of the coexistence of so many religious traditions? It is best to approach them much as the Japanese people have experienced them. In the Japanese religious tradition there is both unity and diversity. Even within the unity of a single tradition, a great diversity of attitudes may be found. For example, both Buddhism and Shinto include a wide range of religious expression, from the most commonly held beliefs to the most abstract philosophy. In earlier ages an illiterate peasant might practice popular forms of Shinto worship and popular Buddhist devotions, while a scholar combined the abstract theories of Shinto and Buddhism. Within a religious tradition there are several levels of religiosity, and an individual finds unity by participating at a particular level in several different traditions. A common person would pick up the popular threads of the Buddhist and Shinto strands to weave a popular world-view; an intellectual would select the theoretical threads of the same strands to develop a more sophisticated world-view. The unity is in the world-view of the individual.

The unity and diversity of Japanese religion is too complex a subject to be explained by the simple metaphor of threads and strands, however. An important aspect of this unity and diversity is the tension between national unity and local traditions. From ancient times, myths and rituals have been deliberately brought together to express national unity under the imperial line; yet the people of every area liked to pride themselves on their unique local rites and usages. This diversity, however, has usually strengthened rather than threatened the overall national unity. The great importance of local custom for Shinto shrines makes the shrines all the more esteemed by the surrounding people as concrete symbols of their involvement in the long

Japanese tradition. Local customs enhance rather than diminish truly national traditions such as reverence for the emperor. Therefore, as we encounter features of diversity and elements of tension in Japanese religion, we should not assume that they signify contradictions. We should ask whether they are part of a larger pattern of unity.

One of the easiest ways to trace the interaction of unity and diversity is to follow the interweaving of the various strands throughout the course of history, and this book takes such a historical approach. As any culture (or religion as part of a culture) moves through time, it maintains an ongoing identity and continuity while constantly undergoing change. Historical study of a total culture (or the religious dimension of a culture) enables us to distinguish the aspects of continuity and change. In this book, Japanese religious history is discussed in terms of three periods, each one a time of major change. (Elements of continuity, or "persistent themes," in Japanese religion will be discussed in Chapter 2.) In each period a complex interaction of tendencies and countertendencies occurred, opening all three periods to various interpretations according to which aspect (continuity or change) and which dimension (economic or political or artistic or religious) are emphasized.

The three periods—discussed respectively in Parts I, II, and III—emphasize the discontinuity in religious institutions. The first period (from prehistoric times to the ninth century A.D.) sets the stage for the formation of Japanese religion. In this initial period, the most important religious traditions all make their appearance. In the second period (between the ninth and the seventeenth centuries), these traditions develop and organize independently and interact with each other. The third period (from the seventeenth century to the present) witnesses the tendency toward formalism, which in turn stimulates renewal. (For a concise overview of the history of Japanese religion, see the "Table of Japanese Religious History," p. xiv.) This brings us down to the present, where we must wait for the next act in the unending drama of Japanese religion. For religious history does not end with the third period; it will continue and be transformed by future events.

SELECTED READINGS

Anesaki, Masaharu. *History of Japanese Religion*. London: Kegan Paul, Trench, Trubner, 1930. Reprint ed., Rutland, Vt.: Charles E. Tuttle Company, 1963. A standard one-volume history, valuable for its balanced treatment of the premodern world.

Earhart, H. Byron. *Religion in the Japanese Experience: Sources and In-terpretations.* Belmont, Calif.: Wadsworth, 1974. See this source-book for the original documents and more detailed scholarly works on which the present book is based.

————. "Toward a Unified Interpretation of Japanese Religion." In *The History of Religions: Essays on the Problem of Understanding.* Edited by Joseph M. Kitagawa. Chicago: University of Chicago Press, 1967, pp. 195–225. This article sets forth the methodological approach to the "unity and diversity" of Japanese religion as presented in this book.

Hori, Ichiro, ed. *Japanese Religion.* Translated by Yoshiya Abe and David Reid. Tokyo: Kodansha International, 1972. A convenient treatment of various Japanese religious traditions in short essays.

Kitagawa, Joseph M. *Religion in Japanese History.* New York: Columbia University Press, 1966. The most up-to-date account of Japanese religion in a single volume, especially valuable for its treatment of the modern period.

CHAPTER 2

Persistent Themes in Japanese Religious History

The unity of Japanese religion is evidenced by a nexus of persistent themes that are present in most historical periods and cut across most of the religious strands. One may be dominant in one period or more prominent in one religious strand, but generally they all interacted to form the total world-view of the traditional person. Six themes whose recurrence may be taken as a sign of the unity of Japanese religion are (1) the closeness of human beings, gods, and nature; (2) the religious character of the family; (3) the significance of purification, rituals, and charms; (4) the prominence of local festivals and individual cults; (5) the pervasiveness of religion in everyday life; and (6) the natural bond between religion and the nation.

THE CLOSENESS OF HUMAN BEINGS, GODS, AND NATURE

In contrast with monotheistic religions such as Judaism and Christianity, Japanese religion emphasizes neither one sovereign God nor a sharp distinction between the several gods and human beings. Mortals and gods alike share in the beauty of nature. The tendency of Judaeo-Christian theology is to think of a hierarchy with God first, human beings second, and nature a poor third. In Japanese religion the three are on more nearly equal terms. Mortals, gods, and nature form a triangle of harmonious interrelationships. Agriculture and fishing, for example, are closely related to the rituals and festivals of Shinto shrines and Buddhist temples. Zen Buddhism in particular, together with Shinto, expresses a love of nature akin to the Taoist sentiments of living in harmony with nature. The harmony between humans, the gods, and nature is a cornerstone of Japanese religion.[1]

In this context, "gods" can be understood as either the *kami* of Shinto or the Buddhas and *bodhisattvas* (Buddhist divinities) of Buddhism. Because there is no exact English equivalent for the word *kami*, it will be used throughout the text without translation. The important thing to remember is that *kami* is much more inclusive than the English word "god." The notion of *kami* is elusive because of the great number of *kami* and their various forms. Early Japanese writings relate that many *kami* participated in the creation of the world and in a mythological age of specialized divinities not too different from the mythological world believed in by the ancient Greeks and Romans. In addition to the *kami* of mythology, in ancient times as well as at present natural objects, animals, and even human beings have been identified as *kami*. In fact, according to one of the greatest Shinto scholars, Motoori Norinaga (1730–1801),

> Generally speaking, (the word) *"kami"* denotes, in the first place, the deities of heaven and earth that appear in the ancient texts and also the spirits enshrined in the shrines; furthermore, among all kinds of beings—including not only human beings but also such objects as birds, beasts, trees, grass, seas, mountains, and so forth—any being whatsoever which possesses some eminent quality out of the ordinary, and is awe-inspiring, is called *kami*.[2]

If they were considered powerful enough, "evil and mysterious things" also rated as *kami*, because the primary consideration was the power to inspire and not "goodness or meritorious deeds." The identity of *kami* is so elastic that perhaps the best general term for understanding *kami* is the notion of the sacred.[3]

Humans are closely related to both *kami* and Buddhas. In fact, men and women can even rise to the status of a *kami* or Buddha. The emperor was considered to be a living *kami*, since he was a direct descendant of the *kami*. Other human beings can attain divinity, too. For example, the military ruler *(shogun)* Tokugawa Ieyasu was venerated as divine or semidivine even during his lifetime (1542–1616). The founders of Buddhist sects have been revered as semidivine or divine, and during the last two centuries founders of New Religions have been viewed as powerful, living *kami*.

THE RELIGIOUS CHARACTER OF THE FAMILY

A second theme of Japanese religious history is the crucial religious function of the family, which is said to include both living and dead members. The dead are so important that the label of ancestor worship has been applied to Japanese religion. Family unity and continuity are essential for carrying out the important rituals honoring the spirits of family ancestors. Even beyond the family, the dead, their burial or cremation, and periodic memorials have great religious significance. The dead can rise to the status of "gods." A dead person is referred to euphemistically as a Buddha *(hotoke)*, and the tacit understanding is that after a fixed number of periodic memorials a dead person joins the company of ancestors as a kind of *kami*. Some shrines are dedicated to the spirits of famous men, such as the great Tokugawa ruler Ieyasu. At present, the religious function of most Buddhist priests and temples is to perform masses and memorials.

The family is important not only for revering ancestors but also for providing cohesion for religious activities. In Japan the family unit has usually consisted of more than one set of parents and their children. The Japanese family has often been an extended family of three or more generations and several sets of related parents; sometimes

Clothing and eyeglasses of family dead are placed on statues of Jizo on Mount Asama, near the Ise Shrines. The custom is to bring objects of clothing, toys, glasses, and even false teeth as a partial means of enshrining spirits of family dead. (New Year's week, 1980)

Paper-thin strips of wood are placed in these racks on Mount Asama, near the Ise Shrines. The strips represent the spirits of the dead and contain the deceased's Buddhist posthumous name, granted by a Buddhist priest during the funeral ceremony. The faithful may "purify" the spirits of the dead by pouring water over the wooden strips. (New Year's week, 1980)

Lighting a candle for the dead is a custom practiced in many traditions. In Japan, the candles are often enclosed in a glass case, as they are here on Mount Asama near the Ise Shrines. (New Year's week, 1980)

Rain does not cancel a trip to visit the ancestors on Mount Asama, near the Ise Shrines. The visitors are flanked on the left by large wooden memorial stupa (distinctive of Mount Asama) and on the right by the more customary stone memorials. (New Year's week, 1980)

workers who were not biologically related to the family members were part of the group. In ancient times, the head of the family line was a priest, and prominent families combined political and religious leadership in their family heads. The home was formerly the center of religious devotion. Traditionally, every home featured a miniature shrine (sometimes called "god-shelf" or *kamidana*) for daily prayers. There was also a Buddhist altar *(butsudan)* for daily offerings to family ancestors in general and periodic memorials for specific ancestors. The *kamidana* are still found in homes, especially in rural areas, and are retained in such places as small shops and even in oceangoing ships. The *butsudan* are found in many homes, even in some modern apartments where the *kamidana* are often missing. These family altars indicate the central religious function of the home. Various semi-religious seasonal activities (notably at New Year's) also take place at the home.

Because the family was such an important social and religious institution, it is not surprising that as Shinto and Buddhism became highly organized their priesthoods developed along hereditary lines. Japanese social as well as religious organization emphasizes a hierarchical ordering based on respect for elders. Even modern businesses and the New Religions are organized in terms of loyalty and belonging that have been compared to the model of the Japanese family.

THE SIGNIFICANCE OF PURIFICATION,
RITUALS, AND CHARMS

A third persistent theme in Japanese religious history is the significance of purification, rituals, and charms. These elements often represent borrowings from Indian and Chinese traditions, but they have become thoroughly integrated into the Japanese religious scene. In front of every Shinto shrine, water is provided for washing the hands and rinsing the mouth before approaching the shrine. The insistence on purification—both physical and spiritual—is basic to Japanese religion. Formerly, many prohibitions and purifications were connected with matters such as death and menstruation. The emphasis on purity carries over into contemporary customs such as the practice of soaking in a hot bath and the provision of a damp face cloth for guests. Purification rituals using salt, water, and fire—all considered to be purifying agents—are found in Buddhist, Shinto, and folk traditions.

Other rituals take care of every conceivable human and spiritual need. Many are connected with agriculture and fishing in order to relate humans, gods, and nature in a beneficial manner. Some rituals meet personal crises such as sickness. Paper charms distributed by shrines and temples include a number of specific boons, like warding off fire or preventing or curing sickness. In modern times, one of the most popular charms is for "traffic safety"—protection against car accidents. Buddhist scriptures (in Chinese translation) are recited by priests as blessings, and phrases from the scriptures are memorized by lay people as semimagical formulas. Taoistic charms and formulas have influenced both Shinto and Buddhism, but Buddhism is the major source of popular prayers and magical formulas.

THE PROMINENCE OF LOCAL FESTIVALS
AND INDIVIDUAL CULTS

A fourth theme of Japanese religious history is the prominence of local festivals and individual cults. Unlike Christian churches, Buddhist temples and Shinto shrines are not the sites of weekly services, but this does not diminish their importance. Because periodic festivals are the expression of the whole village or section of a large city, they are unifying forces that link individual homes with a larger religious group. Social and economic activities of small villages often center on the Shinto shrine. The local festival with its carnival atmo-

Performing the "hundredfold" (ohyakudo) repentance by walking back and forth one hundred times while silently repenting. Usually the path is marked by stone pillars at each end, and even during cold weather the walk is performed barefoot. [At the "sacred land" (goreichi) of the New Religion called Gedatsu-kai, Kitamoto, 1979]

An example of the interrelationship of religious practices: At the left is the stone pillar marking one end of the "hundredfold" repentance path. At the right is a stone basin where visitors are rinsing hands and mouth with water. In the background (behind several trees) is a sacred archway or torii; behind the torii and at the left is seen the outline of a Shinto shrine. Visitors to such religious headquarters are free to perform religious practices at one or more (or all) of these sites. [At the "sacred land" (goreichi) of the New Religion called Gedatsu-kai, Kitamoto, New Year's Day, 1980]

Votive pictures (ema) *bought at a Shinto shrine are inscribed with the person's petition and hung on a special rack near the shrine. (Kyoto, 1979)*

sphere is typical of Japanese religiosity. In this light we can understand why the celebration of Christmas has become popular in Japan, even though Christianity in general has not prospered.

Individual cults, though not organized on a national scale, play a crucial role in religious devotion. The *bodhisattvas* of Buddhism, especially popular *bodhisattvas* such as Jizo and Kannon, have claimed probably the largest following. Statues of these *bodhisattvas* are found in the villages or along the roadside as well as in temples, and they receive the devotion of all those who look to them for spiritual help. Usually priests play little or no role in these devotional cults. Ordinarily a small group of people will form a voluntary association (called *ko*), which meets regularly in the members' homes for devotion to one *bodhisattva*. Various *kami* (including gods of Indian and Chinese origin) are revered by groups of fishermen or other tradespeople. Often the existence of a flourishing cult of this kind at a shrine or temple accounts for most of its visitors and financial income.

THE PERVASIVENESS OF RELIGION IN EVERYDAY LIFE

A fifth theme in Japanese religious history is the importance of religion in everyday life. The Japanese identification with gods and nature, the importance of the family, the significance of rituals and charms, the prominence of individual cults—all bring religion into a natural and close relationship to everyday life. For example, although there is

Fortune papers (mikuji) *are hung on a special rack over small statues of Jizo near a Buddhist temple. (Kyoto, 1979)*

no regular weekly attendance at Shinto shrines and Buddhist temples, there are regular stages in an individual's life when visits to shrines and temples take place. Traditionally, a young infant was carried to the local Shinto shrine and presented to the guardian deity. In case of sickness or special need, one usually visited the shrine or temple that granted an appropriate blessing. Likewise, in recent times the traditional wedding often takes place in a Shinto shrine, and the funeral mass is performed (like the subsequent memorial celebrations) in a Buddhist temple.

Through both formal and informal means, religion has been specifically related to economic activities. Some temples and shrines, for example, are oriented to the fishing communities in which they are found; priests of these institutions pray for large catches, safety on the sea, and repose for the drowned. Some saints are formally considered the patron figures of certain crafts. In an informal sense, many folk practices are inseparable from the various stages of rice cultivation.

Even human sexuality and reproduction are perceived and expressed in religious terms. For example, conjugal harmony of married couples and fertility for rice fields are requested from wayside deities (*dosojin*), who are memorialized on stones on which are carved explicitly sexual symbols or the figures of a man and woman embracing.[4] Religion even pervades the Japanese sense of humor. For example, the great Zen saint of China, Bodhidharma (who sat in meditation until his legs fell off), is remembered in Japan as the legless doll called Daruma, who, as many times as he falls, always rights himself.

THE NATURAL BOND BETWEEN RELIGION AND THE NATION

A sixth theme of Japanese religious history is the close relationship between religion and the Japanese nation—a bond that has existed practically from the birth of the identity of the Japanese people. One of the central mythical tales of ancient Japan relates that the emperor, as descendant of the Sun Goddess, is the sacred leader of the Japanese islands (which were created by the gods or *kami*). In effect the emperor was the symbolic head of ritual and government. Although he seldom ruled the government directly, the rituals he performed were for the benefit of the entire country.

This ancient connection between religion and nation is at the heart of Shinto; yet Buddhism also expressed this theme. Buddhists helped unify and support the government, and the state patronized Buddhism. Buddhist priests prayed for the safety of the imperial family and read special scriptures for the peace and prosperity of the state. Imperial families donated private homes for use as temples, and the state eventually built provincial temples in every province so that Buddhist prayers and scriptures for the state could be read in every area of the country.

Between 1868 and 1945, the natural bond between religion and the nation was used by the state to support nationalism and militarism. Many people, both Japanese and Westerners, feel that this policy was a distortion of the Japanese tradition. In Chapters 17 through 19 of this book we will see how the problem of the relationship of state and religion is being debated in Japan. However this question is resolved, the close tie between religion and the nation at large seems to be an indelible feature of Japanese history.

THE TRADITIONAL WORLD-VIEW

These six themes give us some idea of the dynamics of religious life in Japan. Traditionally people did not belong exclusively to one organized religion but drew upon various traditions as they participated in religious activities. A person wishing to express reverence for nature was not likely to stop and distinguish between the Shinto notion of *kami* dwelling in natural objects, Zen Buddhist ideas of oneness with nature, and Taoist concepts of conforming to the way of nature.

It was more important to venerate nature than to identify and separate the historical influences upon the Japanese view of nature. Similarly, there has not been a clear-cut distinction between separate themes. Veneration of nature and respect for the nation as a divine nation (land of the *kami*), for example, usually have been seen as closely related.

The six themes shape the general view of the world held by most traditional Japanese people. A Japanese person acquires these perceptions of the world by seeing memorials held for ancestors in the home, participating in shrine festivals, and taking part in rituals for the transplanting of rice. More often than not, such a world-view is held unconsciously. Although parts of it may be written down in formal doctrine, the entire world-view is more a matter of personal memory than a written handbook. The world-view is formed as a person gradually develops a sense of identity by participating in cultural life. As we trace the historical formation of Japanese religion, we should keep in mind that this shared world-view has given continuity to religious life.

NOTES

1. A film that captures the Japanese appreciation of nature, especially in the context of Shinto, is *Shinto: Nature, Gods, and Man in Japan,* a 48-minute, 16-mm. color film produced and distributed by Japan Society Films. See also Figure 1, "Nachi Waterfall," in H. Byron Earhart, *Religion in the Japanese Experience: Sources and Interpretations* (Belmont, Calif.: Wadsworth, 1974), p. 20.
2. Quoted in Shigeru Matsumoto, *Motoori Norinaga, 1730–1801* (Cambridge, Mass.: Harvard University Press, 1970), p. 84.
3. Mircea Eliade has elaborated the notion of the sacred as a general feature of all religion, but dominant within cosmic religions. See his *The Sacred and the Profane: The Nature of Religion,* trans. Willard R. Trask (New York: Harcourt Brace Jovanovich, 1959).
4. See Michael Czaja, *Gods of Myth and Stone: Phallicism in Japanese Folk Religion* (New York: Weatherhill, 1974).

SELECTED READINGS

Earhart, H. Byron. *Religion in the Japanese Experience: Sources and Interpretations.* Belmont, Calif.: Wadsworth, 1974. See Part One for a general introduction to Japanese religion.

Kishimoto, Hideo. "The Meaning of Religion to the Japanese People."
In *Religious Studies in Japan*. Tokyo: Maruzen, 1959, pp. 22–28. A
comparison of Japanese and Western religion.

Nakamura, Hajime. *Ways of Thinking of Eastern Peoples: India, China,
Tibet, Japan*. Revised English translation edited by Philip P.
Wiener. Honolulu: East-West Center Press, 1964. The section on
Japan, pp. 345–587, is a comprehensive treatment of the distinc-
tive features of Japanese life and thought.

PART ONE

The Formation of Japanese Religion

The formative period of Japanese religion extends from prehistory to the ninth century A.D. During this stage, the major traditions that were to form and influence Japanese religion first appeared or entered Japan: the prehistoric heritage, Shinto, Buddhism, Confucianism, religious Taoism. The prehistoric heritage is the most difficult to grasp because it is the cumulative result of many centuries of local cultures, which gradually became centralized and unified. Shinto is an easily identifiable successor to ancient beliefs and practices. Buddhism, a foreign religion, arose in India, was transformed in China, and then was transmitted to Japan. China was the birthplace for Confucianism and religious Taoism, both of which entered Japan at about the same time as Buddhism. Folk religion permeated the prehistoric heritage and borrowed from the organized religions, enriching the religious life of the common people. Each tradition made a considerable contribution to the formation of Japanese religion.

The fact that the first period is labeled "formative" does not mean that the formation of Japanese religion was complete by the ninth century. Rather, in this period the major traditions appeared and the general outlines of Japanese religion took shape. Changes that occurred in subsequent periods took this foundation as the point of departure, as we will see in Parts II and III.

CHAPTER 3

The Prehistoric Heritage

Our study begins with the earliest known Japanese religion. Among the several traditions that constitute Japanese religion, the prehistoric heritage is of primary importance. The beginning of religion in Japan, like all other aspects of her early culture, is not well known. We do not know exactly where the Japanese people came from, just as we do not know how the Japanese language was formed. In the absence of certainty in these matters, a number of theories to account for the emergence of the culture and people of Japan have arisen. Japanese culture shows an obvious affinity to the culture of areas both north and south of Japan, but scholars disagree on the interpretation of this affinity. Some have favored a southern hypothesis, seeing the ultimate source of the Japanese tradition in the Ryukyu Islands and farther south. Others have emphasized a northern hypothesis, seeing the main contribution to Japanese culture enter from the Asian continent by way of Korea. Future research will have to take into account both hypotheses.

THE ORIGINS OF JAPANESE RELIGION

Human beings seem to be a comparatively recent arrival to Japan, especially compared to her neighbor China. Some of the oldest human remains and oldest evidence for religion (religious burial), hundreds

of thousands of years old, have been excavated in China. By contrast,
from what is known, religion is a relatively recent development in
Japan. Geologists and archaeologists are still evaluating the evidence
for a Paleolithic (old stone age) culture in Japan. There may never
have been a pure hunting culture in Japan. Decisive evidence places
humans in Japan only as late as the Neolithic age (c. 10,000 B.C.). They
lived in a hunting and gathering or hunting and fishing economy.
Therefore, when we speak of the "indigenous religion" of Japan, we
must keep in mind the relative recentness of the phenomenon.

Another difficult question of early history is the relationship of the
Ainu and their culture to the Japanese. The Ainu, who once occupied
much of Honshu, the main island, were gradually driven east and
north by the advancing Japanese and now survive mainly in Hokkaido. Racially the Ainu are Caucasian and have much body hair; this
places them in sharp contrast to the Japanese, who are Mongolian
and have little body hair. In physical appearance the Japanese are
distinguished by the fold of skin at the corner of the eye, which
Westerners see as a "slant eye." After approximately 250 B.C., the
Japanese depended heavily on rice agriculture; the Ainu traditionally
lived by hunting, fishing, and gathering.

At one time Western scholars thought the Ainu were forerunners of
the later Japanese, and they tried to find the origin of Japanese language, culture, and religion among the Ainu. Now scholars tend to
view the Ainu as an isolated pocket of Caucasians in northeast Asia,
for they are linked with prehistoric northern Asia and Europe not
only racially, but also by their most important traditional ritual, the
bear sacrifice. Nevertheless, there was a great deal of interaction between the Ainu and the Japanese. Especially in northern Honshu and
Hokkaido, place names are borrowed from the Ainu, and some places
formerly sacred to the Ainu have been taken over by the Japanese.
One of the controversial factors relating the religions of the two
peoples is the similarity in the name for "divinity"—*kami* in Japanese
and *kamui* in Ainu language.

From the beginning, Japanese religion represented a combination
of diverse elements. Indeed, the geographical location of the Japanese
islands is a clue to the formation of Japanese religion. The islands
have been in a good position to receive periodic transmissions from
several directions. Especially the recurring influence from the Asian
continent has played a crucial role. However, until recent times there
was no constant contact with the mainland. The span of ocean between Japan and Asia was short enough to allow occasional voyages,

but the difficulty of the trip severely limited their frequency. Consequently, every Asian element that entered Japan was left to ferment in a somewhat isolated setting. This geographical condition is a major factor in the development of a distinctively Japanese religion. The indigenous religion of Japan is a blend of several diverse components.

THE EVIDENCE AND MEANING OF THE EARLIEST RELIGION IN JAPAN

To understand the prehistoric contribution to Japanese religion, we have to synthesize the archaeological evidence that precedes written records. If the very earliest archaeological finds (possibly Paleolithic) are excluded, the bulk of this evidence falls into two prehistoric periods called the Jomon and the Yayoi, followed by a transitional period called Kofun, which shades into early history. These three periods represent successive stages of culture that cannot be dated precisely.

The Jomon period draws its name from distinctive pottery decoration (Jomon or "cord pattern") and may have started as early as 6000 B.C. or as late as 3000 B.C. and continued until about 250 B.C. The main evidence for the culture of this period, usually considered Neolithic, is found in shell-heaps along the seacoast, where shellfish were the main food. There is also some evidence for the existence of mountain dwellers who combined hunting and gathering activities. The Yayoi period is named after the district in Tokyo where a different style of pottery was found. The approximate dates 250 B.C. to A.D. 250 are usually associated with it. The major innovation of the Yayoi period is the cultivation of rice in paddies, utilizing the control of water. It seems that hunting and fishing were continued in addition to the new practice of growing rice.

The Kofun period marks the entrance of a highly defined Asian culture. Stretching from about A.D. 250 to 600, the period is named for the huge earthen mausoleums or tombs erected during this time (*kofun* means "tomb"). These elaborate mausoleums were built for the ruling class, and according to one school of thought this ruling class was a conquering force that swept in from Asia with horses and iron weapons.[1]

These prehistoric developments contain traces of the earliest known religion in Japan, the foundation on which later religion is based. Due to the fragmentary character of the evidence it is impossible to reconstruct the whole fabric of religion in these early periods, but certain features are prominent and have persisted. Although one must recognize the great diversity for different regions and different periods, there were various religious expressions concerned with the dead and afterlife, fertility, and sacred objects. Mythology, rituals, and religious organization can be inferred only by ethnological comparison.

THE RELIGIOUS SIGNIFICANCE OF BURIAL AND THE DEAD

From the earliest records of human life, human beings have shown a religious attitude toward the dead, since they recognize the passage from earthly life to a form of spiritual existence. The early Japanese were no exception, for they practiced several types of burial. The first evidence of intentional burials is the simple burial of bodies in a flexed position or covered with red ochre and stones. During the Yayoi period, the dead were interred in jars. This custom originated in Korea. Gradually the jars were covered with stone slabs (dolmen burial). This seems to have been the forerunner of the large mausoleums called *kofun*. These tombs are often huge mounds covering a stone chamber, all of which is surrounded by a moat. Boat-shaped coffins of wood and stone in the tombs may have been for the voyage of the soul to the next world. In general, with the passage of time, there was an increasing concern for the ritual disposal of the dead: All these practices probably indicate religious passage to an afterlife. The transition to agriculture in Yayoi times probably led to a higher valuation of burial in the earth; the erection of tombs probably was the result of an abrupt intrusion from the Asian continent.

How can we interpret all these concerns for the dead and afterlife? The initial Western scholarship on Japanese religion was confused in asking whether the origin of Japanese religion was ancestor worship or nature worship; there was also the confused controversy as to whether ancestor worship was truly indigenous to Japan or was a Chinese importation. But there is no single origin of Japanese religion. The evidence suggests that the Japanese people have always shown a reverent concern for the dead and that this concern has assumed diverse forms, not only in prehistoric but also in historic times. Much of the archaeological evidence for understanding Japanese religion is found in burials, especially in the elaborate tomb burials of the Kofun period. In later periods the religious significance of the dead is expressed in Buddhist funeral and memorial services.

THE RELIGIOUS SIGNIFICANCE OF FERTILITY

From Jomon times on, objects have appeared that point to a connection between religion and fertility. Large stone clubs suggest a phallic symbol; small clay figurines are probably symbols of female fertility and protection. During the Yayoi period, the figurines took on a definitely female form. Perhaps the burial of metal spears and bells (indicating the intrusion of continental metal-working techniques) was also linked to the notion of fertility. With the introduction of rice cultivation in Yayoi times, we begin to see an increased emphasis on fertility, which colors the agricultural and religious life of all later Japanese history. There were annual rituals that linked religious ceremonies to every aspect of the growing and harvesting of rice.

Archaeology has turned up many sacred objects of prehistoric Japan, such as the phallic stone clubs and clay figurines already mentioned. However, three sacred objects are outstanding because of their importance in historic times: the *magatama* (comma-shaped jewels), swords, and mirrors. In later times a set of these three objects became the sacred regalia of the emperor. Their exact religious significance is unknown, but their similarity to materials from the Asian continent and their connection with the rising imperial tradition are indications of two important trends: an increasing continental influence and a growing consolidation of religion around one center.

THE RELIGIOUS SIGNIFICANCE OF DIVINE DESCENT

From about the first to the eighth century A.D. we cross the border from prehistory to early history. In order to describe this period we must rely upon ethnological comparisons and written records, both Chinese and Japanese. For example, the earliest surviving records about Japan are Chinese accounts suggesting both female rulers and female shamans. Moving back in time from the Japanese records, we find hints of female shamanism and ruling queens, but they are overshadowed by families with a man as the political-religious leader. Probably there was a *kami* (god or spirit) for each family, with rituals performed by the head of the family.

In the light of the "northern" and "southern" hypotheses, several inferences have been made about the pantheon and religious organization in prehistoric Japan in terms of a dual character—both "horizontal" and "vertical." For example, the southern contribution may have been a horizontal cosmology with the conception that the gods come from afar or across the sea, just as the dead go to this distant land. The northern contribution may have been a vertical cosmology in which the gods are thought to descend from heaven and the dead to ascend to heaven. Actually a number of religious elements have been drawn together from diverse areas and periods, so that it is difficult to correlate all these variables. One of the crucial questions is whether the emerging imperial line, which traced its divine descent from the sun, evolved from the earlier Japanese family system or was an intrusion from the Asian continent. Very old stone circles found in Japan may indicate some kind of solar cult. At any rate, in late Kofun times there appeared a greater sense of political and religious unity. The people came to feel political loyalty and religious respect for the major family, the budding imperial family, which traced its divine descent from the Sun Goddess.

At the end of the prehistoric period, Japanese religion already contained many of the themes that would pervade later history, but they were not yet organized into set forms. The imperial line was emerging with a nucleus of mythology and agricultural rituals, all of which would be perpetuated mainly within the framework of Shinto. Up to this point, neither Shinto nor any other clearly defined religion was recognizable. Although Shinto increasingly became the main receptacle for the earlier traditions, none of them was transmitted as a pure element, without receiving the influence of Buddhism and Chinese religion. Most of these elements found their way into one or more of the organized religions, while some continued to exist in folk religion outside any organized religion.

NOTES

1. John W. Hall supports the alternative argument for a "primitive feudalism" arising on Japanese soil; see his *Japanese History: New Dimensions of Approach and Understanding*, 2d ed. (Washington, D.C.: American Historical Association, 1966), p. 25.

SELECTED READINGS

Earhart, H. Byron. *Religion in the Japanese Experience: Sources and Interpretations*. Belmont, Calif.: Wadsworth, 1974. See pp. 186–89 for excerpts from Kidder describing prehistoric religion.

Kidder, J. E., Jr. *Japan Before Buddhism.* Rev. ed. London: Thames and Hudson, 1966. The best single book on prehistoric Japan, with discussions of the religious implications of the diverse archaeological evidence.

Kitagawa, Joseph M. "Prehistoric Background of Japanese Religion." *History of Religions,* Vol. 2 (1963), 292–328. The best summary of prehistoric religion.

Smith, Robert J. *Ancestor Worship in Contemporary Japan.* Stanford, Calif.: Stanford University Press, 1974. Includes a valuable first chapter on the historical origins of ancestor worship.

Tsunoda, Ryusaku, and Goodrich, L. C., eds. *Japan in the Chinese Dynastic Histories.* South Pasadena, Calif.: P. D. & I. Perkins, 1951. Includes the earliest written accounts about Japan. Important passages are reprinted in Ryusaku Tsunoda et al., *Sources of Japanese Tradition* (New York: Columbia University Press, 1958), Chapter 1.

CHAPTER 4

The Formation of Shinto

Shinto is Japan's unique contribution to the history of religion. It arose out of prehistoric practices of the Japanese islands and tended to preserve these practices in modified forms. To a great extent, the religious life within Shinto represents a continuity with ancient customs and therefore has enjoyed a long association with the Japanese nation. However, it would be a mistake to see Shinto simply as the indigenous religion of Japan. A historical tracing of Shinto demonstrates that its organization and much of its content owe a great deal to Chinese and Buddhist influences. The blending of Japanese and foreign religious elements into one great national tradition is the distinctive contribution of Shinto.

Shinto forms the next subject for discussion because, historically viewed, it is the channel through which many of the earliest Japanese religious forms were handed down and preserved. However, in discussing Shinto at this point, we must realize that we are making a chronological jump past the stimulus provided by the entrance of Buddhism. The time span and complex character of the emergence of Shinto can be appreciated just by looking at the origins of the word "Shinto."

For many centuries the religious traditions and practices within the Japanese islands were loosely organized around family lines, with no central organization, without even a common name. Gradually the imperial family and its traditions came to be considered supreme over all other families, but still no name was given to the larger or smaller traditions. Not until Buddhism and advanced Chinese culture entered Japan (about the middle of the sixth century) was there any need to distinguish the old traditional practices from any contrasting cult. Then, because Buddhism called itself the "way of the Buddha" (Butsudo), the traditional religion set itself apart by the counterpart term "Shinto," meaning "way of the *kami.*" The two Chinese characters forming the word "Shinto" originated in an earlier Chinese term pronounced *shentao,* but in Japanese "Shinto" is traditionally understood in the Japanese expression *kami no michi* ("way of the *kami*"). The intention of these words is to indicate the "way of the *Japanese* divinities," even though we recognize various foreign influences upon Shinto as an organized religion.

MYTHOLOGICAL MATERIALS AND THE ORIGINS OF SHINTO

A major difficulty in comprehending the formation of Shinto is that as soon as we pass from prehistory into history, Chinese cultural influence is already evident. In fact, foreign influence is most conspicuous in the written documents because the Japanese had no written language prior to the influx of the Chinese script. Among the first written records in Japan are the *Kojiki* and *Nihon Shoki* (the latter is known in the West as the *Nihongi*), chronicles compiled on court order and completed in A.D. 712 and 720, respectively. These early Japanese documents, mixtures of cosmology, mythology, and chronicle, contain the earliest recorded forms of Shinto. Thus, there is good reason to begin an investigation of the formation of Shinto with these two writings.

The *Kojiki* and *Nihongi* have often been considered the watershed of myth from which all later Japanese religion (particularly Shinto) is derived. This general notion is inadequate, however. In the first place, these scriptures reflect both political and religious motives for unifying Japan. They were compiled by the court elite and did not necessarily mirror the faith of the country at large. In the second place, there is probably no such thing as a foundational myth in Japanese religion. For the Japanese there is neither one sacred myth nor one set of sacred scriptures. Within a primitive tribe a common myth typically defines the world-view or the emergence of reality. In so-called higher cultures, such as India, sacred scriptures like the *Vedas* blend with indigenous motifs to provide the religious base on which later scriptures, commentaries, epics, and even popular dramas are based. In contrast, in Japan no common myth or body of religious scripture (including the *Kojiki* and *Nihongi*) pervades the whole religious scene. It is not a question of foreign influence. It is simply a fact that the *Kojiki* and *Nihongi* were never that popular.

These reservations concerning the *Kojiki* and *Nihongi* have been made not to minimize their importance for Japanese religious history, but rather to set them in the proper perspective so that we may see more clearly their complex character and their relevance for comprehending the formation of Shinto. For example, the opening passage of the *Nihongi* is a creation story that is not Japanese but is a borrowing from a Chinese account of creation (in terms of the Chinese bipolarity of *yin* and *yang*—female and male). It appears that the Japanese writers sought prestige for their own traditions by prefacing them with a Chinese form of cosmology. (Throughout Japanese history there has been a mixture of reverence and respect for the cultural tradition of China, to a much greater degree than Europeans glorify their cultural roots in the Greco-Roman tradition.) From this point— the beginning of recorded history in Japan—all things Chinese tended to have an exalted status in Japanese eyes. Even the notion of possessing a history or tradition and recording it in written form seems to have been borrowed from China. It is important to recognize that these ancient Japanese books begin with a Chinese note and that Chinese elements are sprinkled throughout.

The Chinese cosmological element merely sets the stage for introducing the unorganized Japanese traditions. The Chinese contribution is the notion that the cosmos emerged out of "a chaotic mass like an egg," which then separated into heaven (male) and earth (female). This preface serves as a general explanation for the origin of the world and all the divinities. The first two chapters of these writings, entitled "The Age of the Gods," give a patchwork picture of various traditions concerning the generations of gods and the founding of the Japanese islands. In this mythical period, seven generations of divinities or *kami* culminated in the marriage of Izanagi (a male *kami*) and Izanami (a female *kami*). They brought about the appearance of the Japanese islands by thrusting the "jewel-spear of Heaven" from the bridge of heaven into the briny waters below. Then they descended to the land that had appeared and produced other *kami* as well as other features of the universe.

One major theme of the mythology is the descent of the so-called Sun Goddess Amaterasu from this couple. From Amaterasu comes the imperial line of Japan. This is only one of a number of themes or cycles that have been blended together into a combination of mythology and chronology. In general the other themes have been subordinated to the tradition of an imperial line descended from the Sun

Goddess Amaterasu. One purpose of the two chapters called "The Age of the Gods" is to justify the divine origin of the emperors and empresses whose reigns are recorded in the remainder of the book. As a matter of fact, these chronologies were written on command of the imperial court. According to one tradition, a person who had memorized all the ancient traditions and genealogies recited them for transcribers (who wrote them down by using Chinese characters). Nevertheless, the records in both their intention and their content favor the traditions surrounding the imperial line.

We noted earlier that in ancient Japan there were many large families (or extended families) independent of each other in their religious and political leadership. Probably the imperial line derives from an extended family *(uji)* that became dominant over other extended families and subsequently unified the country both politically and religiously. To unify the religion in pre-Buddhist times apparently meant to orient all the competing traditions around the tradition of the ruling family. After the entrance of Buddhism and advanced Chinese culture, this composite tradition was spiced with Chinese elements for prestige and was written down.

The *Kojiki* and *Nihongi* illustrate two all-important religious notions: first, the divine (or semidivine) descent of Japan and her people, and, second, the proliferation of *kami* intimately related to the land and people. For example, even in these early records we can recognize the characteristic Japanese love of nature as a combination of religious and aesthetic emotion. These themes are not limited to the *Kojiki* and *Nihongi*; rather, they persisted in the life of the people from prehistoric times onward.[1]

Other early Japanese writings are helpful for understanding the religious context out of which Shinto was formed. The *Manyoshu* is a famous anthology of poetry that blends lyric and religious themes. The *Kogoshui* is a valuable document recording a rivalry between several priestly families. Even as early as the seventh and eighth centuries A.D. there were in existence distinct theological and ritual factions. "Shinto" is the name applied to the organized religion that attempted to unify and perpetuate these and similar themes.

In this light, it is much easier to understand how, traditionally speaking, the Japanese could not divorce themselves from Shinto. Until recent times, Shinto has tended to define the character of their cultural and religious heritage. On both the local and national plane Shinto hallows the homeland and the Japanese people, as well as the nexus of the religious, political, and natural order. Given this situation, we can understand why Shinto scholars proudly emphasize that Shinto is a natural expression of Japanese life, rather than the product of a definite set of doctrines or a conscious conversion. Also, we can realize why there has been a close association of religious devotion, patriotism, and reverential respect for the emperor. Indeed, the imperial regalia (sword, mirror, and jewel) were sacred from prehistoric times, as the archaeological evidence proves.

ORGANIZED SHINTO: PRIESTS AND RITUALS IN SHRINES

We have seen that the religio-political combination was present even in the extended families of early Japan. The early government of eighth-century Japan continued this tendency by establishing a powerful department of religion as part of the state's administration. Sir George Sansom described the department of religion:

> It was concerned with the performance of the great religious ceremonies (such as the rites of enthronement and national purification, and the festivals of the first-fruits and harvest thanksgiving), the upkeep of shrines, the discipline of shrine wardens, and the recording and observance of oracles and divinations. It presided over the worship of the national divinities, and had nothing to do with Buddhism.[2]

In Japan as in many early civilizations, religion and the priesthood served as arms of the government: The emperor (as the divine ruler) was responsible for the ritual as well as the administrative propriety of the realm. In many ancient traditions, the perpetuation of the ritual order was necessary for maintaining the whole cosmic order. Therefore, it is important to note the contents of this ritual.

From Yayoi times to the present, Japanese religion, especially Shinto ceremonies, has been linked with every phase of growing rice. Although the planting of rice occasions a festival, this and other phases are overshadowed by the climax of the rice harvest, at which time the new rice is offered up to the *kami* as thanksgiving. Even the enthronement ceremony for a new emperor was patterned after the annual thanksgiving harvest ceremony. Other important annual ceremonies are the public purifications that take place at the midpoint and end of the year.

The ritual prayers (*norito*) for the public ceremonies are recorded in codes called the *Engishiki*. The *Engishiki*, or Codes of the Engi Era, were not written down until 927, but they contain materials that predate this era. In particular the *norito* or liturgies presented in Shinto ceremonies, recorded in the *Engishiki*, are extremely valuable for understanding early Shinto. The priest who read the *norito* served as an intermediary between humans and the *kami*. Usually the priest

The sacred archway (torii) *before a local Shinto shrine. (Kawarayu, 1979)*

"called down" the *kami* at the beginning of the ceremony and "sent them away" at the close of the ceremony. Sometimes this was acted out by opening and closing the doors to the inner sanctum (*shinden* or "*kami* hall") housing the sacred object (*shintai* or "*kami* body"), which symbolized the presence of the enshrined *kami*.

The rites and celebrations of Shinto center on shrines (*jinja*), which are still found in the smallest villages as well as in the largest cities. (In English usage the word "shrine" is the general term for the Shinto building—*jinja* or *miya*; the word "temple" is the general term for the Buddhist building—*tera* or *-ji.*) Normally one passes through a sacred arch (*torii*), which helps define the sacred precincts of the shrine. Devout believers purify themselves by pouring water on their hands and rinsing their mouths. The present shrine buildings betray Buddhist and Chinese architectural influence, but some are still built according to the ancient models. These shrines are built on poles above the ground and have a thatched roof. They can be seen today at Ise, one of the Shinto strongholds that consciously attempted to reject Buddhist influence. (At Ise, the Sun Goddess, Amaterasu, is enshrined.) This ancient shrine architecture seems to have affinities with architecture to the south of Japan. As Shinto scholars like to point out, its natural beauty is accentuated by the use of wood and thatch left bare of decorations.

One theory concerning ancient Japanese religion is that originally there were no shrine buildings; rather, a shrine was simply a sacred precinct set apart in a certain area or around a sacred object such as a

*On May 5, boys' festival, paper or
cloth streamers of carp are flown from
tall bamboo poles next to the home.
Usually there is one carp for each
young son in the family. (Sendai,
1963)*

tree or a stone. Sacred precincts often were the sites where the ancestral spirits dwelled. This is a valuable insight for linking ancestor worship with Japanese notions of *kami* and festivals. Only later did there come to appear the twofold Shinto architecture, with a worship hall (*haiden*) in front and a smaller *kami* hall in back. The worship hall is where the priests (and sometimes the people) directed prayers toward the *kami* hall, which contained the presence of the enshrined *kami* symbolized by a sacred object such as a mirror or sword. As Shinto became organized in medieval times, local shrines were considered to enshrine specific *kami* named in the *Kojiki*.

Religious activities at the Shinto shrine took place in terms of the rhythm of the religious year and an individual's lifespan. The earlier Japanese religious tradition seems to have observed the rhythm of the year, with spring festivals and fall festivals to mark the planting and harvesting of rice. Even today, the spring and fall festivals are still important celebrations in most city shrines. Of great importance, too, have been the purification ceremonies at midyear and New Year's, to wash away the physical and spiritual "pollutions" or "defilements" of the previous half-year.

Five traditional festivals (also revealing Chinese influence) have come to be celebrated throughout Japan: (1) first day of the first month, New Year's festival; (2) third day of the third month, the girls'

festival (or dolls' festival); (3) fifth day of the fifth month, boys' festival; (4) seventh day of the seventh month, star festival; (5) ninth day
of the ninth month, chrysanthemum festival. Although this formal
system of five festivals is a complex mixture of Chinese and Japanese
elements, the festivals have become inseparable from Japanese home
and village life.

Religious activities at the shrine also revolved around the events in
an individual's life. Traditionally, the newborn child was dedicated at
a shrine on his or her first trip out of the house. At other specific ages
a child visited the shrines again. Usually special youth groups helped
carry out the processions of festivals. In more recent times it has
become the custom to be married in a shrine. A visit to a shrine has
always been appropriate in any time of crisis. For example, a soldier
going off to war would pray for safekeeping at his local (guardian)
shrine where he had been carried as a baby. All such visits brought
individuals into contact with the *kami*, the sacred power that sustains
human life.

DISTINCTIVE CHARACTERISTICS OF SHINTO

The preceding discussion of the history and nature of Shinto shows
how native and foreign elements were blended together into one
great national tradition. At the same time the discussion shows that it
is a mistake to view Shinto simply as the indigenous religion of Japan
by falsely contrasting all other traditions as foreign. Nevertheless,
many secondary Western interpretations of Shinto have perpetuated
these misleading notions. Misconceptions arose partly because Western scholars tried too hard to compartmentalize Shinto and Buddhism
into separate religions. Also, the emphatically national character of
Shinto was overexaggerated by Western scholars who studied Shinto
during its nationalistic phase from about 1867 to 1945.[3] It is now time
for a reevaluation of Shinto in more balanced terms. Our treatment of
Shinto in this book has nothing to do with arguments for or against a
national religion; rather we simply want to place Shinto within the
historical context of Japanese religion.

Because Shinto has such a long history and has interacted so much
with other traditions, it is difficult to distinguish Shinto sharply from
all other Japanese traditions. But Tsunetsugu Muraoka, a Japanese
scholar widely respected for his critical interpretations of Shinto history, claims that there are three distinctive characteristics of Shinto.
First, there is Shinto's emphasis on the identity of the Japanese nation

with the imperial family and the descent of this family from ancestral *kami*. Second, Shinto practices a "realistic" affirmation of life and values in this world, accepting life and death, good and evil, as inevitable parts of the world we live in. Third, Shinto features a reverence for the "bright" and "pure" in all matter and thought, attempting to overcome physical pollution with rites of exorcism and bad thoughts with a "pure and bright heart." In Muraoka's interpretation of Shinto and its distinctive features, the first characteristic is political, the second is philosophical, and the third is ethical. The three are interrelated and interact to form the "intellectual strain" that defines Shinto throughout Japanese history.[4] This interpretation is valuable because it locates *distinctive* characteristics of Shinto without claiming that they are the *unique* property of Shinto. As we have seen in the chapters on persistent themes and prehistoric developments, and as we will see later, these distinctive features of Shinto play a large role in Japanese religious history.

A brief summary of the formative period of Shinto will help us focus on the most significant developments. Of greatest importance is the fact that shortly after Buddhism's appearance from China, Shinto arose and assumed its basic shape. Shinto did not create completely new forms, but organized the preexisting heritage into a distinctive tradition. This distinctive tradition included a mythology, pantheon, priesthood, liturgies, and shrines. In the *Engishiki*, an official writing of the tenth century, is recorded a system of over six thousand shrines named in connection with annual offerings from the court. Shinto organized this tradition in reaction to, and partly in imitation of, Buddhist and Chinese importations. Throughout Japanese history, Shinto has manifested a tension between the aim of preserving Japanese traditions and the aim of adopting foreign traditions. Next we will discuss the imported traditions; in Part II we will return to the problem of how Shinto adopted these imported traditions.

NOTES

1. For comments on the *Kojiki* and *Nihongi* by the eighteenth-century scholar Motoori Norinaga, see Chapter 14.
2. Sir George Sansom, *A History of Japan*, Vol. 1 (Stanford, Calif.: Stanford University Press, 1958), p. 68. For a detailed treatment of the department of religion established in A.D. 702, see Sir George Sansom, "Early Japanese Law and Administration,"

Transactions of the Asiatic Society of Japan, Second Series, Vol. 9 (1932), 67–109; Vol. 11 (1935), 117–49.

3. Daniel C. Holtom in his *The National Faith of Japan: A Study of Modern Shinto* (New York: Dutton, 1938; reprint ed., New York: Paragon Book Reprint Corp., 1965) described Shinto nationalism in the questionable terms of "tribal religion." See the more balanced discussion of this problem in Ryusaku Tsunoda et al., *Sources of Japanese Tradition* (New York: Columbia University Press, 1958), Chapter 2.

4. See Tsunetsugu Muraoka, "Characteristic Features of Japanese Shinto: Japan's Uniqueness in Oriental Thought," in his *Studies in Shinto Thought,* trans. Delmer M. Brown and James T. Araki (Tokyo: Ministry of Education, 1964), pp. 1–50.

SELECTED READINGS

Earhart, H. Byron. *Religion in the Japanese Experience: Sources and Interpretations.* Belmont, Calif.: Wadsworth, 1974. See Part Two for selected documents on Shinto, including excerpts from Holtom and the *Kojiki;* see also pp. 128–30 for excerpts from the *Manyoshu* and pp. 162–66 for the translation of a *norito.*

Holtom, Daniel C. *The National Faith of Japan: A Study of Modern Shinto.* New York: Dutton, 1938. Reprint ed., New York: Paragon Book Reprint Corp., 1965. An earlier study of Shinto, still valuable for its historical information.

Muraoka, Tsunetsugu. *Studies in Shinto Thought.* Translated by Delmer M. Brown and James T. Araki. Tokyo: Ministry of Education, 1964. Contains important scholarly essays on Shinto, such as "Characteristic Features of Japanese Shinto: Japan's Uniqueness in Oriental Thought."

Philippi, Donald L., trans. *Kojiki.* Tokyo: University of Tokyo Press, 1968. A recent translation of the earliest written chronicle in Japan, containing practices and mythology that entered Shinto.

Ueda, Kenji. "Shinto." In *Japanese Religion.* Edited by Ichiro Hori. Translated by Yoshiya Abe and David Reid. Tokyo: Kodansha International, 1972, pp. 29–45. A concise overview of the aspects and dynamics of Shinto.

CHAPTER 5

Early Japanese Buddhism: Indian Influence with Chinese Coloration

By the time Buddhism reached Japanese shores, it had been transformed in India as well as in the passage across the Asian continent. In this book we can treat only the place of Buddhism in Japanese religious history. On the one hand, Buddhism made a tremendous contribution to the religious scene in Japan; on the other hand, Buddhism was transformed by weight of the Japanese tradition. The twofold result is that while Japan became a Buddhist nation, Buddhism became a Japanese religion. In the initial or formative period, the Buddhist impact upon Japanese culture and religion was conspicuous. In the second or developmental period, the Japanese transformation of Buddhism became more conspicuous.

Within Buddhist history there have come to be two major divisions along the lines of geography, doctrine, and practice. In southern Asia, in countries such as Sri Lanka (Ceylon) and Burma, there continued the tradition of monastic Buddhism, which emphasized strict adherence to monastic rules or discipline, preservation of the scriptures of the Buddha, and doctrines that made salvation a long and difficult road for lay people. This division is often called Southern Buddhism or Theravada (School of the Elders, or Monks). To the north of India and spreading across China to Japan, there continued the form of Buddhism that placed less importance on monastic discipline and greater importance on later scriptures (such as the *Lotus Sutra*), aspiration to the status of a Buddha, and rebirth in a heavenly paradise. Especially because this Northern Buddhism insisted on the easy path to salvation for all people, it called itself Mahayana (the Large or Great Way) and gave Southern Buddhism the name Hinayana (the Small or Inferior Way). Although there are many similarities between these two divisions of Buddhism, and although the traditions of Southern Buddhism were brought to China and Japan, it was the Mahayana form that made the decisive impact in the Far East.

THE INTRODUCTION OF BUDDHISM
AS A FOREIGN RELIGION

Buddhism entered Japan by way of Korea in the middle of the sixth century. (Most authorities prefer the formal date of A.D. 552 or A.D. 538, even though Buddhist influence may have been present earlier.) The *Nihongi* records the first Japanese reference to Buddhism, when one of the Korean kings sent tribute to the Japanese emperor, including an image of Buddha and Chinese translations of Buddhist scriptures. The Korean king praised Buddhism as the religion of distant India whose doctrine surpasses even the understanding of the Chinese and whose value is without limit. Because it was the first foreign religion to enter Japan, Buddhism provoked a conflict with the preexisting religious tradition. This encounter with a more highly organized religion stimulated the adoption of the name "Shinto" and the formal organization of the preexisting tradition. However, the argument between Shinto and Buddhism was not carried on in terms of abstract doctrine. Instead, the immediate concern was the religious question of whether the nobility should worship the statue of Buddha. Korean immigrants (who had long practiced Buddhism) favored the adoption of Buddha-worship, whereas the Japanese families maintained a firm opposition.

The cult of Buddha underwent some temporary reversals, as in the case when a pestilence was attributed to the wrath of the national gods because the people were worshiping foreign deities. Eventually, however, Buddhism was accepted as one of the religions of the realm and was elevated from the status of a private cult celebrated in private homes to a state religion partly responsible for the welfare of the country. The success of Buddhism as a religious influence on the state is partly due to the fact that the state was in the initial stages of formation, and partly due to the profundity of Buddhist teaching and to the great appeal of its art, ritual, and magic. As a matter of fact, Buddhist magical formulas were brought to Japan together with formal scriptures, and the Buddha was even worshiped as a *kami*. Already in the early period Buddhism presented a religious pattern quite similar to Shinto, with its appeal to divine powers for immediate human needs. Shinto had its shrines, *kami*, ritual prayers *(norito)*, and priests. Buddhism likewise had its temples, Buddhas or Buddhist divinities, scriptures and rites, and priests. Buddhism had its own way of bringing men and women to religious fulfillment or sacred power, conceived in Buddhist terms.

BUDDHISM'S IMPACT ON THE COURT AND THE STATE

The story of early Buddhism in Japan is marked by the unsteady but gradual acceptance of Buddhism by the leading families, then by the imperial court, and finally by the state. Later diplomatic missions from Korea brought more Buddhist images and scriptures, but most important was the arrival of Buddhist priests. At this time the Japanese were just learning to manage the Chinese writing system, so it took a specially trained Buddhist priest to read and expound the Chinese translations of Buddhist scriptures. Also, the Buddhist priests began to serve the religious needs of the court and state.

In the private sphere, Buddhism came to be appropriated for every imaginable occasion, one of the most important of which was the Buddhist memorial service. Already by the first years of the eighth century a Buddhist priest and an empress set the Japanese precedent of having their bodies cremated, a Buddhist innovation. Memorial services were practiced by Buddhist priests as early as 616, when a Shinto shrine oracle "declared that Buddhist priests were the proper persons to perform funeral rites."[1] Eventually Buddhism developed a comprehensive ritual system for the dead: Buddhist priests recited scriptures for the repose of souls, accepted ashes of the dead for safekeeping in their temples, and performed memorial services at regular intervals. Wooden memorial tablets *(ihai)* were enshrined in the family Buddhist altar *(butsudan)*, and often cemeteries with memorial gravestones grew up around Buddhist temples.[2] In addition to memorial services, members of the court had scriptures read for such purposes as relieving sickness and easing childbirth.

While Buddhism was being accepted by the court in the private sphere, it was being accepted by the state in the public sphere. We can even say that Buddhism played a major role in shaping the Japanese state, so great was its influence. The contrast between the acceptance of Buddhism in China and in Japan is worth noting. China possessed such a rich tradition of literature, philosophy, religion, and government that Buddhism had to fight an uphill battle to be accepted. By contrast, Japan had no literature and philosophy to speak of, and her religion and government were only loosely formed. It is no wonder, then, that Buddhism and Chinese culture exerted such a great influence on Japanese culture and religion. The budding Japanese attempts to unify and centralize the country were greatly aided by the stimulus and even some of the models of highly organized Chinese culture. Buddhist priests in early Japan possessed two highly valued treasures: the religious heritage of Indian Buddhism in the garb of Chinese language and custom, and the cultural heritage of China, which included the models for a well-ordered kingdom. Buddhist priests also brought to Japan many technical skills associated with Buddhism, such as carpentry and architecture. For centuries to come, priests played a major role in the importation and implementation of Chinese models of government. A number of Buddhist priests, who went from Japan to China on court order, combined commercial, religious, and governmental functions.

Not only Buddhist priests, but also the emperors themselves were partly responsible for the importance of this religion in state affairs. Of the sixth-century emperor Yomei, it is said that he "believed in the Law of the Buddha and reverenced the Way of the Gods" (Shinto).[3] (Plurality of religions is the rule rather than the exception in Japanese history.) Prince Shotoku (573–621), second son of Emperor Yomei, is traditionally honored as the founder of Japanese Buddhism. He had built at Nara a large temple complex, Horyu-ji, housing many fine examples of Buddhist art. According to his traditional image, Prince Shotoku saw in Buddhism both a profound philosophy of life and a sound foundation for the state. Tradition also credits him with writing several commentaries on difficult Buddhist scriptures; furthermore, he is remembered for declaring Buddhism to be one of the pillars of the state (together with Confucianism) in his famous set of principles or "Constitution" of seventeen articles.[4] This marked the first major recognition of Buddhism's profound message and the outstanding precedent of Buddhism as the rationale for the state.

We must remember that during this formative period the Japanese tried to utilize Chinese models to organize Japanese society. Buddhism was one element in this program of organization and also was an active force in determining how the organizing activity took place. For example, as early as A.D. 624, Empress Suiko regulated the Buddhist priesthood, establishing the supervision of monks and nuns.

The Taiho Code of 702 included several sections dealing with reli- 43
*Early Japanese
Buddhism:
Indian
Influence with
Chinese
Coloration*
gious administration, including the organization of the Shinto bureau and the bureau of religious Taoism.[5] A special section of the
code dealt with the regulation of monks and nuns.[6] Buddhism had
become so flourishing that the state had to step in to curb excesses
and maintain religious uniformity. However, if the state tended
to control Buddhism, Buddhism in turn tended to unify and support
the state.

BUDDHISM AS A STATE RELIGION

During the Nara period (710–84, named after the capital city of Nara),
Buddhism became a state religion, for all practical purposes. Emperor
Shomu (reigned 724–49), one of the most devout emperors, contributed greatly to Buddhism's national status. The greatest symbol of
the unifying power of Buddhism was a magnificent cathedral built at
Nara in 728 on the order of Emperor Shomu. This was the famous
temple called Todai-ji (Todai temple), still a popular tourist attraction
due to the large Buddha statue enshrined there. In the Nara period,
there were six formal schools of Buddhism, and technically Todai-ji
was the headquarters of one of them—the Kegon school. However,
in actuality this central cathedral within the capital protected the emperor and the realm and unified Buddhism throughout the provinces.

In 741 Emperor Shomu ordered two "provincial temples" (kokubunji) to be built in every province: a monastery for monks and a
nunnery for nuns. The monks and nuns would recite Buddhist scriptures, thereby bringing divine protection and blessings to the whole
countryside. In Buddhism the copying and reciting of scriptures—
even thumbing through scriptures or chanting short phrases—has
always been considered a way to accumulate ethical merit or magical
power. The peculiarity in this case is that the nation at large was to be
the recipient of these benefits.

The building of provincial temples and the central cathedral of
Todai-ji, and the religious practices in these institutions, are good
examples of the way in which Buddhism interacted with Japanese
culture and religion: The national prestige of Buddhism grew, and at
the same time Buddhism began to unify the country and spread
among the people. The main temple controlling the provincial temples was Todai-ji, which not only was a geographical and administrative center, but served as a religious focus for the nation as a whole. A
large statue of the Sun Buddha Lochana was erected within Todai-ji.

The funds for the statue are said to have been raised by popular subscription; thus the country was united symbolically by the erection of this statue. Just as Buddhism provided a main national temple and provincial temples to recite scriptures and prayers for the benefit of the state and its people, individuals contributed to the establishment of Buddhism as a kind of national religion.

One might say that the people were able to find an even greater sense of religious and national unity in Buddhism than in Shinto, for in the Nara period the people were not directly related to the emperor. Moreover, Shinto rituals involving the imperial family, although national in significance, allowed little possibility for any sense of participation by the common people. Buddhism had been interacting with Shinto from the time it arrived in Japan (as seen in the previously mentioned controversy over whether to worship the Buddha as a foreign *kami*); from this point on, the mutual influence between Buddhism and Shinto becomes more complex, but Buddhism tends to dominate the scene.

Most scholars feel that by the Nara period Buddhism had overshadowed Shinto as an organized religion. In fact, Shinto tended to borrow on the glory of Buddhism. The continuing interaction between the two traditions is illustrated by two interesting developments at Todai-ji. Worship of the large Buddhist statue was facilitated by invoking the presence of a divinity called Hachiman, who became a tutelary deity of Todai-ji. The origin of Hachiman may be Chinese or Buddhist or both, but by this time Hachiman was considered a Shinto deity or *kami*. However, Hachiman was also called *bosatsu*. *Bosatsu* is the Japanese version of the Buddhist term *bodhisattva* (in Sanskrit), which means here a Buddhist divinity. The word *bodhisattva* literally means "enlightenment-being" and can even refer to a living person or "saint" who has attained a high level of spiritual insight. Hachiman enjoyed a rich history in later Japan but always incorporated both Shinto and Buddhist features.

Also we may note that Lochana, the large statue in Todai-ji, was a form of the so-called Sun Buddha (Dainichi or Birushana in Japanese, Vairocana in Sanskrit). According to one tradition, messengers had to be sent to Ise to gain the approval of the Sun Goddess Amaterasu of Shinto for the erection of this statue. The answer of the oracle seemed to indicate that the Sun Buddha was identical to the Sun Goddess. The tradition of this oracle may not date back to the eighth century, but in later times the two were closely associated, just as so many Buddhist divinities and Shinto *kami* came to be considered counterparts. Several centuries later, in all Japan we find popular conceptions that blended together a local spirit or *kami*, a formal member of the Shinto pantheon, and a Buddhist divinity into one and the same object of worship. The close relationship of Hachiman and Amaterasu to Todai-ji shows how thoroughly Buddhism and Shinto became intertwined.

45
*Early Japanese
Buddhism:
Indian
Influence with
Chinese
Coloration*

Our overall impression of Buddhism up through the Nara period is that it had become firmly entrenched in the hearts of the nobility and the bureaucracy of the state. On the other hand, the popular acceptance of Buddhism was not nearly so widespread. The attempt to propagate Buddhism to the masses was carried out by only a few devoted priests. Gyogi, the most famous of them, not only preached to the people, but also promoted Buddhism through charitable projects such as founding hospitals. He was granted the posthumous title of *bosatsu (bodhisattva)*, equivalent to "saint."

The inclusion of "The Law Concerning Monks and Nuns" in the Taiho Code of 702 was an admission that Buddhist monks and nuns were becoming more numerous and that the masses were beginning to accept Buddhism. It also reflected the state's effort to control the activities of clerics trying to spread Buddhism. We might say that Buddhism already was considered a state religion of Japan and later, with increasing popularity, became a national religion of Japan. Buddhism tended to dominate the whole religious scene but actually paralleled Shinto rather than superseded it.

THE SIX PHILOSOPHICAL SCHOOLS OF NARA BUDDHISM

The general picture of Nara Buddhism suggests a religion of the aristocracy and monks, largely confined to the court and monasteries. During this period numerous sumptuous temples were founded, many of which can still be seen at Nara. Although these wooden structures have been frequently damaged by fires, they are accurately rebuilt and house some of the oldest treasures of Japan, including items from ancient China and beyond. In their flourishing period these temples were overflowing with scholar-monks who frequently catered to the religious needs of the court and state but were primarily committed to scholarship on Buddhist scriptures and doctrines.

In the Nara period the state recognized six divisions within Buddhism. These were more of the nature of philosophical schools than full-fledged religious sects. The six schools transmitted the philosophical heritage of Indian Buddhism in the vessels of Chinese translations; there was no original Japanese contribution at this point. Although these schools are of the greatest importance for tracing Buddhist philosophy from India to Japan, they are of lesser consequence for understanding Japanese religion. Therefore, we will touch on them but briefly in order to illustrate the diversity of the religious heritage in Japan. The six schools and their traditional dates of entry into Japan are Jojitsu (625), Sanron (625), Hosso (654), Kusha (658), Kegon (736), Ritsu (738). Each school focused on one or more of the classic Buddhist scriptures (in Chinese translation), expounding and defining the viewpoint of its distinctive scripture.

According to one Japanese scholar, the Jojitsu and Kusha schools were of minor importance since they did not "have a significant separate existence."[7] The Sanron school (which we will discuss in detail) continued one of the most glorious philosophical streams of Buddhism, including the Madhyamika philosophy of Nagarjuna. The Hosso schools perpetuated the "consciousness-only" philosophy, which played a great role in Chinese Buddhism. The Kegon school has been of great intellectual influence on Japanese Buddhism, as its affiliation with Todai-ji might suggest. The Ritsu school concerned itself with Buddhism's monastic discipline. ("Discipline" is *vinaya* in Sanskrit, *ritsu* in Japanese.) The Ritsu school was important for establishing the rules and actual altars for ordination (one of which was established before the great Buddha at Todai-ji), but in general Japanese Buddhism has not conformed to all the Indian prescriptions of discipline.

These philosophical schools were not mutually exclusive in Japan even in the beginning; priests often studied the doctrines of several of them. A number of the famous old temples, especially those at Nara, are still counted as belonging to one of the six schools, but for the most part the schools live on today as indirect intellectual influences within the later sects of Japanese Buddhism. The schools, although never popular in scope, represent the philosophical resource for Japanese Buddhism and much Japanese thought.

Buddhist philosophy was highly developed in India, and Chinese Buddhists further refined this tradition before passing it on to Japan, where once again some of the best minds were attracted to the subtlety and complexity of Buddhist teachings. Although the majority of Buddhists in any country are more involved in devotional practices and ritual activities, there has always been a small group of priests (usually monks) and more intellectually inclined believers who have

47
*Early Japanese
Buddhism:
Indian
Influence with
Chinese
Coloration*

There is almost no begging for religious purposes in Japan. This young Buddhist priest, apparently as part of his religious training, recites a Buddhist scripture and accepts donations at the gate of the famous Asakusa Kannon temple in Tokyo. (1979)

appreciated the grandeur of Buddhist philosophy. Indeed, the features of Buddhist thought that attracted great minds several thousand years ago are the same features that make it appealing today for many Asian and Western people: Buddhist philosophy possesses a comprehensive world-view combining a profound understanding of the complexity of human existence with a detailed interpretation of the nature of the universe. Such philosophical systems are too complex and elaborate to be summed up quickly, but a brief look at one of the foremost Buddhist schools of philosophy, Sanron, will give some indication of the nature of these systems.

THE SANRON SCHOOL

The Sanron school took its name from the Chinese school San-lun, which in turn was a Chinese elaboration of the Indian school of thought Madhyamika associated with the Indian Buddhist named Nagarjuna. The Buddha discovered the truth of an enlightenment that goes beyond human suffering, but later Buddhists sought a more complete interpretation of the nature of human existence and enlightenment *(nirvana)*. On the question of the nature of human existence, there were two contrary tendencies: One was to view human existence as having material reality (a materialistic argument); the other was to view human existence not as material reality but as a kind of reflection of an ideal (an idealistic argument). The Sanron school boldly rejected both materialistic and idealistic arguments, setting up a fourfold rejection of all known arguments about the existence and nonexistence of life and all phenomena. The Sanron school denied all four of the following arguments about life and phenomena: (1) Their character is (permanent) existence. (2) Their character is nonexistence. (3) Their character is a combination of existence and nonexistence. (4) Their character is neither existence nor nonexistence. Sanron rejected all known arguments about life and existence based on ordinary human reason. Sanron scholars argued that it is much better to rely on the truth of enlightenment that goes beyond mere human reasoning.

At first reading, Sanron's argument may appear to be a play on words. That this argument is quite serious, however, is shown by its treatment of another key problem in Buddhism—the nature of enlightenment *(nirvana)*. From the earliest days of Buddhism, there was difficulty in communicating the nature of *nirvana,* which seemed to be so "absolute," in contrast to the impermanence of human life. There were some positive analogies for describing *nirvana,* such as bliss and security, but many descriptions were negative, such as destruction of desire or "to be extinguished" (as fire is extinguished or "goes out"). Even in the lifetime of the Buddha, as well as today, some critics of Buddhism have called the notion of *nirvana* "nihilistic," for not only was *nirvana* expressed in negative terms, but the goal of *nirvana* was judged to be an "escapist" withdrawal from everyday life to an inexpressible state. Buddhist philosophers tended to be caught on the horns of a dilemma: If they taught that the conventional expressions of life and phenomena in this world were ultimately true, they would be denying the basic Buddhist truth of enlightenment. If they taught that conventional life experiences were simply illusions, then they would be implying a nihilistic destruction of phenomena when *nirvana* was attained.

Sanron arrived at a solution of the dilemma similar to the solution for the problem of explaining worldly phenomena and human existence. Sanron rejected the view of *nirvana* as at the same time a form of both absolute reality (that is, absolute form or being) and nihilism (that is, as a negative kind of nonexistence). Sanron maintained this position by stating that any attempt to grasp *nirvana* as a positive or negative "thing" was a limited viewpoint and must be rejected, because both *nirvana* and conventional phenomena are "empty" of any self-substantiating quality. This means that the only positive statement that can be made about *nirvana* is that it is "empty" of all attributes: *Nirvana* is devoid of particular attributes, so it is characterized as "emptiness."

One of the major concluding points of this brilliant philosophy is that, when viewed from the realization of *nirvana* (enlightenment), both *nirvana* and human life (and related phenomena) in this world are "empty." This enabled Sanron to avoid the one-sided mistakes of materialism and idealism for the questions of both existence and *nirvana*. This is a radical development of the notion that the truth of enlightenment goes beyond any attempt at human reasoning. One of the remarkable features of the argument is its unflinching honesty in denying the absoluteness of any proposition about reality, including its own.

These problems are similar to the questions of the nature of human existence and the nature of the universe that have interested philosophers in all traditions, not only in ancient times but today as well. Because there was no highly developed Japanese philosophical system when these Buddhist schools entered Japan, it is not surprising that they were quickly accepted and continued to attract great minds. Later, as Buddhism assimilated Japanese culture and developed along Japanese lines, these abstract arguments were related to native notions (such as the reverence for nature).

THE DECLINE OF NARA BUDDHISM

If Nara Buddhism became famous for its profound philosophy and glorious temples, it became infamous for its increasing decadence and corruption. Japan is no exception to the rule that money and power tend to corrupt. The Nara temples grew in prestige and wealth by attracting bequests from the nobility and favoritism from the state. In turn, the prestige and wealth of the temples attracted politically ambitious men to the priesthood. In a short time the temples had become so wealthy and their priests so powerful that their interference in the politics of the capital could not be tolerated. This condition seems to have been a primary factor in a decision to move the capital from Nara to Kyoto in the transitional period from 784 to 794. (Before the Nara period, it was the normal custom to move the capital at the death of every emperor, supposedly on the belief that the emperor's death defiled the capital.) This move freed the court from the intrigues of the Nara temples, which were left behind in the former capital; the move also signaled the need for a religious renewal, a need that was met by the new Buddhist sects of Tendai and Shingon, which we will discuss in Chapter 9.

NOTES

1. Sir Charles Eliot, *Japanese Buddhism* (London: Edward Arnold, 1935; reprint ed., London: Routledge & Kegan Paul, 1959), p. 203.
2. For funeral rites, see Arthur Hyde Lay, "Japanese Funeral Rites," *Transactions of the Asiatic Society of Japan*, Vol. 19 (1891), 507–44. An excerpt from this work is included in H. Byron Earhart, *Religion in the Japanese Experience: Sources and Interpretations* (Belmont, Calif.: Wadsworth, 1974), pp. 61–64.
3. *Nihongi: Chronicles of Japan from the Earliest Times to A.D. 697*, trans. W. G. Aston, *Transactions of the Japan Society*, Supplement 1, Vol. 2 (London, 1896; subsequently reprinted separately), p. 106.
4. See ibid., pp. 128–33, for the text of this "Constitution." An excerpt of this work is included in Earhart, *Religion in the Japanese Experience*, pp. 202–03.
5. The bureau of religious Taoism, Onmyodo, is the Japanese version of the Chinese bureau of *yin* and *yang*.
6. See Sansom, "Early Japanese Law and Administration," *Transactions of the Asiatic Society of Japan*, Second Series, Vol. 11 (1935), 127–34, for a translation of "The Law Concerning Monks and Nuns."
7. Shinsho Hanayama, "Buddhism in Japan," in *The Path of the Buddha*, ed. Kenneth W. Morgan (New York: Ronald Press, 1956), p. 315. A brief treatment of the six schools will be found in any general work such as Hanayama or Eliot, *Japanese Buddhism*.

SELECTED READINGS

Earhart, H. Byron. *Religion in the Japanese Experience: Sources and Interpretations*. Belmont, Calif.: Wadsworth, 1974. See Part Three for selected documents on Japanese Buddhism, including excerpts from Lay.

Kitagawa, Joseph M. "The Buddhist Transformation in Japan." *History of Religions*, Vol. 4, No. 2 (Winter 1965), 319–36. Shows how Buddhism was transformed in Japan, becoming related to both national polity and folk piety.

Kiyota, Minoru. "Presuppositions to the Understanding of Japanese Buddhist Thought." *Monumenta Nipponica*, Vol. 22, Nos. 3–4 (1967), 251–59. A technical analysis of Japanese Buddhism in relation to Mahayana philosophy.

Matsunaga, Daigan, and Matsunaga, Alicia. *Foundation of Japanese Buddhism*. 2 vols. Los Angeles: Buddhist Books International, 1974. A detailed survey of the history and doctrine of Japanese Buddhist sects.

Robinson, Richard H., and Johnson, Willard L. *The Buddhist Religion: A Historical Introduction*. 2d ed. Belmont, Calif.: Wadsworth, 1977. A brief survey of Buddhism, from its Indian beginnings to its later expansion; includes a bibliography.

Tamaru, Noriyoshi. "Buddhism." In *Japanese Religion*. Edited by Ichiro Hori. Translated by Yoshiya Abe and David Reid. Tokyo: Kodansha International, 1972, pp. 47–69. A concise overview of the origin and historical development of Japanese Buddhism.

CHAPTER 6

Confucianism and Religious Taoism: Chinese Importations

Confucianism and Taoism developed in China out of a common background of thought and practice and therefore share many features, although they emphasize different aspects of the Chinese heritage. Both traditions were based on early Chinese cosmological notions, such as the "way" *(Tao)* of the universe. Confucianism emphasized the "way" of social action and political order; Taoism emphasized the "way" of mystical practice and natural order. In the lives of the Chinese people, such distinctions were not crucial because most men and women participated in customs that were a blend of Taoist and Confucian (as well as Buddhist) elements. It is not known exactly when Confucianism and Taoism entered Japan, but it is most likely that they arrived with Buddhism by the sixth century A.D. along with a flood of other elements of Chinese culture.

In Japan, neither Confucianism nor Taoism constitutes a formal, organized religion (such as Shinto and Buddhism). Nevertheless, both traditions made important contributions to the life of the people and to the other religious traditions. Confucianism played an explicit role in the religious and ethical foundation of the government and influenced general conceptions of social relations. Religious Taoism started out as a government bureau and ended up as an implicit but pervasive influence on popular beliefs.

CONFUCIANISM: EXPLICIT CHINESE INFLUENCE ON STATE AND SOCIETY

It is not surprising that Confucianism had a great impact in early Japan. Confucianism was the guiding light of the entering Chinese culture, which the Japanese held in the highest esteem. The early attempt to organize the Japanese nation along Chinese lines is recorded in the first great era or name-period of Japanese history, the Taika ("Great Change") period of 645 to 710. By this time, Confucianism was far removed from the person Confucius, having developed into a political philosophy that incorporated various elements and tended to dominate Chinese civilization. In general, Confucianism as a political philosophy was accepted explicitly and implicitly by the Japanese, who were borrowing Chinese models of government.

The great Prince Shotoku (573–621) is credited with recognizing the true principles of Confucianism in his "Constitution" of seventeen articles. Buddhist influence is found in this document, but its main rationale is Confucian political and ethical thought. Indeed, the opening statement of the first clause reads: "Harmony is to be valued," a direct borrowing from the *Analects* (the collection of Confucius's teachings). The Japanese, seeking an effective means to unify their country, found a powerful rationale in the Confucian notion of social harmony: The ruler rules justly; the ministers administer honestly; and, most important, the people are united in their loyalty to the emperor. The Constitution attributed to Shotoku, as well as other adaptations of Chinese bureaucracies and codes, supported the Japanese emperor as a true Son of Heaven—the Chinese notion of a heavenly ordained ruler. This idea supported the theory of the divine character of the Japanese emperor as much as, or more than, the native tradition of his descent from the Sun Goddess Amaterasu. However, the two countries differed on one important point. In China, Heaven appointed the ruler by bestowing a "heavenly mandate"; Heaven could withdraw the mandate from a corrupt dynasty in order to give it to a new dynasty. In Japan, the imperial line was permanently founded as the continuation of the heavenly gods, and it could never be broken.

Although Confucianism was not a separate religion, it was an integral part of the Japanese tradition. The Confucian character permeated the structure of government and official codes (such as the Taiho Code of 702). Even the Confucian precedent of civil service examinations was followed. Confucianism was instilled in the minds of the learned class by means of an educational system that emphasized study of the Chinese classics. It became more directly related to government policy when it reentered Japanese history as Neo-Confucianism about the sixteenth century (this development will be discussed in Chapter 14).

Confucianism also played a crucial role in the formation of social attitudes and the reinforcement of social institutions. The Confucianism transmitted to Japan emphasized a hierarchically arranged class society and compliance to this order. The "harmony" that the Confucian rationale praised was peaceful cooperation between benevolent rulers and obedient people. According to the Confucian model, just as Earth is subordinate to Heaven, so the ruled are subordinate to the ruler. There is a cosmic order that sets the pattern for the social order. Increasingly, Confucianism provided the main ethical model for social action, and the model was interpreted as prescribing loyalty to specific social groups.

One of the most important social virtues adopted from Confucianism was filial piety. In this case, a borrowed ethical model was used to reinforce and expand preexisting Japanese notions about the family. Since prehistoric times, the Japanese had revered the dead, and they openly accepted the Confucian notion of filial piety to idealize and elaborate the practice. (At the same time, they utilized Buddhist memorial rites to sanctify the practice.) Extended families had been important before the arrival of Confucianism, but later most social groups tended to internalize the rationale of filial piety and loyalty. Families drew much of their strength from the fact that they participated as economic units in activities such as farming, but they came to *understand* their unity through Confucian notions. Later, the warrior came to see his relationship to his lord as a combination of duty and privilege defined by absolute loyalty. One can see this hierarchical authority used as a rationale for more recent policies and practices. For example, in the past century of rapid modernization, the government has taken the initiative in telling the people what they must do, and the people usually have complied.

Both Prince Shotoku's "Constitution" of the seventh century and Emperor Meiji's Constitution of the late nineteenth century were handed down on the initiative of the ruler. In Anglo-Saxon history, there are many instances of the people *demanding* their rights from the monarch. In Japan, the people have tended to wait for the imperial rescript or the military ruler's command. Especially during the modernization and military campaigns of the past century, there was an explicit identity of a man's filial piety to his father, his absolute loyalty to the emperor, and his supreme sacrifice for his country. Confucianism was not responsible for the creation of these social attitudes and institutions; rather, such facts demonstrate how well suited Confucianism was to conditions in Japan.

By the Tokugawa and Meiji periods, beginning in the seventeenth century and extending into the twentieth, the notion of filial piety became synonymous with being a good child and a good Japanese citizen. Confucian ideas became closely tied to the process of growing up and becoming a member of society. This can be illustrated roughly by a comparison of recent child-rearing techniques in the West and in Japan. In the West, children are encouraged to become independent and "stand on their own two feet." In Japan, children are brought up to be more dependent on and loyal to the family. In this manner the ideals of Confucianism gradually were woven into the fabric of Japanese society.

RELIGIOUS TAOISM: IMPLICIT CHINESE INFLUENCE ON BELIEFS AND RITUALS

The complexity of Taoism led Chinese scholars to distinguish between the "philosophical Taoism" (Tao-chia) of the mystics and the "religious Taoism" (Tao-chiao) of popular rituals. This distinction gives the impression that the two strands of Taoism were separate entities. In fact they were intimately interrelated from the beginning of the Taoist tradition. Nevertheless, in the absence of more appropriate terminology Western scholars have continued to use these terms.

"Philosophical Taoism" was present in Japan in the form of texts such as the famous *Tao Te Ching* and ongoing intellectual concerns, but it was not a major tradition. "Religious Taoism" refers to the popular aspects of the Taoist movement in China; it incorporated a wide array of religious expressions into one system. In China, popular practitioners of religious Taoism borrowed from several earlier cosmological theories (such as *yin-yang*), continued the Taoist quest for long life, worshiped a large pantheon, practiced alchemy, carried out divination and magic, and generally associated themselves with things occult. In the context of Japanese religious history, the term "religious Taoism" takes on a somewhat broader meaning.

In Japan, religious Taoism is known technically as *Dokyo,* which is the Japanese pronunciation for the Chinese term *Tao-chiao.* This phrase means literally the "teaching of the Tao or way" (the "way" of the universe). But in Japanese religious history the term "religious

Taoism" is usually understood to include Onmyodo (the "way" of *yin-yang*), as well as many popular practices.

Religious Taoism entered Japan by several channels. The books of religious Taoism were brought in at an early date. The practices of religious Taoism were adopted at the court, and in the Taiho Code of 702 a bureau of religious Taoism was organized. In addition, many of the popular divinities and cults of religious Taoism were accepted in early Japan. In an elusive fashion, the love of nature in religious Taoism influenced Japanese arts, especially landscape painting. We cannot trace the complicated histories of these various elements, but a look at some important features of religious Taoism in Japan will indicate its significance in Japanese religious history.

The most conspicuous Japanese example of religious Taoism is the governmental bureau of religious Taoism, Onmyoryo, which existed as early as 675 and was officially organized by the Taiho Code. Sir George Sansom has provided a translation of the original legislation defining the Onmyoryo or "Bureau of Divination."[1] Its responsibility was to regulate divination, astrology, and the calendar. The significance of unusual natural phenomena, for example, was interpreted by the bureau.

To understand the Onmyoryo we have to understand the complex of Chinese thought on which it was based. The word *onmyo* is simply the Japanese pronunciation for the Chinese term *yin-yang*, which refers to two complementary forces that must balance each other if there is to be harmony in the universe. *Yin* is the passive, feminine force; it is associated with darkness, cold, and even numbers. *Yang* is the active, masculine force associated with brightness, heat, and odd numbers. The interaction of *yin* and *yang* produces matter, which consists of five elements—wood, fire, earth, metal, and water. (Originally in China the theory of *yin-yang* and the theory of five elements were unrelated concepts. Before entering Japan, the theories became inseparably related in a unified cosmology.) The forces of *yin* and *yang* interact not only in space, but also in time. In short, religious Taoism presupposes a living universe composed of opposing or complementary forces. Ideally these forces can be harmonized. If they get out of balance, the result is disharmony and catastrophe.

The role of the bureau of divination was to make sure the order of government and society conformed to the cosmic order. Therefore it was only natural that Onmyoryo would regulate the calendar so that human time would correspond to cosmic time. The introduction of the Chinese calendar was of great importance to Japanese religious history, for it seems that earlier the Japanese had only a seasonal

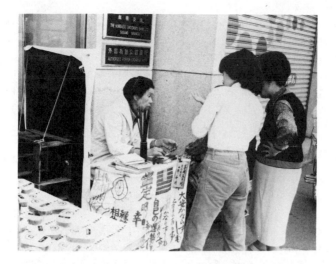

Fortunetelling of all kinds is popular in Japan. This woman has set up her portable stand in front of a closed bank (whose sign is above her head). On her tablecloth are printed examples of her means of telling fortunes: a Chinese hexagram (two sets of three black lines), plus an ear lobe, and a hand. (Tokyo, 1979)

calendar. The Chinese calendar adopted and modified in folk religion, Shinto, and Buddhism—carried with it the cosmological theories and beliefs of religious Taoism.[2]

One way in which religious Taoism filtered down to the masses was through popular diviners. Gradually the official members of the Onmyoryo gave way to popular diviners who served various religious needs. They continued to spread the popular beliefs of religious Taoism, further stimulating the widespread demand for diviners. These popular practitioners of religious Taoism transmitted their beliefs and practices to the wandering semiascetics of "folk Buddhism."

During the Heian period (794–1185), religious Taoism influenced Shinto and Buddhism in the guise of formulas, charms, and cosmological theories. Eventually the various divinities of religious Taoism became accepted within both Shinto and Buddhism, almost losing their Taoist identity. Many of the most typical Japanese beliefs about lucky days and lucky directions came from religious Taoism. In medieval novels the movements of the characters ever and again were determined by the stars and the "unlucky directions." Taoist festivals, legends, and cults became woven into the fabric of Japanese life. Taoist mountain wizards of Chinese origin (*hsien* in Chinese, *sen* or *sennin* in Japanese) were thought to dwell in the Japanese mountains. Another example of Taoist influence is the cult and belief called

Koshin. This cult is typical of Japanese village associations organized to worship specific divinities at regular intervals. From the Heian period onward, the beliefs of religious Taoism became a dominant factor in everyday life. Of course, not many people were aware of the Chinese origin of religious Taoism or completely understood the intricacies of this cosmic system. Nevertheless, it greatly affected their lives.

These two Chinese importations—Confucianism (later Neo-Confucianism) and religious Taoism—were transformed into Japanese traditions. The role of Confucianism is more easily recognized, since it functioned more explicitly as an official philosophy of the learned classes and the state. For example, Confucianism became so thoroughly Japanized that it was used as a propaganda tool for governing both Korea and Manchuria up to 1945. By contrast, Taoism's influence was indirect or implicit and more difficult to recognize.

NOTES

1. See Sir George Sansom, "Early Japanese Law and Administration," *Transactions of the Asiatic Society of Japan,* Second Series, Vol. 9 (1932), 81.
2. For a general picture of the Japanese calendar, see Ernest Clement, "Calendar (Japanese)," *Encyclopaedia of Religion and Ethics,* Vol. 3, ed. James Hastings (Edinburgh: T. and T. Clark, 1908–26), pp. 114–17; and William Hugh Erskine, *Japanese Festival and Calendar Lore* (Tokyo: Kyo Bun Kwan, 1933).

SELECTED READINGS

de Bary, William Theodore, et al. *Sources of Chinese Tradition.* New York: Columbia University Press, 1960. A convenient sourcebook for the Chinese background of Japanese culture.

Earhart, H. Byron. *Religion in the Japanese Experience: Sources and Interpretations.* Belmont, Calif.: Wadsworth, 1974. See Part Four for selected documents on Confucianism, including excerpts from Smith, and Part Five for selected documents on religious Taoism, including excerpts from Saunders.

Saunders, E. Dale. "Koshin: An Example of Taoist Ideas in Japan." In *Proceedings of the IXth International Congress for the History of Reli-*

gions. Tokyo: Maruzen, 1960, pp. 423–32. Analyzes the history of Koshin and its dynamics as a Taoist cult.

Smith, Warren W., Jr. *Confucianism in Modern Japan: A Study of Conservatism in Japanese Intellectual History.* 2d ed. Tokyo: Hokuseido Press, 1973. Treats Confucianism's cultural impact in Japan from 1600 through postwar times.

Tsunoda, Ryusaku, et al. *Sources of Japanese Tradition.* New York: Columbia University Press, 1958. See Chapter 4 for the introduction of Chinese thought and institutions into Japan.

CHAPTER 7

Folk Religion: Religiosity Outside Organized Religion

Every literate culture has a "little tradition" as well as a "great tradition."[1] The "great tradition" within a culture such as Japan's is the written tradition formally recorded and consciously used by major institutions such as the state and organized religion. The "little tradition" is the unwritten sets of customs transmitted orally within contexts such as family, village, and occupation. Organized religion (Shinto, Buddhism, Taoism, and Confucianism) is conspicuous because of its writings, priests, liturgies, shrines, and temples. In Japan, however, much religion is practiced informally. Because of its informal character, folk religion does not lend itself to simple identification and historical tracing; nevertheless, this "little tradition" is an important part of religious experience, particularly in the premodern period.

ASPECTS OF JAPANESE FOLK RELIGION

In Japan there are at least three aspects of folk religion: (1) indigenous folk religion, (2) popular religion, and (3) local customs. Indigenous folk religion is the sum of all the unorganized forms of ancient Japanese religion. These forms often became overlaid with the structures of organized religion, but they existed prior to the organized tradition. One might say that indigenous folk religion "filtered up" into Shinto and Buddhism. An example of indigenous folk religion is the rituals associated with the growing of rice, especially rice-transplanting celebrations, which were never fully incorporated into organized religion.

Popular religion consists of unofficial expressions of organized religion among lay people. Although a religion like Buddhism has its own doctrinal, ritual, and ecclesiastical orthodoxy, it undergoes considerable reformulation as it is accepted by the masses. From a scholarly or ecclesiastical viewpoint, popular Buddhism may diverge from orthodox formulas, but the aim of popular religion is to provide direct access to spiritual resources in the language and style of the people. Popular religion generally can be described as the result of organized religion filtering down to the people. An example of popular religion is the neighborhood club *(ko)* that meets once a month to venerate a divinity, often a Buddhist divinity. Such a practice may borrow elements from Buddhism, but they are expressed and handed down by ordinary men and women in their own homes.

Local customs are peculiar regional and local practices that usually combine features of indigenous folk religion and popular religion. From ancient times, religious practices were heavily influenced by the dominant legends, customs, and activities of the surrounding region. Even Shinto and Buddhism lack the centralized uniformity found in Roman Catholicism and Protestant denominations, allowing Shinto in particular to develop distinctive local practices. This aspect of folk religion contributes much local color to Japanese religion. An example of such a local usage is the preservation of a mythical tale or legend associated only with one region (such as the visit of a specific *kami* to an area in ancient times). The tale may be memorialized in a local shrine or temple and often is dramatized in an annual village festival. Sometimes the occasion for a local custom is a universal religious event, such as the "Buddhist" festival of the dead, *bon,* but there are local variations on the manner of celebration, such as special village gatherings and specially prepared foods.

Indigenous folk religion, popular religion, and local customs cannot be sharply separated from one another, for they form the living fabric of the everyday practice of religion in traditional Japan. For example, folk tales can be found in each as a kind of informal scripture that unifies and preserves religion. It would also be impossible to separate the three folk elements from organized religion, since there is a great deal of mutual influence between the folk and organized traditions. In fact, folk religion is so important that one scholar has stated that "in Japan the little tradition is the great tradition."[2] In premodern times, folk religion was the main channel of expression for religious beliefs and practices, particularly in the countryside and in farm villages.

In more recent times folk religious beliefs and activities have become severely abbreviated because of economic and social changes. The expansion of cities and commerce in the late medieval period and the increasing dominance of an urban-industrial way of life after 1868 greatly disturbed life in rural villages. These changes drew people from the countryside to the city and generally shifted attention from the agricultural lifestyle of traditional Japan to the economic activities of the cities. Thus our description of folk religion refers generally to traditional patterns that were prominent until the late nineteenth century.

FOLK RELIGION IN FAMILY, VILLAGE, AND OCCUPATION

Just as there is no single religion called "Japanese religion," so is there no simple entity called "Japanese folk religion." Rather, folk religion exists informally in family, village, and occupation. Each setting, in its own way, participates in the "little tradition" and serves to transmit it to the next generation, both by word of mouth and by direct example.

The family is an important religious institution for both organized and folk practices. The traditional home is a center of Buddhist worship by virtue of the presence of the *butsudan* (Buddhist altar for the ancestors); it is also a center of Shinto worship by virtue of the presence of the *kamidana* ("god-shelf"). But the family and home do not gain their religious significance merely by borrowing from organized religion; rather they seem to have a religious character that stands apart from organized religion. In the words of one scholar, "Certain types of psychological security found in a relationship to a personal God in the West are found only in relation to the actual family in Japan."[3] Traditional Japanese identified membership in the family with a sense of belonging in the world. The family as a religious institution has at least three levels: (1) the ancestors, semidivine figures who are memorialized and grant blessings; (2) the living, who perform memorial rites and receive blessings; and (3) the unborn, who are the link between the ancestors and living, and the future. Although the religious importance of the family was never fully spelled out by organized religion, it was communicated by and perpetuated in the loose set of beliefs and customs known as folk religion.

A New Year's decoration in the center of the grill of a Tokyo taxi. After a week or so, the decorations are removed. (New Year's week, 1980)

Religious activities centering in the home had their own rhythmic unity. Traditionally most families practiced memorial rites for the family dead, especially on the monthly and annual anniversaries of the death of immediate family ancestors. Daily offerings such as food from the family table might be placed in front of the *butsudan* or, occasionally, on the *kamidana*. In addition, there were important annual celebrations at the home, such as New Year's. Without any priestly help, the family would consecrate the house for New Year's. Family members would place a pine branch on the gate or erect a pine tree in the yard. In the entryway a special New Year's decoration of cooked rice was customary. In the countryside there were distinctive New Year's foods, such as the specially prepared New Year's soup and the pounded glutinous rice. In olden times it was the custom to purify the house at the end of the year by a thorough cleaning, including the use of salt and sacred water; in many locales the fire in the hearth was extinguished and a new fire was obtained from a nearby temple or shrine. The celebration of New Year's is only one example of the family's informal religious heritage.

The village is a larger setting in which folk religion is expressed and handed down. People living in a village or sometimes in a larger region share a special myth or legend that has been preserved and passed down and is celebrated by one or more groups, often in connection with distinctive customs. One legend may serve as an illustration of this aspect of folk religion. In one locale of northern Japan there is a legend that in ancient times the people were bothered by a poisonous insect. Eventually, the insect was driven away by the performance of a ritual in which a mock insect made of straw was burned. According to one version, an imperial prince first began the ritual; in another version, the ritual was revealed to the daughter of a Shinto priest. (In folk religion there is not always one "true" version, as there tends to be in a written scripture.) Every year, the ritual is performed again; but before the mock insect is burned, sections of straw rope around the mock insect are thrown among the youth of the village, who try to grab a piece. The pieces of rope are said to represent the "bones" of the insect. They are taken home by the youths, who hang them under the eaves of their houses. Not only is the ritual said to drive away insects, but the rope sections are believed to prevent fires in the homes where they are displayed.

This is but one example of many local beliefs and practices that endure and touch people's lives with very little help from organized religion. Almost every village in every district makes claim to some more or less distinctive legend and its celebration. The legend may connect a mythological figure to the locale and an annual festival, or it may have to do with the economic life of the region. Often special crafts and distinctive foods are associated with such legends.

Folk beliefs and practices were also closely tied to occupations. Fishermen with small wooden boats had special rites to drive the spirit of the trees out of a newly built boat, at the same time invoking a spirit of the sea. A small altar was often placed by the mast of the boat, and offerings were made at the altar. The spirit of the sea helped protect against drowning and gave large catches but was offended by the presence of women and Buddhist priests, who usually were not allowed aboard the boats. Traditional lumbermen had their own rites for pacifying the spirit of a tree they cut down, and they observed various taboos within their mountain lodges. Certain words offended the tree spirits, and while they were in the mountains the lumbermen had to use a special "mountain language" when referring to the tabooed terms.

A widespread folk tradition among rice farmers was the notion that the *kami* of the rice field alternated with the *kami* of a nearby hill or mountain. Each spring the mountain *kami* descended the mountain and became the rice-field *kami* for the duration of the growing season; in the fall they ascended in the smoke of the rice straw to become once more the mountain *kami*. A number of regions have special celebrations in spring and fall to mark the movement of the *kami*. Rice farmers in other regions believe that the rice-field *kami* resides in the

family home during the winter. Most folk beliefs related to occupations have been strongest in the old traditional forms of work and
have tended to die out as work has become organized on a large scale
in factories.

THE INDIVIDUAL AND FOLK RELIGION

The individual received the "little tradition" informally in his or her
family and village and even during work. Individuals might participate in folk religion within all three of these contexts; yet there were
other ways in which folk religion spoke directly to them. One was the
notion of *yakudoshi*, unlucky or dangerous years in the life of an
individual. These years were ages 25 and 42 for men, and ages 19
and 37 for women. One had to be very careful during these critical
years, and it was a very bad omen if during one's unlucky year an
acquaintance of the same age became sick or died. To offset the omi-
nous character of the critical age, a person was supposed to be diligent
in attending festivals and in using protective amulets. The reverse of
yakudoshi is *toshi iwai*, or years of celebration: Attaining one's sixty-
first and seventieth year of age was considered very lucky and was an
occasion for celebration.

Not only did folk religion supply beliefs and practices for ordinary
individuals, but also it provided specialists who ministered to their
religious needs. The most conspicuous of these specialists was the
traditional shaman (or medium), usually a blind woman who had
undergone extensive training with another shaman and was able to
go into a trance and speak with the dead. In some periods shamans
were brought under indirect control of organized religion, but most of
the time they lived in ordinary homes within villages, carrying out
their role of medium upon the request of another individual. Such
shamans are still found in Japan today.

The person making the request may be concerned about the well-
being of a deceased relative, so he or she visits the shaman with the
customary payment for her to act as medium with the dead. The
shaman makes an offering to her guardian spirit, recites the liturgy
and formulas she learned in her training, and enters into a trance, so
that the voice of the dead can speak through her mouth. The conver-
sation between the grieving person and the dead relative is rather
formal—how the dead relative is faring in the other world, what
offerings might make him or her happy. Nevertheless, this religious
service, performed outside organized religion, speaks directly to the

A blind shaman (itako) is communicating with the dead. The shaman is the woman holding the rosary of black beads. The woman who has requested the shaman's services is to her right, holding a handkerchief to her face and stifling her tears as she hears a message from her dead relative. This is an annual festival of late summer near Mount Osore, and most of the people who come are women of the area. The young woman in the background holding a microphone is a student of linguistics from a Tokyo university recording the distinctive dialect used by these shamans. (Mount Osore, 1963)

relationship between the living and dead, one of the most important aspects in all of Japanese religion. The significance of folk religion is demonstrated by this ability to work within the everyday ordinary contexts of daily life and yet minister directly to the crucial religious needs of the people.

Folk religion has been treated separately here in order to highlight its features. In the lives of Japanese people, however, folk religion blended imperceptibly with organized religion. Just as folk religion often borrowed from organized religion, it was also the case that many popular and folk practices occurred within the context and even the buildings of Shinto and Buddhism. As we will see in the next chapter, this interaction is characteristic of Japanese religion as a whole.

NOTES

1. See Robert Redfield, *Peasant Society and Cultures* (Chicago: University of Chicago Press, 1956), p. 70. For an application of Redfield's notions of "little tradition" and "great tradition" to an example of Japanese religious history, see Ichiro Hori, *Folk Reli-*

gion in Japan: Continuity and Change, ed. Joseph M. Kitagawa and Alan L. Miller (Chicago: University of Chicago Press, 1968), pp. 49–81; an excerpt from Hori's work is included in H. Byron Earhart, *Religion in the Japanese Experience: Sources and Interpretations* (Belmont, Calif.: Wadsworth, 1974), pp. 193–97.

2. Winston Davis, *Toward Modernity: Developmental Typology of Popular Religious Affiliations in Japan* (Ithaca, N.Y.: Cornell China-Japan Program, 1977), p. 6.
3. George DeVos, quoted in David W. Plath, "Where the Family of God Is the Family: The Role of the Dead in Japanese Households," *American Anthropologist,* Vol. 46, No. 2 (April 1964), 307. This article is abridged in Earhart, *Religion in the Japanese Experience,* pp. 148–54.

SELECTED READINGS

Blacker, Carmen. *The Catalpa Bow: A Study of Shamanistic Practices in Japan.* London: Allen & Unwin, 1975. Contains both a historical overview of shamanism and firsthand descriptions of living shamanistic practitioners.

Dorson, Richard M. *Folk Legends of Japan.* Rutland, Vt.: Charles E. Tuttle Company, 1962. A topical collection, with brief introductions for each tale.

Earhart, H. Byron. *Religion in the Japanese Experience: Sources and Interpretations.* Belmont, Calif.: Wadsworth, 1974. See Part Six for selected documents on folk religion, including excerpts from Dorson and Hori.

Hori, Ichiro. *Folk Religion in Japan: Continuity and Change.* Edited by Joseph M. Kitagawa and Alan L. Miller. Chicago: University of Chicago Press, 1968. The best general work on aspects of folk religion; see pp. 181–251 for a good summary of the dynamics of shamanism in Japan.

Miyake, Hitoshi. "Folk Religion." In *Japanese Religion.* Edited by Ichiro Hori. Translated by Yoshiya Abe and David Reid. Tokyo: Kodansha International, 1972, pp. 121–43. A concise analysis of folk religion, describing its annual festivals, rites of passage, and social organization.

CHAPTER 8

Interaction in the Formation of Japanese Religion

We have now seen the major traditions—Shinto, Buddhism, Confucianism, religious Taoism, and folk religion—that contributed to Japanese religious history. After the Nara period, new currents of the older traditions entered Japan, but (with the exception of Christianity) there were no new traditions. By the eighth century, all the major forces in the drama of Japanese religious history had made their first appearance, and the stage was set for the formation of a genuinely Japanese religion. Even at this early point, we can see the future course of action. A general consideration of the five traditions will show their interaction in a common religious milieu.

THE INTERACTION OF RELIGIOUS TRADITIONS

A statement attributed to Prince Shotoku has been used to view the relationship of Shinto, Confucianism, and Buddhism:

> A saying ascribed to Prince Shotoku, the founder of Japanese civilization, compares the three religious and moral systems found in Japan to the root, the stem and branches, and the flowers and fruits of a tree. Shinto is the root embedded in the soil of the people's character and national traditions; Confucianism is seen in the stem and branches of legal institutions, ethical codes, and educational systems; Buddhism made the flowers of religious sentiment bloom and gave the fruits of spiritual life. These three systems were moulded and combined by the

circumstances of the times and by the genius of the people into a composite whole of the nation's spiritual and moral life.[1]

This traditional view of Japanese religion may not have been expressed by Shotoku, but it is quite perceptive.[2] We might add two other traditions to the metaphor without radically changing it— indigenous religion dating back to prehistoric times and religious Taoism. We might say that the earliest (or indigenous) tradition is the native soil in which the roots grew, supporting the tree. Similarly, we might say that religious Taoism is imperceptibly mixed in the sap of the tree, being absorbed into the triad of Buddhism, Confucianism, and Shinto, even seeping into the surrounding soil. This metaphor, in its expanded version, gives a useful overall picture of the interrelatedness of Japanese religion. (Even folk religion and the New Religions, although not fully developed in this early period, fit well into the same metaphor. Folk religion may be seen as the "leafing out" of the tree into full foliage, while the New Religions can be viewed as the new sprouts that emerge after the tree has temporarily died back.)

THE FORMATION OF A DISTINCTIVE JAPANESE RELIGIOUS TRADITION

These traditions mutually contributed to the formation of a distinctive Japanese religious tradition in areas such as ancestor worship, the religious character of the family, and the tie between religion and the nation. Even in prehistoric times there was special veneration of the dead, possibly the dead of particular extended families. Shinto was soon relieved of funeral rites by Buddhism, but even today several important Shinto shrines still venerate the spirits of national heroes. Buddhism greatly emphasized veneration of the dead by means of regular memorial rites, just as Confucianism provided the ethical rationale of filial piety. (Taoism seems to have played no important role in this area.) Therefore, whether we retain the older term "ancestor worship" or adopt a new term such as "veneration of the dead," this typical expression of Japanese religion must be seen as the outgrowth of most of the formative traditions.

A second area, closely related to ancestor worship, is the religious continuity of the family, living and dead. Many important shrines and temples in early Japan were the private sanctuaries of separate clans. Affiliation with Shinto shrines was usually determined either by blood relationship or by geographical boundaries. Families later became linked to a specific Buddhist temple through regular memorials to family ancestors. Confucianism generally stressed social harmony and lines of obedience in the family and country at large. Thus all the formative traditions reinforced the social solidarity of the Japanese people.

A third area in which these traditions shared was the close tie between nation and religion, which has characterized most of Japanese history. The earliest religious tradition was only weakly in support of a centrally unified religion and state—partly because the families combined a political and religious leader in their own family heads or chiefs. Shinto attempted to raise the status of the emperor by the mythological account of his divine descent from the Sun Goddess and was supported by both Buddhism and Confucianism. Buddhism practically became a state religion protecting the ruler and his realm, while Confucianism provided the notion of a Son of Heaven with a divine mandate. Religious Taoism, represented by the divination bureau, promised the proper foundation of nation and society on the basis of cosmic harmony.

Several other areas of Japanese religion that reveal the influence of the five traditions can be summed up more briefly. These areas are pluralism of religions and religious beliefs, emphasis on magical procedures, and religious sentiment in a love of nature. Pluralism has always been a conspicuous feature of Japanese religion. There have been incidents of antagonism between the religious traditions, but they are the exception rather than the rule. Usually it has not been the case that any one religious tradition thought of itself as the true religion to the exclusion of other (false) religions. (The Jodo Shin sect and Nichiren sect of Buddhism are important exceptions to this general rule.) One tradition presupposed the existence of the other traditions and either consciously or unconsciously borrowed from them. Only in this kind of atmosphere could the traditions contribute commonly to ancestor worship and the religious support of the state. And only in this atmosphere could the people participate simultaneously in all the traditions. It is true that the common people might not be aware of an indigenous tradition or of religious Taoism, and might not give second thoughts to the formal teachings of Confucianism. But even when they could see some superficial differences between Buddhism and Shinto, they accepted the two traditions as similar or complementary. It was only natural that the Buddha was first seen by the Japanese people as a foreign *kami*. Later, as Buddhism became more Japanized, Buddhist divinities were worshiped by all with the same fervor that was directed toward the native *kami*.

Magical formulas and charms have been characteristic of each religious tradition. For example, Taoist charms have been adopted by both Shinto and Buddhism. In fact, Buddhism was accepted in Japan because its magical efficacy was believed to surpass that of Shinto. Similarly, shamanistic possession or trance has been recorded in the indigenous tradition, in Shinto, and in Buddhism.

Love of nature is a distinctive feature of the Japanese spirit and is reflected in most artistic and religious expressions, although it is difficult to define. The earliest picture of Japan in the eighth-century poetry anthology *Manyoshu,* and also in the early Shinto rituals, shows a refined appreciation of the religious and creative resources in the natural world. For the sake of contrast we might say that in the Western tradition the tendency has been to define God and human beings apart from nature; in Japan, *kami* and humans are defined in relation to nature or as parts of nature. The Japanese appreciation of nature is found not only within the earliest religious tradition and in Shinto; it is reinforced by the other traditions. The aim of religious Taoism was to be in harmony with nature, and Confucianism drew on this natural harmony for its insistence on social harmony. Buddhism's openness to the natural world later was developed into a return to nature by the Zen sect, which received Taoist influence in China.

This brief survey of the cooperation among the five formative traditions is not an exhaustive analysis of Japanese religion but does provide a basis for understanding its nature and development in the subsequent centuries. These basic elements continued to interact with each other while developing specific religious organizations and while contributing to the wider religious situation. The appearance of new religious currents, particularly Buddhist importations, was of great importance in determining the way in which these elements interacted.

NOTES

1. Masaharu Anesaki, *History of Japanese Religion* (London: Kegan Paul, Trench, Trubner, 1930; reprint ed., Rutland, Vt.: Charles E. Tuttle Company, 1963), p. 8.
2. See Ryusaku Tsunoda et. al., *Sources of Japanese Tradition* (New York: Columbia University Press, 1958), Chapter 13, where this passage is traced to the writings of Yoshida Kanetomo (1435–1511) and a different interpretation is given; Yoshida's purpose for writ-

ing it is to demonstrate the primacy of Shinto over Buddhism and Confucianism: "Thus all foreign doctrines are offshoots of Shinto."

SELECTED READINGS

Earhart, H. Byron. *Religion in the Japanese Experience: Sources and Interpretations*. Belmont, Calif.: Wadsworth, 1974. See Part Eight for selected documents on syncretism in Japan; see pp. 39–44 for excerpts from Matsunaga.

Matsunaga, Alicia. *The Buddhist Philosophy of Assimilation: The Historical Development of the Honji-Suijaku Theory*. Tokyo and Rutland, Vt.: Sophia University and Charles E. Tuttle Company, 1969. Treats the interaction between aspects of Buddhism and aspects of Japanese culture.

Nakamura, Hajime. *Ways of Thinking of Eastern Peoples: India, China, Tibet, Japan*. Revised English translation edited by Philip P. Wiener. Honolulu: East-West Center Press, 1964. The section on Japan, pp. 345–587, deals with the common thought and belief patterns that form the basis for interaction among the several religious traditions.

PART TWO

The Development and Elaboration of Japanese Religion

Part I began the story of Japanese religion with the prehistoric heritage, the development of Shinto, and the importation of the Buddhist, Taoist, and Confucian traditions. The appearance of these religious strands was closely related to political and social developments, such as the creation of a unified nation and a centralized state, and culminated in the political and religious developments at Nara, the capital at the end of the eighth century. By this time the major outlines of Japanese religion were taking shape.

As we enter Part II, we must keep in mind these formative elements and their initial pattern; yet we must also be ready to see new aspects of these formative elements (particularly new importations of Buddhism) and changes within them. The formative elements had not assumed a final shape by the ninth century; they continued to develop through the seventeenth century in ways that further shaped the religious world-view of the Japanese people.

The religious developments to be described in Part II are related to social and political developments. For example, the founders of Tendai and Shingon Buddhism went to China to bring back new emphases in Buddhist teachings and practice. But their trip to China occurred because they were sent as envoys of the Japanese state, in a government ship. Throughout this period religion was closely tied to the brilliant life of the court at the new capital of Kyoto.

The Buddhist sects that developed during this time span constitute the major lines of Buddhist institutions down to the present day. Shinto tended to be overshadowed by Buddhism in this period, but there was a great deal of interaction between Buddhism and Shinto, and Shinto developed theoretical arguments that formed the basis for a renewal of Shinto in the eighteenth and nineteenth centuries. Taoism and Confucianism persevered more as implicit influences than as distinct traditions. Christianity first entered Japan in 1549 and enjoyed a brief popularity before it succumbed to political persecution. Taken as a whole, these additions and changes to the religion of the formative period constitute the period of development and elaboration.

CHAPTER 9

The Founding of a Japanese Buddhism: The Shingon and Tendai Sects

The Heian period (794–1185) was a colorful time in the history of Japan. The Chinese influence continued to be dominant, but more important was the flowering of a distinctive Japanese culture. In many ways Chinese culture was transformed along Japanese lines. Previously there had been some concern with imitating Chinese models, especially in art; from the Heian period on, there was greater freedom to create truly Japanese forms. The writing system, which depended on Chinese ideographs, was modified so that it placed greater emphasis on Japanese phonetics. This gave the Japanese a lighter, freer means of expressing their emotions. The finest example of their new literature is the eleventh-century *Tale of Genji*, a tale of courtly love and sensitivity to the beauty of nature and the passing of the seasons. Poetry and painting, too, developed along more Japanese lines and centered on the glittering life at court. In the countryside the emergence of the manorial system increasingly gave power to large landholders, including Shinto and Buddhist institutions. All these cultural developments are related to the emergence of new forms of Buddhism during the Heian period—new forms imported from China to Japan and brought into close contact with Japanese culture.

THE NEW BUDDHISM OF THE HEIAN PERIOD

The new Buddhism dominated the Heian period. Older Buddhism (the six philosophical schools of the Nara period) was mainly the religion of the nobility and the monks and had become more and more corrupt with its increasing wealth and power. Therefore, it is only natural to expect that a new movement would arise. It is important to understand how the reform of Buddhism occurred, because it affected the whole Heian period and influenced much of later Japanese religious history.

Politically, the Heian period was ushered in by the shift of the capital from Nara to Kyoto, which remained the imperial capital until 1868. It is thought that one reason for moving the capital from Nara was the intolerable corruption and the political interference of the six schools of Nara Buddhism. The move freed the capital from the grip of Nara Buddhism and set up the possibility for a reform of Buddhism. Religiously, the Heian period is distinguished by two new Buddhist sects, each of which was founded by an outstanding religious leader. The Shingon sect was founded by Kukai (774–835), known posthumously as Kobo Daishi. The Tendai sect was founded by Saicho (762–822), honored posthumously as Dengyo Daishi. (*Daishi* is an honorary term meaning "great teacher.")

The two sects and their founders share many features in common. Not only were the founders contemporaries, but they went to China by imperial sanction at the same time in their quest of an authoritative Buddhism. Both were Buddhist priests who, dissatisfied with Nara Buddhism, traveled to China in search of the true Buddhism. Even more important, both seem to have been committed to the ideal of establishing a genuinely *Japanese* Buddhism. That is, they wanted actively to propagate a kind of Buddhism that would provide all the Japanese people with the teachings of Buddhism. We will also see some important differences between the two movements. For example, the two founders differed in their choice of sects of Buddhism in China and in their organization of the sects upon their return to Japan.

SHINGON: ESOTERIC BUDDHISM IN JAPAN

Kobo Daishi, the founder of Shingon, is one of the most illustrious figures in Japanese history. Formally, he is remembered for founding the Shingon sect. On the popular level, he is honored as the creator of the Japanese phonetic system of writing, and he still is venerated in many places he is supposed to have visited.[1] However, his historical significance is best seen in his transmission of esoteric Buddhism from China to Japan.

The terminology of Buddhism is rather complex, and that of Shingon Buddhism is especially complex because it is related to an elaborate symbolic and ritual system originating in India. Generally, the

79
*The Founding
of a Japanese
Buddhism:
The Shingon
and Tendai
Sects*

*A statue of Kobo Daishi, the founder of Shingon Buddhism, here shown as a protector
of children. By borrowing a pilgrim's staff and circling his statue, a person acquires
the same religious benefit as if he or she made a distant pilgrimage. (Kyoto, 1979)*

expression "esoteric Buddhism" refers to highly symbolic and even
secret formulas and practices. More specifically, the phrase refers to
the Buddhism arising out of the Tantric tradition of India from about
the third to seventh centuries A.D.[2] The Tantric tradition, which influenced both Hinduism and Buddhism, takes its name from the
Sanskrit word *tantra*, a group of writings emphasizing occult rituals to
control the mind and body for the purpose of realizing ultimate truth.

The Tantric tradition emphasized unconventional practices, such as
the use of mystic diagrams and mystic syllables *(mantra)*, and elaborate meditation techniques (which for initiated students might in-
volve symbolic and actual sexual union). A result of such extremes
was that the Tantric tradition was sometimes viewed with disfavor
by Hindus and Buddhists alike. Nevertheless, Tantric Buddhism
developed a very rich iconographic, ritual, and meditative practice,
especially in Tibet, where in combination with local practices it
formed the major Buddhist tradition.

Tantric Buddhism also found its way directly from India to China,
where it was known as Chen-yen, a translation into Chinese of the
Sanskrit term *mantra*, or "true word." The formal tradition of Chen-
yen did not survive severe persecution by the government in the year
845, but by that time Kobo Daishi had already transmitted this tradition to Japan. In Japanese, *Chen-yen* is pronounced *shingon*. Thus, the
Shingon sect is literally the True Word sect, meaning the sect that

employs esoteric Buddhist practices such as the invocation of "true words" or mystic syllables.

During Kobo Daishi's stay in China (804–06), he learned all there was to know of esoteric Buddhism and obtained crucial Buddhist scriptures (in Chinese translation) and ritual paraphernalia. His transplantation of the esoteric Buddhist tradition was a radically new contribution of Buddhism to Japan, one that was more strongly Indian than Chinese. Equally important is what Kobo Daishi did with it on Japanese soil. He dissociated himself both from the old Buddhism of Nara and from the new capital in order to establish a monastery on the secluded mountain called Koyasan. In part, Kobo Daishi imitated the mountain monasteries of China, but he also emphasized the need to make Buddhism native to Japan. Even though he established his monastery far from the capital, the esoteric doctrines—and especially the rites—soon were sought after by both laity and priests.

Shingon teaching divides Buddhism into the exoteric (or public) and the esoteric (or secret). Exoteric or public teachings are not wrong but are limited to inferior knowledge; by contrast, esoteric or secret teaching reveals the heart of the cosmos and enables one to draw upon this higher power. The key to esoteric knowledge is the *Great Sun Sutra (Mahavairocana Sutra* in Sanskrit, *Dainichi-kyo* in Japanese), which is the basic scripture for Shingon. In it is a description of the cosmos as an emanation from the Sun Buddha (Vairocana, or Dainichi in Japanese).

The esoteric knowledge of Shingon reveals the higher unity in the Sun Buddha, which transcends the apparent dualities of the world. Ordinarily we experience life in terms of dualities such as male and female, dynamic and static. To the ordinary person, the dualities of the world appear hopelessly split, but the esoteric knowledge of Shingon reveals that there is a higher unity to all things within their original source in the Sun Buddha. All the doctrine, art, and ritual of Shingon is based on the premise of the Sun Buddha as the original source of the cosmos.

Kobo Daishi developed Shingon teaching in an attempt to "solve the paradox of human existence" as he experienced it. In his view, human beings must face the meaninglessness of life and the futility of human knowledge. This is seen in one of his writings:

Unknowable, unknowable
    It is completely unknowable,
About the Buddha and the non-Buddhists
    There are millions of scrolls;

Dark, dark, it is very dark
  Of the Way that is spoken there are many paths.
What is left
  When the copying and chanting of scriptures stop?
No one knows, no one knows
  And I too do not know,
Though they consider and speculate
  Even the wise do not know.[3]

81
*The Founding
of a Japanese
Buddhism:
The Shingon
and Tendai
Sects*

Here Kobo Daishi emphasizes the critical predicament of men and women but goes beyond this dark analysis of the human situation to pose a promising solution. Although human beings are faced with a meaningless existence and even though the exoteric or public teachings of Buddhism do not hold absolute assurance, nevertheless, there is hope. Shingon teaching, based on esoteric doctrine and practice, reveals the integration of humanity with the cosmic Buddha (or Sun Buddha). Shingon developed the Mahayana Buddhist notion that Buddha-nature is inherent in every person and, therefore, every person can become a Buddha (or enlightened person) during one's own life and can even become a Buddha within the limits of one's own physical body. This teaching is at the heart of Shingon doctrine and practice.

Shingon doctrine, because of its highly symbolic and esoteric character, is one of the most complex in all of Japanese Buddhism. It is easier for the average lay person and Westerner to grasp the artistic expressions of Shingon than to comprehend its theology. The dualities of the world are often expressed in two contrasting *mandala* (in Sanskrit), symbolic representations of the cosmos. The *mandala* usually feature a square border enclosing symmetrical patterns of squares within circles and circles within squares. Literally hundreds of Buddhist divinities are found within the smaller circles and squares, each identified by its particular iconographic attributes and mystic gestures. (Sometimes the divinities are represented by the mystic letters associated with them.) Such a *mandala* presents a panorama of the Buddhist cosmos. The *mandala* were sometimes used in Shingon ordination rites: A blindfolded priest threw a flower on the *mandala* and thereby became directly linked with the particular Buddhist divinity on which the flower fell. There was also the practice of meditating upon the *mandala* and thereby uniting one's life with the higher cosmic truth.[4]

Even for the average person who did not perform the most difficult practices, merely to behold the splendor of the *mandala* was to be given a glimpse of the cosmic vision to which Shingon held the key. The same can be said of the fearful statues of Shingon, which to Western eyes appear grotesque. These statues feature menacing countenance, glaring eyes, sharp teeth, and brandished weapon; but they are simply the malevolent side of various deities, the counterpart of the benevolent side. Shingon does not deny the existence of evil and violence but seeks first to comprehend the duality of the world and then to affirm the higher unity that transcends worldly duality. Although many people did not necessarily comprehend the full plan of the cosmic vision, they readily brought devotion and offerings to the awesome statues.

The practice of Shingon centers on the sect's great ritual treasures. Kobo Daishi brought back from China both ritual paraphernalia and the actual liturgies for performing the rituals. Within a few years, he and his followers were in demand for performing rites at court. Especially popular were rites for healing and for childbirth. Rather quickly such rites came to be practiced by all Buddhist priests as requests came from the court and nobility and eventually from ordinary women and men. Perhaps the most fascinating of all Shingon rituals is the fire rite called *goma,* which is thought to be related to the Indian *soma* sacrifice. In the *goma* rite the priest builds up layers of wood and ignites it, pouring on various substances such as sesame oil. (In Japanese, "sesame" is *goma*.) The symbolism of the rite pertains to the basic elements of the universe, burning defilements and purifying the self, and becoming transported by the wisdom of fire to the higher truth of Shingon. To sit in a dark temple, listening to the chanting of the priest and watching the flames leap up, illuminating the gilded statues, is an experience that elevates the viewer to another world.

The quest for cosmic power in Shingon may seem alien to early Buddhism, but it was totally consistent with Tantric Buddhism. The Indian bent for elaborate iconography and complex symbolism in doctrine and ritual is expressed more within Shingon Buddhism than in any other form of Japanese Buddhism. In fact, Shingon is closer to the esoteric Buddhism of Tibet, with which it shares the common historical foundation of Tantric Buddhism, than to other sects of Japanese Buddhism. However, the general principle that Buddhism provides power for solving immediate problems was accepted as soon as it reached Japanese shores.

The major contribution of Kobo Daishi was to bring to Japan the whole range of the esoteric art, doctrine, and ritual in a systematic form. For the aesthetically inclined, the artistic expressions and elaborate rituals of Shingon were overwhelming. For the intellectual, there was a comprehensive system explaining the nature of the world and criticizing all other philosophical systems. (Kobo Daishi developed a philosophy of religion that ranked all religions then known on a scale of ten levels. Esoteric Buddhism occupied the highest level.) The devotionally minded could utilize the meditation, divinities, and ritual to achieve personal fulfillment and to experience the unity of Shingon's cosmic vision. The magical formulas of Shingon provided easy access to cosmic power. So attractive were these dramatic aspects of Shingon that they were quickly borrowed and used by other Buddhist sects and gradually filtered down to the ordinary people. However, Shingon did not generate new Buddhist sects in the fashion of Tendai, the other major Buddhist sect in the Heian period.

TENDAI: FAITH IN THE *LOTUS SUTRA* AND AMIDA

After the Heian period, the Tendai sect, founded by Dengyo Daishi, became increasingly more important than Shingon. Historically, Tendai can be considered the more important of the two sects, for it spawned most of the later Buddhist developments in Japan. Although Dengyo Daishi went to China at the same time as Kobo Daishi, his experience there was quite different. Dengyo Daishi viewed the esoteric Buddhism of China merely as one important Buddhist tradition along with Ch'an (the Chinese term for the Zen sect). For Dengyo Daishi the T'ien-t'ai sect was superior to the other Buddhist traditions. (*Tendai* is the Japanese pronunciation of *T'ien-t'ai*.) Dengyo Daishi spent most of his time in China at the headquarters of the T'ien-t'ai sect, on a mountain called T'ien-t'ai.

The T'ien-t'ai sect, established by the Chinese monk Chih-i (538–97), focused on the *Lotus Sutra* and the teachings of the great Buddhist scholar Nagarjuna (c. A.D. 150). Chih-i considered the *Lotus Sutra* the culmination of the Buddha's teaching and used it to synthesize most previous Buddhist doctrine into one grand system. He emphasized the notion that all life was present in the mind of the historical Buddha from the moment of his enlightenment, and he related this idea to Nagarjuna's philosophical insistence on the emptiness of all phenomenal existence (that is, life here and now). Chih-i's doctrine is a threefold analysis of existence that both denies and at the same time affirms phenomenal existence.[5] For the lay person, this means that even daily life, if properly perceived and meditated on, can be the road to Buddhahood (becoming Buddha or attaining the level of a Buddha). In both China and Japan this sect emphasized that proper Buddhist practice is dependent upon proper meditation.

When Dengyo Daishi returned to Japan, he went to the mountain called Hieizan, overlooking Kyoto. There he established the Tendai sect, emphasizing the *Lotus Sutra* and the necessity of monastic retreat for proper meditation. Of course, the *Lotus Sutra* already had a considerable history in Japan: Even Prince Shotoku is supposed to have written a commentary on it, and the Buddhist schools of Nara had recognized its profundity. Dengyo Daishi's contribution was to teach the primary importance of the *Lotus Sutra*. He criticized earlier interpretations of it as false and proposed as the true interpretation that "all forms of life stand on an equal basis in attaining Buddhahood,"[6] emphasizing the notion in the *Lotus Sutra* that all life has the potential for becoming enlightened.

Dengyo Daishi was uncompromising not only on doctrinal matters, but also in matters of training and ordination. His criticism of corrupt Nara Buddhism and his concern for proper meditation led him to prescribe a twelve-year period of training for monks on Hieizan, during which time they were not allowed to leave the mountain. His insistence on establishing the proper rite of ordination (which he had received in China and wanted to install in Japan) involved him in a lifelong struggle, which received governmental approval only after his death. Under his guidance, Hieizan became the center of Buddhist studies in Japan.

The mountain headquarters of Hieizan symbolizes Dengyo Daishi's great plans for Japanese Buddhism. He was concerned that Buddhism in Japan be orthodox in ordination rites, scriptures, doctrine, and devotion. Having received proper ordination himself (in China), he felt qualified to lead orthodox Buddhism in Japan. Convinced that the *Lotus Sutra* was the essential teaching of Buddhism, he upheld it as the foremost scripture. For doctrine he transmitted the T'ien-t'ai teachings based on the *Lotus Sutra*, that every phenomenal aspect of the world is filled with Buddha-nature. Determined that his monks be properly devout and disciplined, he required long periods of meditation. History rewarded Dengyo Daishi's efforts, for Hieizan became the monastic and scholastic headquarters of all Japanese Buddhism, regardless of sect affiliation. In spite of the ravages of time and warfare, much of the glory of this monastic headquarters survives today and is a popular tourist attraction just outside Kyoto. One of the peculiar architectural structures at Hieizan is the chapel with an image of Amida in the center of an empty room, so that priests could circumambulate Amida while in devotional meditation. The faith in Amida nurtured within Tendai later blossomed in the practices of the Pure Land sects.

The impact of Tendai on popular life is not so clear as that of Shingon. One of Tendai's greatest contributions is the placing of the *Lotus Sutra* in the center of attention, for this is probably the single most influential Buddhist scripture for China and Japan. In it we find the most direct and dramatic expression of the gist of Mahayana Buddhism: All beings may easily attain enlightenment through simple acts of devotion. In the words of the *Lotus Sutra*, whoever memorizes or recites but a single stanza of this scripture "and who honours that book with flowers, incense, perfumed garlands, ointment, powder, clothes, umbrellas, flags, banners, music, joined hands, reverential bows and salutations . . . must be held to be accomplished in supreme and perfect enlightenment."[7] This compassionate rendering of Buddhism summed up the meaning of the tradition to the majority of the Japanese people. Tendai teaching so emphasized the penetration of Buddha-nature within the phenomenal world that in medieval times it preached the inherent Buddha-nature of the natural world: "Not only the grass and trees but also rivers, mountains, and the earth are themselves Buddhahood already possessed intact."[8] Here we see how the Japanese appreciation of the natural world became part of Tendai teaching.

The founders of the Shingon and Tendai sects were contemporaries, but they led different careers and made contrasting contributions to Japanese Buddhism. Some scholars feel that Dengyo Daishi would have been more successful if he had been more compromising, like Kobo Daishi. Both men founded headquarters of mountain Buddhism in Japan; yet their fortunes were quite different. Although Kobo Daishi's fame was immediate and lasting, his sect was of lesser importance for religious history, as a covert influence. In contrast, Dengyo Daishi has enjoyed less personal fame, but his sect is of the utmost importance for subsequent religious history as the source of all later Buddhist sects. Two elements that Dengyo Daishi brought to Japan along with Tendai were faith in the *bodhisattva* named Amida and Zen practices. For a while these two elements had only a minor role within Tendai because Tendai gradually became heavily laden with Shingon ritualistic influence. However, with the passing of Shingon's golden age, these two dormant elements woke to new life. They became so active that they burst the bonds of Tendai and gave rise to new sects.

THE DEVELOPMENT OF JAPANESE BUDDHISM
AND JAPANESE RELIGION

The Heian period was a strong affirmation of the Japanese creative ability to mold innumerable continental borrowings. Nara Buddhism had remained in essence a foreign religion. Kobo Daishi and Dengyo

Daishi were in agreement about the reason for searching out authoritative Buddhism in China: to mold it into a truly Japanese Buddhism. Because of their efforts, Buddhism in Japan took on a decidedly Japanese character.

At the outset of this chapter we indicated that the period of development and elaboration was characterized by two trends: the continuation of general patterns that had taken shape in the formative period, and the appearance of new influences such as the new Buddhism. Thus far we have surveyed only the new influences. The Tendai and Shingon sects, however, were not signs of discontinuity; on the contrary, they reinforced the earlier religious patterns. Both Shingon and Tendai deliberately emphasized the Japanese character of Buddhism. The headquarters of both were founded with full cooperation of the *kami* who were considered the patron deities of the two mountains on which the monasteries were located. Thus, the rapport between the Buddhas and *kami* became even more intimate. The Tendai and Shingon sects also tended to spread Buddhist teachings and build temples in areas distant from the capital.

In addition, although the two new sects had reacted against the state Buddhism of Nara, eventually both the ritualism of Shingon and the ecclesiastical authority of Tendai were used to protect and bless the state. The artistic and magical heritage of esoteric Buddhism and the Tendai emphasis on the *Lotus Sutra* gradually blended with the characteristically Japanese emphasis on purification and ritualism. Many Buddhist divinities *(bodhisattvas)*, such as Kannon, Amida, and Jizo, became increasingly important as objects of popular piety. Magical charms and Buddhist divinities were not confined to organized Buddhism—to temples and priests—but became part of the living faith of the people. "All through the Nara and Heian periods, almost all the sects of Buddhism aimed at tangible rewards in this world and they mainly depended upon incantation and magic."[9] All in all, the Heian period saw Buddhism take on a decidedly Japanese character as it increasingly penetrated the life of the people.

Meanwhile, the religious elements described in Part I coexisted with the new sects. In fact, the beliefs of religious Taoism were more active in the Heian than any other period. Medieval novels such as the *Tale of Genji* show how the movements of the people were determined by the "unlucky directions" learned from religious Taoism. The age was pervaded by all the implications of the *yin-yang* cosmology. The charms and incantations of earlier Buddhism, reinforced by both Shingon and its Taoistic coloring, penetrated all classes of society. The seventh-century precedent of having Buddhist priests per-

87
*The Founding
of a Japanese
Buddhism:
The Shingon
and Tendai
Sects*

*Kannon is one of the most popular Buddhist divinities in Japan. People "worship"
Kannon by ladling water over the statue and using brushes (bought inside the temple
grounds) to scrub the part of the statue corresponding to the part of their body that is
ailing. On one fine September Sunday in Tokyo, about seventy-five people (mostly
women) were patiently lined up waiting their turn to ladle water on and scrub the
statue. (Tokyo, 1979)*

form burial services had become widespread. The Buddhist festival
of *bon* for honoring the return of the souls of the dead, probably with
the help of ancient Japanese practices, became popular throughout
the country. Various religious practitioners—diviners, exorcists,
ascetics—drew on all the previous traditions to serve the religious
needs of the people. Shinto became more fully organized, as was
evidenced by the compilation of the *Engishiki* of 927, but tended to
lean on the prestige of Buddhism. The many *kami* of Shinto became
even more closely identified with the Buddhas and *bodhisattvas,* and
we will see that Shinto became organized around the complex philosophies of religious Taoism, Shingon, and Tendai. Folk religion too
showed its vitality.

An example of the uniquely Japanese interrelationship of these
elements is the movement called Shugendo, little known in the West.
Shugendo became highly organized during and after the Heian period.
Building on the ancient theme of sacred mountains and festivals performed on mountains, Shugendo developed a "mountain religion"
that emphasized pilgrimage to the mountains and ascetic retreats

within the mountains. It combined the Shinto notion of local *kami* dwelling on mountains with the Buddhist notion of local *bodhisattvas*. In addition, it borrowed the theories and charms of religious Taoism. The legendary founder of Shugendo gained religious power by combining the aspects of several traditions: He practiced Buddhist asceticism on a Japanese sacred mountain while taking over features of the Chinese mountain wizard (*hsien* in Chinese, *sennin* in Japanese). Many popular religious practitioners gained their religious powers by training in the mountains before descending to minister to the people. In later periods, while Shingon languished as a separate sect, Shugendo practitioners (called *yamabushi*) were instrumental in spreading the charms and incantations of esoteric Buddhism (mixed with Taoistic charms and Shinto elements) to the people. The *yamabushi* were important in spreading Buddhism to northern Japan. This is but one illustration of the complex religious interrelationships within the Heian period and later periods.

NOTES

1. See the folk legend "Saint Kobo's Well" in H. Byron Earhart, *Religion in the Japanese Experience: Sources and Interpretations* (Belmont, Calif.: Wadsworth, 1974), p. 100.
2. For a brief treatment of Tantric Buddhism, see Edward Conze, *Buddhism: Its Essence and Development* (New York: Philosophical Library, 1951; reprint ed., New York: Harper & Row, 1959), pp. 174–99.
3. *Hizo-hoyaku*, as translated and quoted by Minoru Kiyota, *Shingon Buddhism: Theory and Practice* (Los Angeles: Buddhist Books International, 1978), p. 30.
4. For a lavishly illustrated book on esoteric Buddhist temples and art, see Takaaki Sawa, *Art in Japanese Esoteric Buddhism*, trans. Richard L. Gage (New York: Weatherhill/Heibonsha, 1972).
5. For a brief interpretation of this doctrine, see Ryusaku Tsunoda et al., *Sources of Japanese Tradition* (New York: Columbia University Press, 1958), Chapter 6.
6. Shinsho Hanayama, "Buddhism in Japan," in *The Path of Buddha*, ed. Kenneth W. Morgan (New York: Ronald Press, 1956), p. 325.
7. *Saddharma-Pundarika or The Lotus of the True Law*, trans. H. Kern (New York: Dover Publications, 1963); see p. 215. An excerpt

from this scripture is in Earhart, *Religion in the Japanese Experience*, pp. 44–47.

8. Hajime Nakamura, *Ways of Thinking of Eastern Peoples: India, China, Tibet, Japan* (Honolulu: East-West Center Press, 1964), p. 360.
9. Ibid., p. 363.

SELECTED READINGS

Earhart, H. Byron. *A Religious Study of the Mount Haguro Sect of Shugendo: An Example of Japanese Mountain Religion.* Tokyo: Sophia University, 1970. A detailed study of one Shugendo sect, treating the relationship of esoteric Buddhism to folk practices.

Hakeda, Yoshito S., trans. *Kukai: Major Works.* New York: Columbia University Press, 1972. A scholarly introduction to the life and thought of the founder of Shingon Buddhism, with translations of his works.

Hurvitz, Leon Nahum. *Chih-i (538–97): An Introduction to the Life and Ideas of a Chinese Buddhist Monk.* Brussels: Institut belge des hautes études chinoises, 1962. A detailed account of the founder of T'ien-t'ai (Tendai) Buddhism.

Kiyota, Minoru. *Shingon Buddhism: Theory and Practice.* Los Angeles: Buddhist Books International, 1978. The only concise interpretation of Shingon doctrine in English; it presupposes some acquaintance with Buddhism and Buddhist terms but provides a valuable glossary of technical terms.

Tsunoda, Ryusaku, et al. *Sources of Japanese Tradition.* New York: Columbia University Press, 1958. See Chapter 6 for translated documents concerning Tendai and Chapter 7 for translated documents concerning Shingon.

Ui, Hakuju. "A Study of Japanese Tendai Buddhism." In *Philosophical Studies of Japan.* Vol. 1 (1959), pp. 33–74. A detailed analysis of Tendai doctrine, comparing its Chinese origins with its Japanese developments.

CHAPTER 10

Elaboration Within Japanese Buddhism: The Pure Land, Nichiren, and Zen Sects

Buddhism went through many changes in India and other countries before arriving in Japan, but the Indian and Chinese developments were most important for Japanese Buddhism. During the Heian period (794–1185), the grand philosophical systems of India were continued in the six schools of Nara Buddhism, and Shingon and Tendai were freshly imported from China. In the face of so many varieties of Buddhism, we may wonder why the Kamakura period (1185–1333) saw such a vigorous expansion of Buddhist sects.

The elaboration of new Buddhist movements during Kamakura times seems to be related both to the previous history of Buddhism in Japan and to the rise of creative Buddhist founders. As Shingon and Tendai became successful, they tended to attract money and power from the nobility and court, and they became closely tied to the political and social elite. Shingon priests spent more and more time performing colorful rituals for the wealthy, and Tendai priests became involved in political interference in the new capital of Kyoto. The three great Buddhist sects of the Kamakura period—Pure Land, Nichiren, and Zen—arose in reaction to these developments. The three new sects were somewhat critical of Tendai and Shingon, which were primarily mountain centers of Buddhism not directly related to the life of the people. Also, Tendai and Shingon had not exhausted the richness of Chinese Buddhism. The Kamakura sects selected different aspects of the Chinese Buddhist heritage to develop in order to make simpler Buddhist practices available to more people. Because the new Kamakura sects usually were set up on the plains, rather than on secluded mountains, they are sometimes referred to as "plains Buddhism." The Pure Land, Nichiren, and Zen sects are the largest and most distinctively Japanese Buddhist institutions, and they reflect both the long history of the Buddhist tradition and the social conditions of the Kamakura period.

91
*Elaboration
Within
Japanese
Buddhism:
The Pure
Land,
Nichiren, and
Zen Sects*

FROM HEIAN BUDDHISM TO KAMAKURA BUDDHISM

Following the relative peace of the Heian period came the troubled times of the Kamakura period (1185–1333), in which there was a major shift in political power from the court at Kyoto to ruling feudal groups headed by a generalissimo *(shogun)*. The period draws its name from the site of Kamakura where this feudal government was first established. Actually, struggles between rising feudal powers had occurred in the Heian period, but in the Kamakura period they dominated the entire scene. The large Buddhist temples also figured as major economic and military forces, contributing to the general unrest of the times.

The shift from the Heian period to the Kamakura period had two immediate consequences for Japanese Buddhism. First, the decline of the court and nobility led to the withdrawal of patronage and financial support of Shingon and Tendai. Second, the uncertainty of life in these trying times called for a more immediate resolution of religious problems and questions of salvation.

One of the Buddhist theories that resounded through the Kamakura period was the theory of the "decline of the law." Here "law" *(dharma* in Sanskrit, *ho* in Japanese) means the Buddha's teachings, or Buddhism. This theory presupposed three major Buddhist ages of increasing degeneration: first, the ideal age when people followed the teaching of the Buddha and could attain enlightenment; second, a rather degenerate age when people practiced the teaching of Buddha even though they knew enlightenment was impossible; and third, a completely degenerate age when no one bothered to practice the Buddha's teachings. Japanese Buddhists, following the Chinese interpretation of this theory, understood that the first two ages were already past and they were living in the third and final age.[1] The people who lived through the all-too-frequent warfare and bloodshed of the Kamakura period feared an imminent end of the world. Moreover, they realized that in this age of the decline of the law, organized Buddhism itself was of little help to the lay person seeking salvation.

This crisis within Buddhism, however, did not bring about its extinction. On the contrary, the philosophical schools of Nara survived, and the Heian sects of Shingon and Tendai continued to develop. Furthermore, this new situation in the Kamakura period stimulated latent features of Japanese Buddhism, which flourished as never before. If the contribution of the Heian period was an authentic *Japanese* Buddhism, then the Kamakura contribution was Buddhism for the Japanese *people*. Kamakura developments marked the first time in Japanese history when Buddhism captured the attention of large numbers of the common people, and it is these same sects that today claim the majority of Buddhist temples and Buddhist adherents. In Kamakura times Buddhism emphasized not so much the formal notion of enlightenment or salvation *(nirvana)* as simpler religious goals such as rebirth into Amida's pure land.

Neither Shingon nor Tendai could fully meet the new religious needs. Tendai, however, contained the germs of the three major Buddhist developments of the Kamakura period: the Pure Land sects, the Nichiren sect, and the Zen sects.

THE PURE LAND SECTS: FAITH IN AMIDA AND THE RECITATION OF THE *NEMBUTSU*

The term "Pure Land" (or "Pure Realm") is a translation of the Japanese term *Jodo*. It can refer to one particular group of Buddhist sects, the Pure Land sects, but in a broader sense it refers to the Pure Land of Amida in the Buddhist pantheon. Amida (Amitabha or Amitayus in Sanskrit) was an important Buddha even in Indian Buddhism and became one of the most important objects of Buddhist devotion in China. Amida has compassion on and wants to save all human beings. To rescue them Amida brings humans to the Buddhist realm called the Pure Land. All people can avail themselves of Amida's saving grace simply by invoking or chanting the name of Amida. In Japan this practice is known as *nembutsu:* The actual phrase is *namu Amida* or *namu Amida Butsu*, meaning "I put my faith in Amida Buddha." Originally the *nembutsu* meant meditation on Amida, but the element of meditation was soon replaced by fervent devotion and endless repetition. The development of the Pure Land sects expressed the shift from meditation to faith. In China and then in Japan the cult of Amida became closely associated with memorials for the dead.

The simplicity of faith in Amida helped spread this cult throughout the land. Although all people yearned for their own salvation and the repose of their ancestors, only a few could spend the time and money for Shingon rituals and Tendai meditation. Furthermore, no comprehension of subtle doctrines was required in Pure Land Buddhism. The founders of the Pure Land sects were thoroughly trained in the monasteries of Hieizan and elsewhere, but they emphasized the availability of salvation for even illiterate peasants. Amida Buddhism did not win the day because people chose to follow Pure Land doctrine instead of Tendai and Shingon doctrine. It was not a matter of choosing one intellectual system over another so much as it was a matter of choosing popular devotion to Amida over the former Buddhist systems. Faith in Amida became more important for the people than all the earlier Buddhist movements combined—the philosophical systems of Nara Buddhism, the rituals of Shingon, and the meditation of Tendai.

93
*Elaboration
Within
Japanese
Buddhism:
The Pure
Land,
Nichiren, and
Zen Sects*

A number of Buddhist priests within the Tendai sect stimulated belief in Amida, but the one who is most remembered as the founder of Pure Land as a separate sect is Honen (1133–1212). Most of the earlier priests who preached faith in Amida did so within the context of Tendai, without establishing a separate sect. The career of Honen is a good example of the changing religious atmosphere. Honen studied Buddhism at Hieizan and gained fame as a scholar. Even though he devoted his life to studying the many systems of Buddhist thought, he did not see how these complex doctrines could help a person attain religious peace during such troubled times. At the age of 42 he became convinced of the truth of the Pure Land teachings.

Honen was able to make a clear distinction between the earlier Buddhist teachings in Japan and the newer teaching of faith in Amida. In doing so, he followed the precedent of an earlier Japanese Amidist by calling previous Buddhist teachings of right conduct and religious exercises the "holy path" and ascribing them to the first two ages of Buddhist history. However, Honen, who lived during the third and final age, believed that it was too much to expect women and men to achieve salvation through their own efforts. The only hope in such evil times was the possibility of rebirth in Amida's Pure Land. Like his Amidist forerunner, Honen distinguished sharply between the overly "difficult" holy path of earlier sects and the need for an "easy" means of salvation in the age of the decline of the law. Honen proposed an easy means of salvation available to all: rebirth in Amida's Pure Land by means of invoking Amida's name. Honen maintained that all human beings were so wicked that they could never win their own salvation, even if they followed the holy path perfectly. They would be much better off to acknowledge their imperfection and throw themselves upon the mercy of Amida.

Salvation would be effected by the power of Amida. Interpretations of Amida's saving power differed considerably, however. There was disagreement over whether good works were a necessary precursor of the *nembutsu* or whether good works were unimportant for salvation. Another area of disagreement was whether a person was saved absolutely by just one recitation of the *nembutsu* or whether one's salvation depended upon constant repetition of the *nembutsu*.

Several priests following Honen elaborated different themes of Pure Land teaching but did not found separate sects. One who did establish a new sect was Shinran (1173–1263), who rivals Honen in Pure Land history and was considered by his followers to be the founder of the Amidist sect called Jodo Shin. Shinran, too, received his Buddhist training at Hieizan but became converted to Honen's teaching of faith in Amida. Shinran was even more zealous than Honen in propagating Amidism. He said that the all-important thing was faith in Amida. With his emphasis on the importance of *faith*, Shinran tended to deemphasize repetition of Amida's name. He maintained that even "one calling" on the name of Amida was sufficient for salvation, in opposition to Honen's teaching that emphasized repetition of Amida's name.

In every aspect, Shinran turned Honen's teaching to the extreme of absolute trust in Amida, completely deprecating the ability of men and women to work for their own salvation. Honen had said, "Even a bad man will be received in Buddha's Land, how much more a good man." Shinran placed such trust in Amida and such distrust in human goodness that he turned this saying around: "Even a good man will be received in Buddha's Land, how much more a bad man."[2] Shinran's emphasis on faith in Amida alone led his followers to reject other Buddhist divinities and especially Shinto divinities *(kami)*. Families belonging to the Jodo Shin sect were exceptional in that their homes featured only the Buddhist altar *(butsudan)* and excluded the customary Shinto altar *(kamidana)*.

The followers of Honen became the Jodo (Pure Land) sect; the followers of Shinran became the Jodo Shinshu (True Pure Land sect), which is usually known by its abbreviated name Shinshu (True sect). The Pure Land movements experienced varying degrees of success. After the death of Shinran, the Jodo Shinshu tended to decline. One of Shinran's successors, Rennyo (1414–99), is credited with "restoring" the sect by helping to shape its doctrine and organizational structure. Shinshu became the largest Buddhist sect.

Shinran's importance is not limited to his status as a founder of Jodo Shinshu. According to tradition, Shinran was contemptuous of

95
*Elaboration
Within
Japanese
Buddhism:
The Pure
Land,
Nichiren, and
Zen Sects*

the celibate life required of monks because that lifestyle presupposed the individual monk's ability to attain salvation on his own and, furthermore, the monastic life implied a lack of faith in the Buddha's grace, which could erase all imperfection. Shinran supposedly wanted to show that the Buddhist life could be practiced by even the ordinary householder, so he married and raised a family. One account says that Honen himself arranged the marriage. Whether or not this story is true, Shinran is popularly venerated for establishing the precedent for a married priesthood. In later times, all the Buddhist sects allowed priests to marry. This is a distinctive feature of Japanese Buddhism, one that sets it off from the Buddhism of countries such as Sri Lanka (Ceylon) and Burma, where Theravada Buddhism adheres to a celibate monasticism.

Amidism is one of the most pervasive of all religious movements within Japanese history. Faith in Amida preceded the founding of the Pure Land sects and overflowed the boundaries of those sects. The *nembutsu* was something that people accepted and practiced regardless of their own temple affiliation. Amida was responsive to all who called on the name of Amida, and men and women and children looked to Amida for help in time of need. It is said that on medieval battlefields the dying warriors sent up their loud pleas for Amida to take them to the Pure Land.

Pure Land priests were active both in spreading Buddhist faith in the heart of the cities and in building temples in rural areas. Even the pattern of temple organization was an innovation to Japanese Buddhism. In the past, temples had been founded and maintained mainly by government sponsorship. Shinran gathered together practitioners of the *nembutsu*, along the lines of popularly organized congregations. Rennyo and others later solidified this network of believers into a tight organizational system. It is no accident that Pure Land groups in general and Jodo Shinshu in particular possess one of the largest memberships and are among the most tightly organized of all Japanese Buddhist groups.

NICHIREN: FAITH IN THE *LOTUS SUTRA* AS THE EXCLUSIVE NATIONAL BUDDHISM

Nichiren (1222–82) is one of the most forceful personalities in Japanese history. By his opponents he was despised; by his followers he was emulated. Nichiren began his career, as did most eminent Buddhists of his time, at Hieizan. However, Nichiren's religious experience at Hieizan was radically different from that of his contemporaries. At an early age he became convinced that the *Lotus Sutra* contained the essence of the historical Buddha's teachings. Eventually he believed himself to be the only reformer who recognized the true teaching of Tendai and its founder Dengyo Daishi. In fact, "Nichiren called himself the reincarnation of the Bodhisattva Jogyo to whom the Lotus Sutra had been entrusted."[3] In his critique of the existing schools and in his reinterpretation of the *Lotus Sutra,* he founded a new, powerful sect.

Several passages in the *Lotus Sutra* make the claim that the *Lotus Sutra* is the one true channel of Buddhism. Nichiren accepted this theme and established the *Lotus Sutra* as the basis of his inspiration and as an object of veneration. He interpreted the turmoils of the times and the very age of the decline of the law as a falling away from the truth of the *Lotus Sutra,* which teaches that the Buddha is revealed in three bodies: the historical Buddha (Sakyamuni), the cosmic or universal Buddha, and the Buddha of bliss, which appears in various forms. Nichiren used his understanding of the Buddha-concept to criticize the central doctrines of both Shingon and Amidism as fragmentary. He thought that they neglected the historical Buddha and overlooked the threefold character of the Buddha. His religious convictions also clashed with the other sects on the basic issues of the true object of worship and the true goal of religious life. Nichiren ridiculed the esotericism and ritualism of Shingon as superstitious folly. He was especially critical of Shingon ritualism because it had invaded Hieizan and overshadowed the original Tendai teaching.

Nichiren criticized Amidism for several reasons. In the first place, he objected to the cult of faith in Amida Buddha and repetition of the *nembutsu.* This was not simply a doctrinal criticism, for Nichiren said the true object of worship was the *Lotus Sutra* itself. Later he composed a graphic representation, or *mandala,* of the title of this sutra, making this *mandala* a primary object of worship. He encouraged his followers to venerate and praise this scripture with the phrase "namu Myoho Renge Kyo" (praise to or faith in the wonderful *Lotus Sutra*). In other words, Nichiren did not really object to the principle of gaining religious power from magical pictures *(mandala)* or from devotional recitation. His real objection was that Shingon and Amida Buddhism did not recognize the proper object of devotion, which was the *Lotus Sutra,* and the recitation of faith in the *Lotus Sutra.*

Nichiren was also contemptuous of the Pure Land stress on absolute trust in Amida at the expense of human initiative. He was just as convinced as the Amidists about the decline of the law, but he reacted in a different way. He emphasized the active responsibility of every person to change this decadent situation by a return to faith in the *Lotus Sutra*. Some other Buddhist priests thought the disturbed times and corrupt Buddhism could be corrected by a return to the proper monastic rules—a revival of the Ritsu (Vinaya) expression of Buddhism. Nichiren dismissed this movement, too, for he measured everything in terms of the *Lotus Sutra*. At the same time, Zen was becoming a major factor in Japanese Buddhism. Nichiren had no use for the Zen form of Buddhist meditation.

Nichiren's uncompromising character is evident in his unbending criticism of other contemporary Buddhist groups, but this trait is even more strongly accentuated in the founding of his own movement. In Japan, religion and country have always been closely associated. Nichiren did not stop with criticism of other sects; he went so far as to say that the religion of the *Lotus Sutra* should be adopted as the state religion and all other Buddhist sects should be annihilated. This is perhaps the most extreme expression of the Japanese association of religion and nation. In fact, Nichiren was as much a patriot as a religious leader. His whole life can be seen as a valiant attempt to save Japan, making use of the teachings of the *Lotus Sutra*. He suffered severe persecution for his outspokenness, several times narrowly escaping execution. But he thought little of this, since it was in the service of Buddhism and his country. He is well remembered for having made the prediction that the Mongols would attempt to invade Japan, a prediction that came true in his lifetime. The Mongol invasion was interpreted by Nichiren as a punishment for Japan's (Japanese Buddhism's) evils and a sign of the age of the decline of the law.[4]

Although the Nichiren sect is not the largest Buddhist group, it has been one of the most active. Not every follower of Nichiren had the founder's sense of mission, but this peculiar development had great significance for later history. It fed into nationalistic streams before World War II and also gave rise to important New Religions, such as Soka Gakkai, which focus on the *Lotus Sutra*. Nichiren Buddhism can be seen both as a distinctive Japanese development of Buddhism and also as a Buddhism for the Japanese people.

THE ZEN SECTS: ENLIGHTENMENT THROUGH MEDITATION

Zen is the most publicized but not necessarily the most understood aspect of Japanese Buddhism. Many Westerners have been led to believe that Zen tells the whole story of Japanese Buddhism and the Japanese spirit. In this short work, the treatment of Zen must be limited to its role in Japanese religious history. There is already a vast popular literature for Westerners dealing with contemporary Zen as a personal philosophy of life, to which the reader may refer. However, to understand Zen historically, we must recognize that in Japan it first rose to prominence during the Kamakura period. Therefore, it existed in the same religious and cultural atmosphere as Pure Land and Nichiren Buddhism.

Zen cannot be divorced from its Indian and Chinese origins. As one Japanese scholar has described the subject, "Zen combined with the intellectual culture of India, the pragmatic culture of China, and the esthetic culture of Japan."[5] The word *zen* derives from the Sanskrit word *dhyana,* meaning "meditation." However, the practice of meditation did not form the basis of a separate school until this stream had entered China, where it became related to Taoist conceptions and practices. The Chinese sects of Ch'an (Chinese for *dhyana*) formed the basis for the Japanese sects of Zen (the Japanese pronunciation of *Ch'an*).

Zen was known in Japan several centuries before Kamakura times without becoming a major movement. Several of the priests who went to China on imperial order brought back Zen. Dengyo Daishi, the founder of Tendai, visited Zen monasteries in China and brought back the Zen practices of meditation. Nevertheless, Zen at Hieizan could not hold its own against Dengyo Daishi's teaching of the *Lotus Sutra,* the dominant Shingon esotericism, which overshadowed Heian times, and the emerging Amidist beliefs. In effect, Zen had to be reimported by forceful personalities who made a special effort to propagate it. The two most important figures are Eisai (1141–1215) and Dogen (1200–53).

Eisai received a thorough training in Buddhism at Hieizan but was not satisfied with the contemporary forms of Buddhism. He wanted to go to India to search out the true Buddhism but traveled only as far as China, making two trips there. In China, Eisai was converted to the Lin-chi sect of Ch'an (Zen) Buddhism and received the full training of this sect. His return to Japan marks the beginning of the Japanese Zen sect of Rinzai. (*Rinzai* is the Japanese pronunciation for *Lin-chi*.) There is a tradition that he was responsible for the introduction of tea into Japan. Eisai had little luck in advocating Zen around the capital city of Kyoto, where the older sects were still entrenched. However, he found continuing support from the military warlords at Kamakura.

In China, too, Zen (Ch'an) had been partly a reaction against the scholasticism and formalism of some imported forms of Indian

Buddhism. In place of innumerable abstract doctrines, Zen set forth a simple notion that every person could attain enlightenment by insight into his or her own experience and the surrounding world. The Lin-chi (Rinzai) sect placed emphasis on a sudden enlightenment that might be triggered by an accidental circumstance. It is not surprising that Zen made a good showing in the Kamakura period, when Buddhism was appealing to the masses in simpler terms. Whereas the Amida cults stressed faith in Amida and Nichiren advocated faith in the *Lotus Sutra*, Zen priests replaced complicated doctrines with a notion of immediate enlightenment in the course of one's everyday life. It is no wonder that Kamakura military leaders found this notion appealing. Eisai, however, had to make certain compromises to the military rulers and to established Buddhists in order to have Zen recognized as a separate sect.

DOGEN: SITTING IN MEDITATION

Dogen (1200–53) reportedly went to see Eisai after being disappointed in his own studies of Buddhism at Hieizan. After Eisai's death, Dogen traveled to China but could gain no satisfaction from the Buddhist teachings there. Finally he attained enlightenment under the guidance of a Chinese Zen master and received the training of the Ts'ao-tung sect. He returned to Japan to spread this new version of Zen. (*Ts'ao-tung* is pronounced *Soto* in Japanese.) However, Dogen was more uncompromising than Eisai and could not bring himself to serve the military rulers. This made his life difficult, but eventually his Soto sect of Zen flourished.

The difference between Rinzai Zen and Soto Zen is roughly the same in China and Japan. Rinzai favors the use of techniques such as meditation on *koan* (which are comparable to riddles) to achieve sudden enlightenment. The Soto sect gives some weight to study of the scriptures and emphasizes the gradual entry into enlightenment. The Soto sect is famous for its practice of *zazen*, "sitting in meditation." Because of Dogen's two emphases "on scriptural authority and on faith in Buddha . . . the Soto Zen school in Japan was Dogen's unique creation."[6] Within Japanese society, Rinzai came to be identified with the ruling class, Soto with the common people.

Dogen's system of thought is considered by Japanese scholars to be one of the most creative developments within Japanese Buddhism, and increasingly Western scholars have become attracted to Dogen's analysis of human existence and the nature of time. A distinctive feature of Zen teachings, both in China and in Japan, has been to

emphasize a direct, intuitive transmission of the Buddha's enlightenment, and this is equally true for the transmission of Buddhist teaching about enlightenment from one master to his disciple.
Dogen's meeting in China with the Chinese Zen (Ch'an) master Ju-
ching was all-important in bringing Dogen to a realization of the
direct, intuitive nature of enlightenment. According to tradition,
Dogen was enlightened when he heard Ju-ching scolding a monk
sleeping. Ju-ching said that instead of sleeping, the monk should
"drop off the body and the mind." This brought home to Dogen the
fact that true enlightenment meant leaving behind completely both
mind and body. When Dogen set up his own monastic retreat, he
emphasized loyalty to one's Zen master and meditation that went
beyond thinking.

Dogen was critical of the Rinzai tradition of Zen Buddhism, which
stressed meditation on *koan*. He feared that monks meditating on *koan*
would become so engrossed in intellectual reflection on the *koan* that
they would be deluded into thinking about enlightenment. For Dogen, the attaining of enlightenment was not a rational process or a
solution to an intellectual puzzle. Enlightenment was more likely to
be achieved by the total realization of the whole person than by intellectual activity. Instead of the *koan*, Dogen emphasized *zazen*. Although even sitting in meditation requires the use of the body and
mind, Dogen stressed that the disciplining of body and mind in meditation facilitated the dropping off of body and mind. In other words,
enlightenment is beyond matter and spirit. In fact, according to Dogen, one can enter enlightenment only after any thought of attaining
enlightenment, or even any thought about enlightenment, has been
eliminated. The way to free oneself from any such thoughts is just
"to sit," to practice *zazen*. In a sense, one does not actually attain
enlightenment, for there is no enlightenment to attain.

From the time Dogen first studied Buddhism at Hieizan, he had
pondered the apparent contradiction of "original enlightenment" and
"attained enlightenment." A person had to have some original potential for enlightenment or else one could not become enlightened. But
if a person possessed the original enlightenment, then why did Buddhists find it so hard to strive to attain what they already possessed?
Dogen's solution, reached through his own enlightenment experience, was that the contradiction appears because people think about
enlightenment rather than practicing the way to enlightenment, *zazen*. A person who meditates in the proper fashion realizes that the
practice of meditation and enlightenment are the same. In proper
zazen, body and mind disappear automatically.

Dogen emphasized the importance of *zazen*, saying it superseded everything else. The experience of enlightenment within *zazen* reveals that the entire world is filled with the Buddha-nature. This is something that the unenlightened eye does not see but the enlightened eye is able to grasp immediately and intuitively.

101
Elaboration
Within
Japanese
Buddhism:
The Pure
Land,
Nichiren, and
Zen Sects

Dogen stressed the primacy of *zazen* to the extent that he set forth a radical view of time. According to Dogen, only the moment of enlightenment has "reality," and both past and present are contained within the essence of this crucial moment. This did not mean that a person who attained enlightenment could stop practicing meditation. On the contrary, for Dogen believed that life is most important and most real when a person sits in meditation. His creative genius brought the discipline of meditation to a mature conclusion.[7]

ZEN: INSTITUTIONAL AND ARTISTIC DEVELOPMENTS

Zen eventually assumed major importance in the Buddhist world. One landmark of Zen's success was the *shogun*'s decree of 1338, "which led to the building of Zen temples in sixty-six localities."[8] The temples, called *ankokuji*, or "temples to pacify the country," were similar in function to the earlier *kokubunji*, or provincial temples. Just as the *kokubunji* of the Nara period spread Buddhist teachings, so did the *ankokuji* of the fourteenth century help to spread Zen to the various regions of the country and to people of lower classes. The government recognized the top-ranking Zen temples (of the Rinzai sect), and the priests of these temples led the way in the study of Chinese classics and Neo-Confucianism.[9]

Even Zen was no exception to the general tendency of Buddhist sects to undergo fluctuating periods of strength and weaknesses. For example, Dogen's thought and practice were very lofty, and he trained important disciples, but the development of Soto Zen into a major Buddhist denomination in Japan was mainly the work of Keizan (1268–1325), who lived shortly after the time of Dogen. Keizan was more willing than Dogen to compromise and blend with Zen other ritual practices. The simple funeral and memorial practices that he developed helped Soto Zen spread among the people much more thoroughly than Rinzai Zen. Later, the aristocratic Rinzai tended to lose its vigor, but in the eighteenth century, Hakuin (1686–1769) did much to revive Rinzai and meditation on *koan*. Hakuin is the author of the famous *koan* "Listen to the sound of the single hand"[10]—that is, to realize the sound of one hand clapping.

The seventeenth-century poet Basho (1644–94), who also practiced Zen Buddhism, did much to further the aesthetic expression of Zen in his beautiful short poems called *haiku*. During Basho's last illness, while he was on a trip, his followers asked him to give them a final poem or "death poem." At first, Basho refused. But he lived through the night, and the next morning he gave them a poem based on his dreams during the night:

> On a journey, ill,
> and over fields all withered, dreams
> go wandering still.[11]

Zen has its roots in India, emerged as a sect in China, and first flourished in Japan as the imported Rinzai and Soto sects. But Zen is much more than a sectarian expression of Buddhism or a personal experience of enlightenment. In both China and Japan, Zen had a strong impact on the arts. Shingon had made some contribution to the graphic arts; Zen pervaded the whole culture. Zen (colored by Taoism's love of nature) is the spiritual inspiration of much Chinese and Japanese painting; its influence can be seen in the art of flower arranging *(ikebana)*. Unlike Shingon art, which favors the esoteric and borders on the grotesque, Zen favors a quiet simplicity.

It is difficult to say whether the Chinese tradition of Ch'an (Zen) taught quiet simplicity to the Japanese or whether the Japanese brought a cultural tradition of quiet simplicity to their understanding of Zen. However, from ancient times the Japanese have had a peculiar tradition combining aesthetic and religious appreciation of nature. This can be seen as early as the eighth-century anthology of poetry, *Manyoshu*. Many Westerners have come to appreciate Zen through translations of *haiku*, which express the spirit of Zen. Also, the drinking of tea and the cult of tea have been closely associated with Zen.

Zen has pervaded Japanese culture even beyond the realms of what Westerners ordinarily understand as art. Zen practitioners cared less for subtlety of doctrine than they cared for the complete training of mind and body. There was a relationship between emphasis on the instant of enlightenment and tuning the mind and body to every instant of experience. Therefore, military techniques or sports such as swordsmanship, archery, and wrestling were pursued for the sake of Zen. The object was not simply to defeat the opponent, but to tune one's whole being to a naturalness and freeness that transcended the formalities of prescribed movements. Kamakura warriors adopted Zen both for its utilitarian and its spiritual benefits. In the modern period, Zen continues to be a major inspiration for philosophical thought and religious cultivation.

103
*Elaboration
Within
Japanese
Buddhism:
The Pure
Land,
Nichiren, and
Zen Sects*

Offering incense at temples is one of the most common acts of religious devotion in Japan. On the top is the courtyard of a large Zen temple in Tokyo. In the top photograph, people are offering incense in a large metal brazier in front of a seated statue of Jizo (featuring a large pilgrim's hat). Below, people take advantage of the curative powers of incense at another nearby temple by placing their hands in the smoke and rubbing the afflicted parts of their bodies. The woman in front is holding her hand into the smoke, while the women behind the incense brazier are rubbing their bodies. (Tokyo, 1979)

In order to explain the development and elaboration of Buddhism, it has been necessary to describe new sects and doctrinal variations. However, one should not infer that all the Japanese people who accepted Buddhism were aware of all these developments. Buddhism made its impression on the lives of ordinary lay people in a direct fashion. We must not forget, amid these discussions of doctrine, that Japanese Buddhism has always been important for carrying out indispensable memorials for family ancestors. Even Nichiren, seen by some as a religious fanatic and superpatriot, is said to have spent much time in prayer for the departed souls of his parents and teacher. One way of viewing the development of sects is to recognize that they created special channels within which practical functions could be carried out. In addition to the memorial services, temples held regular festivals and issued various protective charms. The people who had memorial services performed at a temple or went there for other reasons might not be familiar with the peculiar doctrines of that sect. The sects that came into being in the Kamakura period are the major Buddhist institutions of the modern era, and since their founding they have combined theoretical doctrine with popular practice.

NOTES

1. The third and final age is known in Japan as *mappo*, a compound term formed by the two words *matsu* (last or final) and *ho* (the Buddha's teachings).
2. Masaharu Anesaki, *History of Japanese Religion* (London: Kegan Paul, Trench, Trubner, 1930; reprint ed., Rutland, Vt.: Charles E. Tuttle Company, 1963), pp. 182–83.
3. Hajime Nakamura, *Ways of Thinking of Eastern Peoples: India, China, Tibet, Japan* (Honolulu: East-West Center Press, 1964), p. 451.
4. The Mongol fleet was destroyed by a storm that proponents of Shinto chose to interpret as a "divine wind" *(kamikaze)*. Thus, the Shinto interpretation stressed that native gods had driven out the foreigners. In World War II, the airplanes of the suicide pilots who crashed their planes into Allied ships were also called *kamikaze*.
5. Reiho Masunaga, *The Soto Approach to Zen* (Tokyo: Layman Buddhist Society Press, 1958), p. 34.
6. Joseph M. Kitagawa, *Religion in Japanese History* (New York: Columbia University Press, 1966), p. 129.
7. A film that illustrates meditation and also social activities within two Soto Zen temples is *Zen in Life*, a 25-minute, 16-mm. color film produced by a Soto university and distributed by Hartley Productions.
8. Heinrich Dumoulin, *A History of Zen Buddhism*, trans. Paul Peachey (New York: Pantheon Books, 1963; several reprints), p. 178; the localities were different provinces.

9. The actual system of ranks (of five temples or *gozan*) is probably Chinese in origin. See Toshihide Akamatsu and Philip Yampolsky, "Muromachi Zen and the Gozan System," in *Japan in the Muromachi Age,* ed. John Whitney Hall and Takeshi Toyoda (Berkeley: University of California Press, 1977), pp. 313–15.
10. Philip B. Yampolsky, trans., *The Zen Master Hakuin: Selected Writings* (New York: Columbia University Press, 1971), p. 163.
11. Haiku from the book *An Introduction to Haiku,* translated by Harold G. Henderson. Copyright © 1958 by Harold G. Henderson. Reprinted by permission of Doubleday & Company, Inc.

SELECTED READINGS

Anesaki, Masaharu. *Nichiren the Buddhist Prophet.* Cambridge, Mass.: Harvard University Press, 1916. An early publication but still the standard biography of Nichiren in English.

Bloom, Alfred. *Shinran's Gospel of Pure Grace.* Tucson: University of Arizona Press, 1965. A concise study of Shinran's thought.

Coates, Harper Havelock, and Ishizuka, Ryugaku. *Honen the Buddhist Saint: His Life and Teaching.* Kyoto: Chion-in, 1925; several later reprintings. A careful study of Honen.

Dumoulin, Heinrich. *A History of Zen Buddhism.* Translated by Paul Peachey. New York: Pantheon Books, 1963. The best historical treatment of Zen; includes a convenient bibliography.

Earhart, H. Byron. *Religion in the Japanese Experience: Sources and Interpretations.* Belmont, Calif.: Wadsworth, 1974. See pp. 52–61 for materials related to Pure Land Buddhism and pp. 131–44 and 197–200 for materials related to Zen.

Foard, James H. "In Search of a Lost Reformation: A Reconsideration of Kamakura Buddhism." *Japanese Journal of Religious Studies,* Vol. 7, No. 4 (December 1980), 261–91. A reassessment of early Japanese Buddhist groups in sociological terms, reserving the label of "sect" for Jodo, Jodo Shinshu, and Nichiren groups.

Tsunoda, Ryusaku, et al. *Sources of Japanese Tradition.* New York: Columbia University Press, 1958. See Chapter 10 for translated documents concerning the Pure Land sects, Chapter 11 for translated documents concerning the Nichiren sect, and Chapter 12 for translated documents concerning the Zen sect.

CHAPTER 11

The Development of Medieval Shinto

In Chapter 4 we saw how Shinto became organized partly in reaction to the influx of continental traditions such as Buddhism. In later chapters we discussed the development of Buddhism, Confucianism, and religious Taoism. Chapters 9 and 10 demonstrated the vitality and innovation within Japanese Buddhism from the ninth through the thirteenth centuries. It may seem that Shinto has been crowded out of the historical picture by the attempt to discuss foreign importations such as Buddhism. As a matter of fact, Shinto had been overshadowed by the flourishing of Buddhism. Most of the emperors and the nobility favored Buddhism, and the court was mainly concerned with Buddhism. Thus, if we look at the capital and the formal organization of the state, Buddhism seems to have overwhelmed the native religion.

However, the "great tradition," which dominated political and literary life, is only one side of Japanese religious history. There is also the "little tradition," which expressed the cultural and religious life of the people. The common people outside of the capital lived their religious lives primarily in terms of annual festivals connected with agriculture and other vocations. Many shrines and festivals existed before the entry of Buddhism and continued naturally with or without the influence of Buddhism. While Buddhism dominated the court, Shinto with its loosely organized religious life centering on local shrines remained the prevailing religion of the countryside.

MEDIEVAL BUDDHISM AND MEDIEVAL SHINTO

107
*The
Development
of Medieval
Shinto*

Buddhism never completely superseded Shinto. Even at the capital, Shinto lived on in the cult headed by the emperor. In fact, as long as Buddhism was centered at the capital, it tended to remain the religion of the aristocracy. Nara Buddhism made very little impact on the people. Even the Tendai and Shingon sects of Heian Buddhism fell short of their goal of developing a Japanese Buddhism. Buddhism would become a religion of the people only when it entered the life of the people. In part, Shinto's appropriation of Buddhist systems enhanced Buddhism's popular appeal. People eventually came to accept various Buddhist *bodhisattvas* on the same level as their Japanese *kami*. Therefore, although Buddhism seemed to triumph on the surface, the religious life of Shinto persevered—even within Buddhist forms. While Buddhism was being transformed into a Japanese movement, Shinto was quietly incorporating the various strands of continental influence.

BORROWING BY MEDIEVAL SHINTO

The further development of Shinto is the result of more than a simple encounter with Buddhism. In the Heian and Kamakura periods, when Chinese culture was so highly esteemed, Shinto tended to draw into itself elements of Confucianism, religious Taoism, and Buddhism—especially speculative philosophy and cosmology from Buddhism. In general, Shinto borrowed various religious expressions from the three traditions. Ethical concepts came from Confucianism; religious Taoism provided cosmology, a religious calendar, divinities, festivals, and charms; Buddhism furnished philosophy, cosmology, rituals, objects of worship, and formulas.

Shinto's practice of borrowing must be seen from two viewpoints in order to be understood. On the one hand, Shinto never ceased to be the perpetuator of the older Japanese traditions; borrowed foreign concepts usually complemented or explained Shinto traditions. In this sense, Shinto remained Shinto in spite of the borrowings. On the other hand, the borrowings became so much a part of Shinto that eventually their foreign origin was forgotten. In this sense, the complexity of Shinto increased to the extent that Shinto cannot be called simply the indigenous religion of Japan. Borrowed traditions added to the richness of Shinto and enabled it to become more systematically organized.

"Medieval Shinto" is an approximate term referring to Shinto when it was actively borrowing from other traditions and organizing itself on borrowed patterns, especially from about the twelfth through the sixteenth centuries. The outside limits of medieval Shinto are difficult to set, for Shinto never was completely isolated; the precedent for Shinto's borrowing from other traditions was already established in the Nara period. Perhaps it may be said that medieval Shinto took shape and flourished from the Heian period onward. The terminal date for medieval Shinto is officially 1868, the date of the Meiji Restoration, when Shinto and Buddhism were forcibly separated. Shinto purists, however, had been working for this separation for several centuries before 1868.

Perhaps the best way to introduce medieval Shinto is to discuss it in terms of the traditions that influenced it. Although Buddhism was not the only influential tradition, it was undoubtedly the most influential. The Buddhist theory of *honji-suijaku* ("original substance manifests traces") pervaded practically the whole of Shinto. The theory of *honji-suijaku,* transmitted from China to Japan, became the theoretical foundation for considering Japanese *kami* as "manifest traces" *(suijaku)* or counterparts of the "original substance" *(honji)* of particular Buddhas and *bodhisattvas.* In the Nara period Hachiman was considered both a *kami* for Shinto and a *bodhisattva* for Buddhism. In later periods almost every Shinto shrine considered its enshrined *kami* as the counterpart of some Buddha or Buddhist divinity. It was customary to enshrine statues of these Buddhist counterparts in Shinto shrines, and this practice further encouraged the interaction of Buddhist and Shinto priests. It should be noted that the mixing of Buddhism with local Japanese religion is not unique in the history of Buddhism. The Buddhist pantheon had been closely associated with other divinities in India, and then in China it developed counterparts of various Chinese deities.

One reason medieval Shinto is difficult to outline is the fact that it was never uniformly systematized. For example, the theory of *honji-suijaku* was put into practice in many local shrines throughout the country, but there was no uniform set of counterparts for Shinto *kami* and Buddhist divinities. Shinto shrines might be dedicated to the worship of divinities that were Buddhist, Chinese, Korean, or Indian in origin. Shinto priests (and Buddhist priests and the people) could participate religiously in this ambiguous context without making any precise relationships or sharp distinctions. We have seen that this informal sense of harmony among the several religious traditions is present throughout Japanese religious history.

THE RELATION OF TENDAI AND SHINGON TO MEDIEVAL SHINTO

When the "way" of Buddha (Butsudo) entered Japan, it stimulated the formation of the "way" of *kami* (Shinto). Thereafter Buddhism and Shinto were in informal contact with one another, but not until the Heian period did the Tendai and Shingon sects openly favor cooperation between Buddhism and Shinto. Medieval Shinto arose in the Heian period and borrowed from the Tendai and Shingon sects for two main reasons. First, these two Buddhist sects actively assumed a Japanese character, making them acceptable to Shinto. Second, both sects possessed the richer cosmology, philosophy, and ritual that Shinto apparently desired. There were early precedents for Shinto-Buddhist cooperation, which Shinto scholars could use in the Heian period to justify borrowing from Tendai and Shingon in building up a more glorious Shinto system. This set the stage for significant cross-fertilization between Shinto, and Tendai and Shingon.

The first elaborate system of borrowing between Shinto and Buddhism was at Hieizan, the mountain headquarters of Tendai. To a certain extent the basic mode of borrowing was similar at Koyasan, the mountain headquarters of Shingon. In the Heian period, Shinto shrines and Buddhist temples stood side by side, and priests of Shinto and Buddhism sometimes participated in each other's rites. The founders of the two Buddhist sects, Dengyo Daishi and Kobo Daishi, thought it only natural that shrines should be erected to honor the local *kami* of their respective mountains. Gradually there emerged at each locale individual forms of thought and practice that related the Shinto *kami* and Buddhist doctrine. Since the Tendai headquarters was modeled after the Chinese mountain headquarters by the same name (*T'ien-t'ai* in Chinese), the Tendai scholars had a precedent to follow in recognizing the local deity. The name for the local deity, adopted from the Chinese, was "mountain king" (pronounced *Sanno* in Japanese). The theoretical foundation of the system, according to Tendai, was found in the highly revered *Lotus Sutra*. In this text is a statement that all the Buddhas that come into the world are only "one reality" *(ichi jitsu)* — the Tendai concept of an absolute reality behind the whole universe. The theory was used to argue that the various *kami* are Japanese historical appearances that correspond to Buddhist divinities, all of which are subsumed in the "one reality." This form of Shinto was called either Sanno Shinto or Ichi-jitsu Shinto. The *honji-suijaku* theory set up a general framework of correspondences between *kami* and Buddhist divinities; Ichi-jitsu Shinto developed a particular theory of correspondences based on Tendai teaching.

This brief presentation may have given the impression that borrowing was mainly intellectual. The contrary, however, is true: At the popular level, there was a ritual and devotional union of Shinto and Buddhism. Officially Shinto was separated from Buddhism after 1868, but even today many Sanno shrines survive. Although explicit Buddhist influence has been removed from the shrines, the very existence of Sanno shrines is a continuing reminder of the earlier Shinto-Buddhist intermixture.

In the same vein, we can see Shinto absorbing the Shingon notion that the whole world can best be understood through two *mandala.* The symbolic pictures of the cosmos represented the bipolar character of existence apparent in the mutually opposing forces of matter-mind, male-female, and dynamic expression—static potential. With this ideological framework, Shinto priests could coordinate Japanese *kami* and Buddhist divinities, for they could place some *kami* within the womb *mandala* and other *kami* within the diamond *mandala.* Because this syncretistic style of Shinto emphasized the two *mandala* of Shingon, it was called Ryobu Shinto. *Ryobu* means "two parts" or "dual," and sometimes Ryobu Shinto has been called "Dual Shinto." A famous example of the rationale of Ryobu Shinto is found at the Ise Shrines, the most venerated shrines in Japan. Amaterasu, the Sun Goddess and ancestress of the imperial family, is enshrined at Ise. In later times the Sun Goddess came to be equated with the Sun Buddha of the *Mahavairocana Sutra,* which is the main scripture of Shingon. The Ise Shrines, which include the Inner Shrine and Outer Shrine, came to be considered representations of the two *mandala* of Shingon.

It should not be overlooked that Shinto influenced Buddhism, even in the highly developed religious art form of the *mandala.* A Shinto version of the *mandala* appeared. Often it portrayed a kind of aerial view of a shrine compound. Shinto borrowed the form of the *mandala* but gave it a typically "this-worldly" Shinto coloring.[1] Shinto transformed the abstract Buddhist *mandala,* which represented an ideal other world, into a picture of the actual Japanese landscape. This is a good example of how Shinto emphasis on the sacredness of nature and the presence of *kami* in this world influenced the abstract Buddhist symbolism that it borrowed.

Shinto also borrowed from Shingon—rituals such as the fire rite, architectural forms, and theoretical elements. A shrine that received the influence of Ryobu Shinto can be identified even today by the peculiar *torii* (sacred arch) in front of it. There are various kinds of Shinto *torii*, all of which feature two upright poles with a crosspiece connecting the poles. In Ryobu Shinto the *torii* was modified so that each upright pole had attached to it two smaller poles. The two smaller poles indicate the dual character of the world, which is transcended by an overarching unity.

MEDIEVAL SHINTO: INDIVIDUAL SCHOLARS
AND FAMILY TRADITIONS

Tendai and Shingon influenced Shinto most strongly in places where their temples stood near shrines. However, the interpenetration experienced by some Buddhist and Shinto centers is not the whole story. Medieval Shinto can be said to have developed in at least two other ways. One was through the traditions maintained by hereditary Shinto priestly families. Another was through individual Shinto scholars. For example, the Japanese tradition of religious Taoism (Onmyodo) entered medieval Shinto through the Shinto families who had carried on the traditions formerly within the government bureau of divination. Naturally, this school emphasized the important role of divination. Even outside these hereditary families, the *yin-yang* notion of religious Taoism was already available as early as the writing of the eighth-century *Nihongi*. Medieval Shinto received the influence of religious Taoism from its earliest traces in Japan, both directly from these hereditary families and indirectly from the Taoistic traditions incorporated within Shingon. The charms and divinities of religious Taoism penetrated both Buddhism and Shinto. Confucianism was an indirect influence on Shinto thinkers, since their education was still heavily Confucian.[2]

From the very moment when Shinto arose, we see a general picture of Shinto appropriating as much as it could of the continental traditions. Shinto was not a passive recipient of these influences; rather, it actively adapted the new elements. The reason for this appropriation and adaptation was to strengthen and organize Shinto. As Shinto became more self-confident, it attempted to reassert its distinctiveness and superiority.

The best example of Shinto adaptation is the Yui-itsu (or Yui-ichi) school of Shinto. This movement reversed the former interpretation of *honji-suijaku*, making the Japanese *kami* the "original substance" *(honji)* and the Buddhist divinity the "manifest trace" *(suijaku)* and giving the superior position to the Japanese *kami*. The Yui-itsu school of Shinto, sometimes named after the Yoshida or Urabe family, developed a comprehensive pantheistic system on this basic principle, making Shinto into an all-embracing philosophy and religion. The Yui-itsu school and other Shinto scholars used similar schemes to try to set themselves apart from Buddhism, Confucianism, and Taoism. However, from our historical vantage point we can see that they could not escape from the borrowed influence. The pantheistic system was pervaded by the very Buddhist influence they were trying to escape. Nevertheless, these movements are important for understanding the growing Shinto concern to "purify" itself and to regain its former position of glory.

A long line of writers from medieval times onward supported the cause of a purified Shinto. The most famous of the early writers is Kitabatake Chikafusa (1293–1354), who supported the theory of the divine descent of the imperial line and argued for the superiority of Shinto over the foreign traditions. A more systematic writer, the foremost proponent of Yui-itsu Shinto, is Yoshida Kanetomo (1435–1511). One Japanese scholar of Shinto has written, "From this inexhaustible intellectual fountain-head of Kanetomo's theology almost every later Shinto theological school of the Tokugawa period takes its source."[3] Kanetomo depended heavily on *Gobusho,* a thirteenth-century writing of the Ise priests. The *Gobusho,* a collection of five writings, is a good example of how Shinto became organized partly in reaction to Buddhism. Shinto writers composed the *Gobusho* so that they, too, would have a scripture. The writing drew heavily on foreign themes.

A number of nebulous Shinto schools formed themselves around one or more of these borrowed traditions. But they remained schools (lines of teaching) and did not become separate sects (organized religious institutions) until about the nineteenth century. The Shinto schools never had the distinct existence that Buddhist sects enjoyed. Perhaps this is a significant clue to medieval Shinto. Shinto possessed unique Japanese traditions that were very important for the life of the country, yet Shinto lacked a unified system by which to express these traditions. Shinto lacked the philosophical subtlety and completeness of Buddhism. The motive for Shinto's borrowing was not to create a tradition, but to elaborate the Shinto tradition into a full-blown system equal to any foreign tradition.

We must never forget the vitality and broad base of Shinto. As early as 927 the Institutes of the Engi period *(Engishiki)* recorded more than six thousand Shinto shrines where annual offerings were made by officials of the court or provincial government.[4] This was a big step in organizing and ranking the loosely affiliated shrines. Gradually local shrines became more closely related to the regional community and more directly related to the formal Shinto pantheon. Although many early shrines were practically the possession of individual families and their blood relations, these shrines eventually became places of worship for all the people of that area. This set the pattern for the traditional village shrine with the village (or village subdivisions) as the geographical parish. During medieval times when powerful families began to open up the northern part of Japan, they established branch shrines of their famous shrines in their new homes in the north. The branch shrines, too, became important regional worship centers for the surrounding people. At the same time there was a tendency for Shinto scholars to insist that the object of worship in local shrines had to correspond to one of the *kami* in the *Kojiki* or *Nihongi*. Although these *kami* were specified as the official objects of worship at local shrines, this change did not really alter the rituals at the shrines and the faith of the worshipers.

The true power of the shrine system is seen in the times leading up to World War II, when Shinto was used by the government to inculcate patriotism in the guise of venerating the emperor. Throughout the medieval period, political power rested almost completely in the hands of the military rulers, but the emperor was still held in high regard by the people and was at least respected by the military rulers. The emperor had an important role in continuing Shinto ceremonies on behalf of the nation. At the same time, the emperors were deeply concerned with Buddhism, and it was often the custom for the emperor to abdicate after a short reign and become a Buddhist monk.[5]

NOTES

1. For a lavishly illustrated book on Shinto art, including Shinto *mandala*, see Haruki Kageyama, *The Arts of Shinto*, trans. Christine Guth (New York: Weatherhill/Shibundo, 1973).
2. Much later, in the nineteenth century, several Shinto sects were formed around Confucian doctrines.
3. Genchi Kato, "The Theological System of Urabe no Kanetomo," *Transactions of the Japan Society of London*, Vol. 28 (1931), pp. 149–50. (Yoshida and Urabe refer to the same family line; it is customary to refer to such famous scholars by their given names. In the text of this book all Japanese names follow the Japanese practice of giving the family name first.)

4. See Ryusaku Tsunoda et al., *Sources of Japanese Tradition* (New York: Columbia University Press, 1958), Chapter 13. For a translation of the *Engishiki*, see Felicia Gressitt Bock, trans., *Engi-shiki: Procedures of the Engi Era, Books I–V* (Tokyo: Sophia University, 1970); *Engi-shiki: Procedures of the Engi Era, Books VI–X* (Tokyo: Sophia University, 1972).

5. For a fascinating excerpt from a fourteenth-century emperor's diary and a glimpse of other religious aspects of the medieval age, see Sir George Sansom, *A History of Japan*, Vol. 2 (Stanford, Calif.: Stanford University Press, 1961), pp. 127–40.

SELECTED READINGS

Earhart, H. Byron. *Religion in the Japanese Experience: Sources and Interpretations*. Belmont, Calif.: Wadsworth, 1974. See pp. 39–44 for excerpts from Matsunaga.

Holtom, Daniel C. *The National Faith of Japan: A Study in Modern Shinto*. New York: Dutton, 1938. Reprint ed., New York: Paragon Book Reprint Corp., 1965. See pp. 30–52 for a historical treatment of the transition from early to medieval Shinto.

Kato, Genchi. "The Theological System of Urabe no Kanetomo." *Transactions of the Japan Society of London*, Vol. 28 (1931), 143–50. Treats the general significance of the medieval Shinto theologian Kanetomo.

Matsunaga, Alicia. *The Buddhist Philosophy of Assimilation: The Historical Development of the Honji-Suijaku Theory*. Tokyo and Rutland, Vt.: Sophia University and Charles E. Tuttle Company, 1969. Provides an interpretation of the "unification of gods and Buddhas" from the viewpoint of Buddhism.

Tsunoda, Ryusaku, et al. *Sources of Japanese Tradition*. New York: Columbia University Press, 1958. See Chapter 13 for an introduction to medieval Shinto, with translated documents.

CHAPTER 12

The Appearance of Christianity in Japan

By the middle of the sixteenth century, all the basic traditions within Japanese religion had interacted to a great degree and had developed distinctive lines of transmission. In 1549 Christianity was introduced into the Japanese islands by Roman Catholic missionaries. The Japanese, being rather self-conscious of their own distinctive blend of traditions into a Japanese culture, did not at first understand Christianity and viewed it as a foreign religion. It may be argued that Christianity (unlike Buddhism) did not become transformed into a Japanese religion. Nevertheless, an examination of "the Christian century in Japan," as one scholar has described the period of about one hundred years when Christianity first flourished in Japan,[1] gives us many insights into Japanese religious history.

The first Christian missionary to Japan was Saint Francis Xavier, later called the Apostle of Japan. Xavier was drawn to Japan by favorable accounts of the country, and his first impression verified the rumors. In a few years he saw an encouraging number of converts and foresaw a glorious future for the Roman church in Japan. He did not underestimate the faith of the most sincere converts, but neither did he suspect the great trials to which their faith would be subjected. Within a century's time the foreign priests and Japanese Christians experienced a persecution that some scholars say is unparalleled in the history of the Christian church. By about 1650 Christianity ceased to exist as a public religion, surviving only on a small scale as a secret cult.

THE INTRODUCTION OF CHRISTIANITY INTO JAPAN

The motives for missionary work, both Christian and Buddhist, have usually included a mixture of religious, economic, and cultural factors. The entry of Christianity into sixteenth-century Japan was no exception. The earliest missionaries were chiefly Portuguese Jesuits, and the ships that brought the Jesuits carried European goods for trade. The economic support of the Jesuits was closely related to this trade, and it was no secret that the Japanese feudal lords desired the presence of a Jesuit priest in order to attract trade with the Portuguese ships. (The ships brought highly prized Chinese silk to Japan.)

Xavier at first traveled to the capital with the purpose of speaking to the "king" of Japan and discovered that in the midsixteenth century the emperor was only a figurehead; real political power was held by a military ruler and local feudal lords. In Europe, Jesuit missionaries first tried to convert members of elite groups such as the nobility. This pattern was repeated in Japan. The Jesuits learned that without the cooperation—or at least the tolerance—of the feudal lords, they could do nothing. A feudal lord often would declare for Christianity more or less superficially, and his subjects would follow suit. The Jesuits were well aware of the expediency of these conversions, but they accepted the situation because it enabled them to work for genuine converts.

Xavier left Japan reluctantly after two years. A handful of priests remained to carry on the work. Gradually other Roman Catholic orders were represented, but there never was a great number of priests in Japan. (The unfriendly rivalry between Jesuits and other Catholic orders constituted a major obstacle to effective missionary work and may have made the military rulers suspicious of all foreigners.) However, there was an increasing number of conversions, and the attraction to Christianity cannot be explained simply in economic terms. In accounting for these conversions to Christianity, we can understand something about the nature of Christianity itself, the contemporary religious scene in Japan, and the Japanese people.

THE JAPANESE ACCEPTANCE OF CHRISTIANITY

Generally speaking, when a foreign religion enters a new area, its acceptance or rejection hinges on a host of complicated factors that are not directly related to religion. A religion is never accepted or rejected solely on the basis of its message. In Japan as elsewhere, an important factor influencing the acceptability of a foreign religion has been the relative instability of the social and political situation. Japanese scholars have pointed out that during periods when there was great social unheaval and the Japanese people were eager to receive a new message, the foreign character of Christianity was to its advantage in gaining Japanese converts. Christianity was most successful during three periods of radical social change: (1) the latter part of the period of civil wars (1482–1558), (2) the Meiji era (1868–1912), and (3) the post–World War II period of occupation (1945–52). But when the national mood swung back to emphasize national and cultural unification, the foreignness of Christianity invited criticism and even persecution.[2]

The acceptance of Christianity during the first half of the Christian century (from 1549 to 1597) was stimulated by great social changes. Japan was suffering from civil wars, which had resulted in much bloodshed and sudden swings of loyalty. In the midst of this confusion there was a great deal of immorality, particularly on the part of the warriors. Buddhism suffered from its own participation in these bloody wars, as well as from sharp sectarianism. These conditions helped to persuade the Japanese to look for a new, foreign faith.

The difference that the Japanese perceived in Christianity was not simply its foreign origin, but its contrast with the tradition of Japanese religion. The contrast can be highlighted by focusing on some central features of the two heritages. Christianity emphasizes absolute faith in a transcendent deity (to the exclusion of other religious commitments). The Japanese tradition accepts the existence of many *kami* and Buddhist divinities as well as multiple affiliations by one person. The Christian tradition sees a great distance between human beings and the deity; the Japanese notion stresses the close harmony among mortals, *kami* (or Buddhist divinities), and nature. Crucial to Christian faith is the idea of human sinfulness and the need for redemption; the Japanese tradition has a higher opinion of human nature and eliminates impurities and corrects mistakes through purification ceremonies. And, to take one final example, Christianity stresses individual responsibility before God, whereas the Japanese tradition values group loyalty and group participation in religion. These differences, which were recognized by both Christian missionaries and Japanese, were not so great as to make it impossible for Japanese to accept Christianity; but they played a role both in the initial acceptance and in the subsequent rejection of Christianity.

It is well to remember that the historical circumstances of the sixteenth century sharply limited Japanese perception of Christianity.

Christianity had the advantage of presenting to the Japanese a unified system of faith and practice, because only Roman Catholicism entered Japan at this time and at first it was introduced only by the Jesuit order. The Jesuits deserved their reputation as the intellectual leaders of Catholicism. Their military style of organization enabled them to recruit able men and train them as well-disciplined defenders of the Church in the attempt to rebuild Catholic strength following the Protestant Reformation in Europe. Of course, most Japanese were not aware of the Protestant-Catholic confrontation and Protestant sectarianism in Europe, and the Jesuits chose not to tell them. All that the Japanese knew about Christianity, they learned from the Roman Catholic missionaries.

In the context of these general historical considerations, what was the attraction of Christianity? According to one scholar, "Christianity represented a double attraction: ethical to the *bushi*, the leading class of Japan; and salvationist to the masses." For the *bushi*, or warrior, who was brought up on the notion of absolute loyalty to his feudal lord, "the step to Christianity was not a large or an illogical one,"[3] because the relationship between human beings and the Christian God was also taught by the Jesuits to be one of absolute loyalty. In fact, the Jesuit preaching in Japan, which stressed both a self-sacrificing ideal and an uncompromising moral code (with stinging criticism of immorality in Japanese society), appears to have been very attractive to these highly disciplined warriors. The Jesuits, with their blend of religious and military discipline, appealed directly to the Japanese warriors.

In northern Kyushu, in particular, common people were the mainstay of the Church, and they seem to have been drawn by the combination of a guarantee of a transcendent salvation and a strong moral code. (It is worth recalling here that each of the most successful Buddhist movements in Japan—the Pure Land, Zen, and Nichiren sects—had stressed an assurance of salvation in a distinctive fashion. Thus it is not surprising that some Japanese would accept a foreign variation of the notion of assurance of salvation.) Some feudal lords seem to have been more concerned with patronizing Christianity (especially by allowing missionaries to preach in their domains) or with converting to Christianity for the economic benefit of attracting the Portuguese trading ships in which the Christian missionaries had a financial interest. In some cases when the feudal lord converted, he had his whole domain convert to Christianity.

As the foregoing considerations demonstrate, the historical circumstances and personal motivations leading to acceptance of Chris-

tianity were complex. (The same is true of almost all instances of
religious conversion.) But whatever the circumstances and motivations, many Japanese overcame the obstacles of difference and
foreignness to gain a deep and lasting commitment to Christianity,
even to the point of martyrdom. Although the exact degree of personal commitment cannot be determined, by 1579 there were about
130,000 Christians in Japan. What is surprising is that this large
number of Christians was served by only fifty-five members of
the Jesuit order (twenty-three of whom were priests).

At first, the Jesuit missionaries in Japan required Japanese converts
to adopt Christian (and European) customs and refused to ordain
Japanese as priests. This policy was soon changed, so that both the
European priests and their Japanese converts followed Japanese customs wherever possible, and Japanese men were eventually ordained. The inability of the Christian mission to spread throughout
Japan was not the result of ineffective policy; it was due to limited
manpower and meager finances. It was impossible for the Jesuits to
gain enough replacements for the European priests (the journey to
Japan was lengthy and hazardous), and the training of Japanese assis-
tants was a painfully slow process. The missionaries created their
own dictionaries of Japanese, for even the simplest tract had to be
translated from a European language, such as Latin, to Japanese. In
terms of money, the mission field was not yet self-supporting, and the
only income was the profit from the annual trading ship (which might
be lost at sea). The miracle of the Christian century is that, in the face
of all these difficulties, Christianity made as much progress in Japan
as it did. The Christianity of this early period is still remembered
by the Japanese term *Kirishitan*, a Japanese pronunciation of the
Portuguese word *Christao*, for "Christian." The Japanese perception
of Christianity as a foreign religion had helped Christianity gain
members. Later the foreign character of Christianity would make it
the object of suspicion by the government.

THE EXPULSION OF CHRISTIANITY

The fortunes and misfortunes of Roman Catholicism in medieval
Japan were closely linked to the careers of three great military leaders
and unifiers of Japan: Oda Nobunaga (1534–82), Toyotomi Hideyoshi
(1536–98), and Tokugawa Ieyasu (1542–1616). During Nobunaga's
rule, Christianity flourished with his consent. It is said that Nobunaga
was motivated not so much by his love for Christianity as by his

hatred for Buddhism. Nobunaga, in trying to unify the country politically, saw the large Buddhist headquarters as political and military threats. Several times he saw fit to punish the Buddhist strongholds with military force. In 1571, for example, he completely devastated the Tendai mountain of Hieizan, massacring all monks, laymen, and even women and children. It is thought that Nobunaga may have allowed Christianity to grow only with the ulterior motive of having it check the strength of Buddhism.

Nobunaga's successor Hideyoshi turned into a persecutor of the Christian church. The reasons for this change are veiled by the passage of time. The reversal of policy, however, may be connected with a general suspicion that the Catholic fathers had secret plans to take over Japan. Hideyoshi had destroyed the strongholds of Pure Land Buddhism, which threatened his secular power, and he did not hesitate to ban a foreign religion that seemed to demand too much loyalty of his subjects. To a pragmatic ruler like Hideyoshi, there was no room for absolute loyalty outside the state—whether it was to Amida and Pure Land priests or to Christ and Catholic priests. Hideyoshi's 1587 order expelling the Catholic priests was really neither antiforeign nor anti-Christian. "It was part of Hideyoshi's program for the restructuring of Japan under central authority."[4] At any rate, Hideyoshi still encouraged trade with the Portuguese while proscribing the Christian faith. In actuality, his edict against Christianity was not rigorously enforced, and the result was that more converts were added to the church during this period of mild persecution.

Ieyasu, the next ruler, made good the threats of his predecessors by actually driving the foreign missionaries from Japan. Whereas Nobunaga and Hideyoshi had been antagonistic toward Buddhism, Ieyasu's personal life was influenced by Buddhist piety and his government policy was supported by Confucian ideals. Ieyasu is one of the most imposing figures in all Japanese history. He was so revered that he was deified by his own priestly adviser as the Sun God of the East.[5] An imposing shrine serves as his tomb of enshrinement at Nikko, and branch shrines dedicated to him are found throughout Japan. His decree of 1614 meant the physical deportation of all foreign missionaries, including some leading Christians.

Although Ieyasu did not shed any blood, his successors provided many martyrs for the church. Priests who had defied the edict to stay in Japan, and the loyal Japanese Christians who hid them, were executed. The most hideous tortures were devised to make these foreign priests and Japanese Christians recant their faith and refute Christianity publicly. The tortures were only partially successful in gaining formal renunciation of the faith among the people. Gradually the foreign priests were all hunted down, and later attempts to land missionaries resulted in immediate capture.

One of the decisive events in the downfall of Catholicism was the Shimabara Revolt of 1637–38 by Japanese Christians in Kyushu. Because of the hardships of peasant life and oppressive government policy, many peasants and some warriors occasionally revolted against the government. In fact, Pure Land and Nichiren groups had become involved in social and economic protest. In the bloody Shimabara Revolt (as in previous revolts), "The revolt was not primarily a religious uprising, but a desperate protest against the oppressive rule of feudal lords in a remote and backward region."[6] Nevertheless, in this feudal context any rival faith represented a threat to social stability, and the feudal government used the Shimabara Revolt (when many thousands were killed) as a justification for abolishing Christianity. This led to the final exclusion order of 1639, which strictly prohibited any future visits by Portuguese ships on penalty of the destruction of ship and crew. In 1640, when a Portuguese ship came to Japan on a diplomatic mission to negotiate this decree, the ship and almost all of the crew were destroyed.

Japan in the 1640s was more highly unified and centralized than in the 1540s, when Christianity first arrived. The mood of the midsixteenth century was relatively favorable to a foreign religion, but in the midseventeenth century the emphasis on national unification made Christianity's foreign character a serious disadvantage. Just as complex social and political factors affected the acceptability of Christianity, there were also complex reasons for its rejection. At any rate, by about 1650 Christianity had become an underground religion. The Japanese authorities thought they had completely abolished this foreign religion, but in reality it was handed down as a secret tradition within certain families, particularly in the Kyushu region where it had gained its strongest foothold.

THE SIGNIFICANCE OF THE CHRISTIAN CENTURY

It is ironic that Christianity took on a Japanese character only when it was deprived of ordained priests and went underground. Japanese customs and beliefs became naturally mixed with Christian beliefs. Interestingly enough, one of the persistent arguments against Christianity in the exclusionary edicts was that Christianity was anti-Japanese and against the Japanese religious traditions. Christianity was considered anti-Japanese because a Japanese Christian was loyal to foreign gods and to foreign priests, rather than to native *kami* and to the local Japanese feudal lord.

Christianity certainly presented a contrast to the general theme in Japanese religion that traditions harmonize with one another rather than making exclusive claims to absolute truth. The Jesuits were very effective in their active policy of acquiring the language and customs of the country, but in matters of religious doctrine and practice they were not so flexible. It is curious that Buddhism, once seen by the Japanese as a foreign religion and for that reason opposed as offensive to the native *kami*, had become thoroughly assimilated within Japanese culture. Although they lost much of their original Indian and Chinese features, both Buddhism and Confucianism were considered full-fledged Japanese traditions having the right to oust the foreign Christian religion. By contrast, Christianity has never become Japanized to the extent that it could be considered a Japanese tradition to oppose foreign traditions.[7]

The Christian century in Japan may seem a relatively unimportant interval in the long stretch of Japanese history, but it is very important for understanding later developments. The success of the Catholic missionaries is nothing to gloss over. The number of Catholic priests was always small, never exceeding two hundred, and yet they succeeded in gaining as many as 300,000 converts by the first decade of the seventeenth century. If the population of this period was between 20 million and 25 million, then a higher percentage of the population was Christian at that time than Japan has ever known since. This is remarkable in light of the large numbers of Catholic and Protestant missionaries who have spent great sums of money during the past century, only to achieve a lower percentage of Christian converts, Protestant and Catholic combined.

The Christian century in Japan influenced later developments in Japan. Some scholars feel that the threat of Christianity—real or imagined—directly affected Japan's decision to impose a "closed-door" policy, which isolated Japan from foreign influence between the midseventeenth and midnineteenth centuries. Furthermore, in order to stamp out Christianity, every family was required to belong to a Buddhist temple. In effect, this made Buddhism an arm of the government, giving it a great advantage over Shinto. We must be aware of this imbalance in order to comprehend religious developments during the Tokugawa period (1600–1867), which will be discussed in Part III.

1. See C. R. Boxer, *The Christian Century in Japan, 1549–1650,* rev. ed. (Berkeley: University of California Press, 1967).
2. See Norihisa Suzuki, "Christianity," in *Japanese Religion,* ed. Ichiro Hori (Tokyo: Kodansha International, 1972), pp. 71–73.
3. George Elison, *Deus Destroyed: The Image of Christianity in Early Modern Japan* (Cambridge, Mass.: Harvard University Press, 1973), pp. 45–46.
4. Ibid., p. 117.
5. See "The Sun God of the East" in Ryusaku Tsunoda et al., *Sources of Japanese Tradition* (New York: Columbia University Press, 1958), Chapter 15. For remarks on this pattern of "immanental theocracy," see Joseph M. Kitagawa, *Religion in Japanese History* (New York: Columbia University Press, 1966), pp. 154, 161.
6. Sir George Sansom, *A History of Japan,* Vol. 3 (Stanford, Calif.: Stanford University Press, 1963), p. 38.
7. The relative success or failure of a religion may be closely connected with the political fortunes of the people supporting the religion. When Buddhism was first introduced and in subsequent centuries, the families and territories supporting Buddhism gained political power; in contrast, the feudal territories supporting Christianity lost political power, as seen in the Shimabara Revolt.

SELECTED READINGS

Boxer, C. R. *The Christian Century in Japan, 1549–1650.* Rev. ed. Berkeley: University of California Press, 1967. A scholarly survey of early Roman Catholicism in Japan, with translations of European documents.

Earhart, H. Byron. *Religion in the Japanese Experience: Sources and Interpretations.* Belmont, Calif.: Wadsworth, 1974. See pp. 106–11 for excerpts from Boxer describing the Jesuit experience in Japan and pp. 121–23 for Hideyoshi's "Letter to the Viceroy of the Indies," in which he rejects Christianity.

Elison, George. *Deus Destroyed: The Image of Christianity in Early Modern Japan.* Cambridge, Mass.: Harvard University Press, 1973. A detailed, scholarly analysis of the "acceptance" and "rejection" of Christianity during the Christian century, with extensive translations of anti-Christian documents from this period.

Suzuki, Norihisa. "Christianity." In *Japanese Religion*. Edited by Ichiro Hori. Translated by Yoshiya Abe and David Reid. Tokyo: Kodansha International, 1972, pp. 71–87. A concise overview of the "foreignness" of Christianity in Japan and its major developments.

Tsunoda, Ryusaku, et al. *Sources of Japanese Tradition*. New York: Columbia University Press, 1958. See Chapter 15 for information concerning Nobunaga, Hideyoshi, Ieyasu, and their policies with regard to Christianity.

CHAPTER 13

The Five Traditions: Development and Mutual Influence

From earliest times, the five basic traditions of Japanese religion have interacted with one another. In the period of development and elaboration, discussed in Part II, these traditions developed unique forms within the general context of Japanese religion. Buddhism received from China new waves of influence that were restructured into forms of Japanese Buddhism. Likewise, Confucianism and Taoism continued to be Japanized. Confucianism, along with Buddhism and Shinto, provided a semiofficial rationale for existence of the state. Religious Taoism played an equally important role, but on the level of popular religion. Folk religion interacted with the more organized traditions and persisted in the beliefs and customs of the people. Shinto was busy borrowing from all these religious streams with the motive of becoming systematized and strengthened so as to compete with the other systems.

This period has been called one of development and elaboration because, with the exception of Christianity, no new religious traditions were introduced. Only new streams of the older traditions were introduced, such as the newer sects of Buddhism. Buddhism became elaborated into a truly Japanese phenomenon: Buddhist practices became more thoroughly interrelated with Shinto practices; distinctively Japanese developments of Buddhism such as Nichiren Buddhism appeared; and the largest Buddhist sects developed.

Shinto underwent development and elaboration when it appropriated foreign traditions and, by incorporating them, produced a more complete religious system. Study of Confucian classics led Shinto scholars to a study of the Japanese classics, which in turn led them to support a revival movement for "purifying" Shinto.

Religious Taoism, which entered Japanese history mainly in the form of a government bureau controlling the calendar and divination, spread through the countryside. The cosmology of religious Taoism provided a rich resource for cosmological speculation, especially within Shinto. On a more popular level, Taoist notions within the adopted Chinese calendar gave rise to many widespread beliefs about what was lucky and unlucky. These Taoist thoughts and beliefs were carried to the people by *hijiri*, a kind of popular successor to the earlier officials in the government bureau of religious Taoism (the Onmyoryo). The *hijiri*, a combination of sage, saint, and fortuneteller, were wandering practitioners who went directly to the people to meet all kinds of religious needs.[1] Unattached to shrines or temples, they drew on Shinto and Buddhist usages as well as those of religious Taoism in their fortunetelling, divination, and purifications.

One popular cult that drew heavily on the influence of religious Taoism and the activity of *hijiri* was the Koshin cult. The mythological background of the cult had become mixed with Buddhist elements in China and was blended with Japanese folk practices by people such as the *hijiri* and by local village cults. The village cults were independent associations organized for the purpose of lengthening life through all-night vigils. They met especially on the six Koshin days of the Chinese calendar, revering an image or painting of the Taoist-Buddhist divinity while holding a festive banquet. During the all-night vigils they abstained from sexual relations, because on that night a divinity observed them and reported on their conduct to a heavenly superior. These cults, their beliefs, and their practices became so thoroughly ingrained in village life that the devotees took for granted the Japanese character of the Koshin cult, completely forgetting its foreign origins.[2]

Folk religion continued in the many customs and beliefs associated with seasonal rhythms and the home, but in increasing interaction with the organized religions. The beliefs and festivities of the Chinese calendar were inseparable from Japanese seasonal and agricultural customs. For example, the New Year festivities came to be celebrated especially through Buddhist and Shinto usages. Popular religious observances connected with the growing season, too, were related to the organized religions. Often a farmer visited a shrine or temple in order to obtain a paper charm, which he would place in his rice field as a blessing for his crop.

127
*The Five
Traditions:
Development
and Mutual
Influence*

The home continued to be a major focus for folk religion. This is especially well illustrated by the religious decorations around the home at New Year's. Each household became a repository of the various elements of the Japanese religious tradition. For example, each family knew that physical and spiritual sickness could be caused by evil forces, which could be warded off through the help of benevolent divinities. The afflicted family might visit a temple or a shrine, or an itinerant *hijiri* or Shugendo practitioner might visit the afflicted family. These popular practitioners resorted to Buddhist rituals and formulas as well as Taoistic purifications in order to effect healing. Some popular religious figures specialized in the art of trance and possession for the purpose of communicating with the dead. Often a blind woman, a female shaman, communicated with the dead. All these practices illustrate the way in which folk religion continued to exist outside of organized religion while various elements of the organized traditions came to be the common property of the people.

Christianity's appearance on the Japanese scene was an unexpected interruption of the process of development and elaboration. Indeed, in this early period Christianity could hardly be considered a *Japanese* tradition. Those who did not accept Christianity saw it as a threat to all the Japanese traditions. Buddhism, Confucianism, and Shinto took a stand and jointly challenged the threat of the anti-Japanese, or at least non-Japanese, tradition of Christianity.

The process of development and elaboration ran into something of a dead end after the sixteenth century. The vital religious motives that had impelled the founders of the newer Buddhist sects became crystallized in rather rigid institutional forms. The problem of institutionalization appears in the history of any religious tradition and calls for a renewal of the wellsprings from which the tradition flows. At this particular juncture, formalism became a widespread problem in Japanese religion—especially in Buddhism—and yet there appeared no new religious geniuses such as the founders of the newer Buddhist sects. Because no renewal took place, organized religion tended to become formalistic. We will see how this formalism became a great problem before it finally provoked movements of renewal.

NOTES

1. For an account of the *hijiri,* see Ichiro Hori, *Folk Religion in Japan: Continuity and Change,* ed. Joseph M. Kitagawa and Alan L. Miller (Chicago: University of Chicago Press, 1968), pp. 83–139.

2. See E. Dale Saunders, "Koshin: An Example of Taoist Ideas in Japan," in *Proceedings of the IXth International Congress for the History of Religions* (Tokyo: Maruzen, 1960), pp. 423–32. An excerpt from Saunders' work is included in H. Byron Earhart, *Religion in the Japanese Experience: Sources and Interpretations* (Belmont, Calif.: Wadsworth, 1974), pp. 76–80.

SELECTED READINGS

Earhart, H. Byron. *Religion in the Japanese Experience: Sources and Interpretations*. Belmont, Calif.: Wadsworth, 1974. See Part Eight for selected documents on syncretism in Japan; see also pp. 39–44 for excerpts from Matsunada and pp. 76–80 for excerpts from Saunders.

————. *A Religious Study of the Mount Haguro Sect of Shugendo: An Example of Japanese Mountain Religion*. Tokyo: Sophia University, 1970. Demonstrates the blending of most Japanese religious traditions, both organized and folk, within the life of Shugendo.

Hori, Ichiro. *Folk Religion in Japan: Continuity and Change*. Edited by Joseph M. Kitagawa and Alan L. Miller. Chicago: University of Chicago Press, 1968, pp. 83–139. Treats the popularization of organized religion through the medium of "holy men."

Matsunaga, Alicia. *The Buddhist Philosophy of Assimilation: The Historical Development of the Honji-Suijaku Theory*. Tokyo and Rutland, Vt.: Sophia University and Charles E. Tuttle Company, 1969. Interprets interaction among religious traditions from the viewpoint of Buddhism.

Saunders, E. Dale. "Koshin: An Example of Taoist Ideas in Japan." In *Proceedings of the IXth International Congress for the History of Religions*. Tokyo: Maruzen, 1960, pp. 423–32. Shows how a Taoist cult became thoroughly Japanized.

PART THREE

Formalism and Renewal in Japanese Religion

Part I introduced the formative elements of Japanese religion and their initial interaction; Part II treated the further development and elaboration of these formative elements and described the reception accorded Christianity upon its introduction to Japan in the sixteenth century. Part III discusses subsequent changes in Japanese religion in terms of formalism and renewal.

Every religious tradition experiences periods of growth and decline. New traditions may emerge gradually out of previous ones or spring suddenly from the teachings of a great leader. Some new traditions soon disappear. Those that endure embody the original spark of inspiration in lasting forms—that is, they become institutionalized. Religious institutions usually try to preserve the original inspiration. Then, either gradually or suddenly, comes the realization that forms are being preserved for their own sake and the inspirational spark has been lost. The continuation of institutional trappings out of a sense of their appropriateness rather than out of feelings of enthusiasm and dedication is a kind of formalism. Renewal, the opposite of formalism, is characterized by the rediscovery of an earlier tradition or the birth of a new tradition.

Signs of formalism and renewal may be seen in almost any culture at any time. In the history of Japanese religion, they are especially apparent in the period extending from about 1600 to the present.

Buddhism, dominant for so long, became formalistic for two reasons: First, its institutional ideas, rituals, and practices became rather rigid, and, second, it increasingly served as an arm of the government rather than as a source of spiritual support for the people. Buddhism had experienced renewal in the Heian and Kamakura periods because of the efforts of vigorous founders of new institutions, but from the Tokugawa era (1600–1867) Buddhism tended to live on more through earlier forms than because of new developments. Many lay persons and priests were content to live within these forms; and although there were some attempts at reform, the great religious changes that took place after 1600 did not occur in Buddhism.

The most dramatic changes of the Tokugawa era took place in Confucianism and Shinto. These traditions were rediscovered as means of stimulating large numbers of people to a new sense of commitment. Neo-Confucianism defined the major rationale for the Tokugawa government in achieving the unification of Japan, thereby creating the foundation on which modern Japan rests. Confucianism had been present in Japan more than a thousand years earlier, but Japanese scholars rediscovered this tradition in the writings of Neo-Confucianist Chinese scholars. Ironically, this interest in Chinese classics encouraged Japanese scholars to study Japanese classics and resulted in a rediscovery of the ancient Shinto tradition. Renewed interest in Shinto helped to shape the climactic events marking the end of Tokugawa feudalism and the rise of a modern nation-state.

From late Tokugawa times to the present, another form of renewal has been conspicuous. The formation of so-called New Religions is an example of renewal through the creation of new traditions. Usually established by charismatic founders outside the framework of organized Buddhism and Shinto, the New Religions have gradually developed into the most dynamic religious force on the contemporary scene.

As we enter the third and final period, it is proper to acknowledge the overlap among the three periods and the flexibility of the terms characterizing them. The first period, from prehistory through the late eighth century, has been called formative because that is when the basic elements of Japanese religion first appeared and a distinctive religious tradition first can be recognized. The word "formative" is not meant to imply that by the end of the eighth century the formation of Japanese religion was complete; rather, it means that the most significant feature of the period is the formative process.

Because Japanese religion is an identifiable tradition that continued to undergo change after the eighth century, we may say that the process of formation continued into subsequent periods. The second period, from the late eighth century to the seventeenth century, has been called the period of development and elaboration because this is when the formative elements interacted more thoroughly and assumed definite shapes. The phrase "development and elaboration" is not meant to imply that the development and elaboration of Japanese religion occurred only in this time span; rather, it means that the most significant features of the period are development and elaboration. The second period is directly related to the first and third periods.

Development and elaboration emerge from the formative process in the first period and continue into the pattern of formalism and renewal.

The final period, from the seventeenth century to the present, has been characterized as an era of formalism and renewal because during this time the dominant tradition of Buddhism became formalistic and major trends were started by the rediscovery of Confucianism and Shinto and by the emergence of New Religions. The expression "formalism and renewal" is not meant to imply that formalism and renewal occurred only during this period; rather, it means that the most significant features were formalism and renewal. The third period represents an extension of the processes of formation, development, and elaboration that occurred earlier. In other words, the three periods should be viewed not as separate compartments but as three related acts of one continuous historical drama.

CHAPTER 14

Buddhism, Neo-Confucianism, and Restoration Shinto in the Tokugawa Period

The Tokugawa period (1600–1867) was very important for unifying Japan and establishing the basis on which a modern nation would be developed in Meiji times (1868–1912). Just prior to the Tokugawa period, political and social conditions were unstable. Each feudal territory was like a separate kingdom, and there was a constant threat that one feudal lord would use force to acquire neighboring territories. Even religious institutions, especially Buddhist temples, had become armed camps as priestly soldiers struggled to protect their own territories. The great achievement of the Tokugawa period was the bringing together of the separate feudal territories under the power of one military leader, thereby unifying the country and creating political stability. Several military leaders began the process of subduing the individual feudal territories and large Buddhist monasteries, but the Tokugawa line of military rulers completed the unification and carried out a thoroughgoing policy of social control. In this chapter, we will examine the important changes experienced by Buddhism, Confucianism, and Shinto during the Tokugawa period.

THE TOKUGAWA GOVERNMENT AND RELIGION

The head of the military government was the *shogun*,[1] or military dictator, theoretically the highest general in the emperor's army but in actuality the top military leader in control of the government. The title was passed down in the Tokugawa family after Tokugawa Ieyasu seized control in 1600 and unified the country. The family gained control of the country through warfare but later maintained its control through a centralized government. Administration of government policies was efficiently carried out, and the entire society was carefully organized. In general people were separated into four classes—*samurai* (warrior), farmer, artisan, and merchant. The status of the warriors was much higher than the status of the three other classes, for warriors were seen as the protectors of the realm. They alone had special privileges such as the right to wear swords, and they received stipends of rice. The other three classes were the economic mainstay of the country. Especially important were the farmers, who provided rice, which was the measure of economic income.

The political stability achieved by the Tokugawas lasted for two-and-a-half centuries and made possible considerable social and economic development. With the cessation of warfare, life in the cities and industry generally flourished. Early in the seventeenth century, the Tokugawa rulers severely curtailed trading with Europe, so there was no extensive trade with foreign countries. Within Japan, however, trade and commerce developed so rapidly that commerce soon outranked agriculture in economic importance. Life in the cities began to determine new cultural styles. The wealth of merchants supported popular theater, and generally cities gave rise to art forms for the masses, such as woodblock prints. Many impoverished farmers risked punishment to leave the country and work for wages in the city. The increasing secularism of the cities is seen in the popularity of ribald novels and woodblock prints featuring both daily life and sensual delights.[2] Both the rich merchant and the average worker were at least as interested in the sensuality of this world as in the spirituality of the other world.

Religion was not unaffected by the Tokugawa policies of unification and social control. The great religious centers, especially the powerful Buddhist monasteries, had been subdued in bloody fighting of the sixteenth century that preceded the Tokugawa rise to power. From the midseventeenth century, as part of a program to eliminate Christianity and control the people, every family had to belong to a Buddhist temple. The Tokugawas used the temples for purposes of social control. The major rationale for social control came not from Buddhism, however, but from the Chinese commentaries on Confucian teaching known as Neo-Confucianism.

Japanese thinkers not only adopted Neo-Confucian teachings but also adapted them in terms of a practical rationalism in tune with the social and economic developments of the time. The overall social stability was apparent even in the villages, which developed residential patterns of affiliation to local Shinto shrines.

TOKUGAWA BUDDHISM: STATE PATRONAGE AND WEAKENED VITALITY

The Tokugawa period was a time of peace and order thanks to the unification of the country achieved by Oda Nobunaga, Toyotomi Hideyoshi, and Tokugawa Ieyasu. Government policy was characterized by stability and unification rather than by innovation and creativity. The tone of the period was set by the need to safeguard unification with a strong central government. A consistent Tokugawa goal was to eliminate religious strife, which threatened to divide the country into warring factions. Whereas Nobunaga had favored Christianity, partly in order to counteract the power of Buddhism, later in the Tokugawa period Buddhism was patronized and Christians were persecuted.

During the Tokugawa period, when Christianity was a proscribed religion, the government used Buddhism to enforce the proscription. Every family had to belong to a Buddhist temple and had to be questioned periodically by the temple priest. Births were registered and deaths were recorded in the local temple to which the family belonged. (Prior to the Tokugawa period, there was individual membership in temples.) The Tokugawa government was even responsible for rebuilding many temples destroyed in earlier warfare, including temples at the Tendai headquarters of Hieizan, which had been ruthlessly razed by Nobunaga. However, the state money that flowed freely into the Buddhist temples cost them their autonomy and some of their religious vitality. Nobunaga and Hideyoshi had punished the large temples with military force because the temples were their most powerful political rivals. The Tokugawa government, by unifying the country, controlled all the Buddhist sects from the top. Buddhist priests became government servants, and the government strictly forbade any intersect quarrels. Buddhism was practically the established religion of Japan; the separate sects remained under direct government supervision.

This situation stifled religious devotion. The Japanese historian Anesaki has aptly described the general reaction: "For the people at large religion was rather a matter of family heritage and formal observance than a question of personal faith."[3] To the present day, the organized sects of Japanese Buddhism have not been able to escape completely the unfavorable stigma of disinterested affiliation. Both enlightened priests and devout lay people have often deplored the inertia of Tokugawa "feudal" patterns of Buddhist ancestor worship and have lamented the lack of a strong, personal Buddhist faith.

137
Buddhism,
Neo-Confucianism,
and
Restoration
Shinto in the
Tokugawa
Period

NEO-CONFUCIANISM: POLITICAL STABILITY AND SOCIAL CONFORMITY

The Neo-Confucianism of the Tokugawa period must be distinguished from the Confucianism of earlier Japan. Before Tokugawa times, Confucianism had always played a subordinate role, contributing to the national tradition but not existing as a separate school. In fact, Confucian scholarship had been kept alive within the Buddhist temples, where Buddhist priests studied Chinese Buddhist scriptures and Confucian classics. From the thirteenth to seventeenth centuries, the scholars of the Zen sects were most influential in preserving and transmitting the traditions that emerged in Neo-Confucianism.

Neo-Confucianism is a general term for the Confucian revival that took place in China especially during the Sung dynasty (960–1279). Confucianism in China underwent various periods of development. During the Sung dynasty, it borrowed from Taoism and Buddhism to create a comprehensive philosophy for interpreting every aspect of the world and of human life in the world. This philosophy, called Neo-Confucianism, offered a profound understanding of cosmology, humanistic ethics, and political ideals in a unified system. It enjoyed great success not only in China, but also in Korea and Japan. Although there were several schools within Neo-Confucianism, the Chinese philosopher Chu Hsi (1130–1200) developed the most famous system of thought. (In Japan, Chu Hsi is called Shushi.)

According to Chu Hsi, there is a rational principle in the universe, and this principle works in the material world to give rise to human beings and all things. This Neo-Confucian teaching provided Japan with a rational and secular philosophy that would serve to both unify the country from within and provide a unified front for dealings with foreign countries. The feudal order of Tokugawa times, with its agrarian economy and hierarchical social system, would be reinforced by this Neo-Confucian world-view.

In early Japan, Confucian classics were adopted as a solid foundation for education, and they were studied from Nara times up to the Tokugawa period. However, these studies became very formal and scholastic because they continued to depend upon Chinese commentaries composed many centuries previously. Gradually the tradition of Neo-Confucianism maintained within the Japanese Zen temples began to attract attention outside Buddhist circles, influencing even Confucian scholars. The preeminence of Neo-Confucian philosophy became official early in the Tokugawa period when the emperor commanded Confucian scholars to use the commentaries of the Sung dynasty and disregard the earlier commentaries. This official pronouncement recognized as the prevailing rationale of the state the philosophy of Chu Hsi (Shushi). The importance of Neo-Confucian philosophy derives not from its connection with the Japanese imperial line, but from its foundational character for the Tokugawa feudal regime.

The Tokugawa government was interested more in the organizational powers of Neo-Confucianism than in its cosmological theories. Tokugawa Ieyasu apparently saw in Neo-Confucianism a suitable philosophy for stabilizing and ordering the state. What the Neo-Confucian tradition amounted to was a heavenly sanction for the existing political and social order. Neo-Confucianism in this period served as the intellectual rationale justifying the existence of the four social classes and their support of the Tokugawa government. The rulers or superiors were advised to be just and benevolent; subordinates were cautioned to be obedient and respectful.

The harmony of the universe was said to depend upon a reciprocal relationship of justice from the superior and obedience from the subordinate. One venerable Confucian scheme for ensuring this harmony was based on the bond of five human relationships: (1) ruler and subject, (2) parents and children, (3) husband and wife, (4) elder and younger, and (5) friend and friend. The last relationship, friendship, is characterized by mutuality; the other four are characterized by the obedience of subordinates to superiors. This philosophy gave support to the feudal ethics of Tokugawa times. Neo-Confucianism did not create the feudal situation, but it provided a rationale.

The political use of the Confucian (or Neo-Confucian) tradition to justify the status quo has been criticized. There is no doubt that Neo-Confucianism in Japan helped to maintain peace during this time. It contributed especially to social mores and education. A famous example is the Neo-Confucian contribution to the philosophy of life called Bushido, the "way of the warrior," a scheme of training and a code of ethics that emphasized self-control and duty to one's master. Bushido also included the aspect of self-cultivation. At first it was limited mainly to the warrior class, but this combined sense of frugality and unswerving loyalty later had wide influence among the people. However, the personal qualities of loyalty and filial piety had been stressed in earlier Japanese history; Neo-Confucianism only reinforced them. The Japanese *samurai* (warrior), too, drew upon several traditions simultaneously. "The typical Tokugawa samurai saw some value in each of the three world views that competed for his allegiance. Buddhism and Shinto provided for his religious needs; Confucianism gave him a rational cosmology and a social ethic; Confucianism and Shinto both contributed to his conceptions of the political order."[4]

139
*Buddhism,
Neo-Confucianism,
and
Restoration
Shinto in the
Tokugawa
Period*

Under Tokugawa patronage, Neo-Confucianism became a combination of state cult and state educational system. By this time there were independent scholars of Neo-Confucianism outside the Buddhist temples. Some of these scholars were given land on which to found Neo-Confucian schools, which not only studied the Chinese classics by means of the Neo-Confucian commentaries but provided bureaucrats for the Tokugawa government. The cult aspect is seen in the fact that these scholars were ordered to perform old Confucian ceremonies such as the annual sacrifices and Confucian temples were built for the sacrifices. Eventually, the Chu Hsi school of Neo-Confucianism enjoyed such privileged protection by the government that other schools of Neo-Confucianism were outlawed. In general, Neo-Confucianists exerted a widespread influence, tending to move away from Buddhism and combine forces with those who were attempting to purify Shinto. In late Tokugawa times, in spite of government opposition, popular teachers established new schools in which great numbers of the middle class were instructed in a heavily Neo-Confucian philosophy of life.

NEO-CONFUCIANISM: THE DEVELOPMENT
OF PUBLIC AND PRIVATE ETHICS

Although Neo-Confucianism generally served as the official government rationale for the status quo, it was much more than a rubber stamp of government policies. A long line of creative thinkers was attracted to several kinds of Neo-Confucian thought, and these minds were instrumental in developing systems of public ethics and personal philosophies of life. One of the first was Fujiwara Seika (1561–1619), who had studied Confucian teachings while he was a Buddhist priest. Seika was the first Buddhist priest to give up Buddhist orders and concentrate his life solely on Confucianism. His shift from

Buddhism to Confucianism is symptomatic of Tokugawa times generally, for during this period leading thinkers became concerned more with secular rationales for the social and political order than with religious solutions such as Buddhist enlightenment. Fujiwara Seika met with the great ruler *(shogun)* Tokugawa Ieyasu. One result of their meeting was the establishment of the Chu Hsi form of Neo-Confucianism as the official rationale for the Tokugawa government.

One of Fujiwara Seika's students, Hayashi Razan (1583–1657), was the first of a three-generation line of hereditary Confucian advisers to the *shogun*. The Hayashi family was faithful to Chu Hsi (Shushi) philosophy in pursuing a rational and secular order, in the process severely criticizing Buddhism as being antisocial. However, the direction and results of Confucian teaching were not easy to control. For example, Neo-Confucianists emphasized a study of Chinese classics and a dislike for Buddhism as a "foreign" tradition. Eventually this emphasis was reinterpreted by Japanese scholars to mean a study of *Japanese* classics and a dislike for *Confucianism* as a tradition foreign to Japan.

One of the transitional steppingstones to the revival of the Japanese tradition was Yamazaki Ansai (1618–82), who took a moderate position, balancing Confucianism with the native Shinto tradition. Yamazaki Ansai attempted to blend the ethical teachings of Confucianism with the religious aspects of Shinto. He equated Shinto stories of creation with Chinese cosmology. Later Shinto scholars such as Motoori Norinaga (1730–1801) were extremely critical of Yamazaki's compromising of the Shinto tradition with Neo-Confucian rationalism, but Yamazaki in his own way helped build a bridge from Confucianism to Shinto and thereby helped promote the rediscovery of Shinto.

That Neo-Confucianism was much more than formal philosophy is seen in the life and work of Kaibara Ekken (1630–1714). This man lived a simple life and tried to convey to common people the principles of Neo-Confucianism in rather informal Japanese language (rather than in the highly formal style of early Neo-Confucianists). Instead of stressing abstract metaphysical doctrines, he taught people that they should obey their parents and respect Heaven and Earth as their parents on a grander scale. For Kaibara Ekken, respect for nature meant not just love of nature but the actual study of nature. His extensive studies of plant life were pioneering works that attracted Western attention. He enjoyed a happy married life, but his views on women were rather narrow. He wrote *Great Learning for Women*, a classic feudal statement of the subjugation of women to men; it had a strong influence on the popular mentality and helped to shape women's sense of themselves as subordinate and inferior to men.

141
*Buddhism,
Neo-Confucianism,
and
Restoration
Shinto in the
Tokugawa
Period*

The Tokugawa rulers had brought unity and order to a Japan that had been torn by strife and disorder, and they felt their destiny was to continue in power and maintain their control. Neo-Confucianism was seen generally as a rational and moral force in society (particularly in politics) that corresponded to the rational force in the universe and life generally. Therefore, the government's support of "orthodox" (that is, Chu Hsi) Neo-Confucian teachers and advisers was a political duty, in the interest of preserving the social order. The government, by supporting an official school of orthodox Neo-Confucianists who taught people the nature of the moral order, would help produce moral citizens and thereby preserve social stability. The government sought to tie the political system and social stability to support for orthodoxy and officially prohibited Confucian teachings other than the Chu Hsi brand of Neo-Confucianism.

However, currents of thought generated by the new social conditions of Tokugawa times and stimulated by Neo-Confucian scholarship could not be stopped by government order. The Neo-Confucian teachers of the early Tokugawa period, especially the Hayashi family, had set forth a rather slavish restatement of Chu Hsi's philosophy, which through repetition became viewed as formalistic. A number of thinkers dared to challenge the government prohibition of unorthodox teaching.

Even in China, the Neo-Confucianism of Chu Hsi was criticized by contemporaries and later Chinese philosophers. One of the most influential later critics of Chu Hsi was Wang Yang-ming (1472–1528), who first studied Chu Hsi philosophy and then rejected Chu Hsi's notion of abstract reason in favor of a more subjective or intuitive reason within the human mind. The philosophy of Wang Yang-ming (known as Oyomei in Japan), with its emphasis on a strong moral sense and actual deeds (rather than intellect and words), appealed to Nakae Toju (1608–48) so much that he advocated it rather than Chu Hsi's rational philosophy.

Nakae Toju is considered the founder of the Wang Yang-ming (or Oyomei) school in Japan, but his fame was due not so much to his brilliant intellect as to his example of a highly moral life. He resigned a government post to return to his native village and care for his aging mother, thus putting into action his teaching about filial piety. He took very seriously the notion of cultivating the mind, not only by scholars and officials, but by all men and women. In contrast to Kaibara Ekken, who thought a woman's education should be limited to serving her future husband and in-laws, Nakae Toju held that cultivation of mind is important for both men and women, and he favored the proper education of women.

Other followers of the Wang Yang-ming school opposed Neo-Confucian orthodoxy, but a more significant break was proposed by Yamaga Soko (1622–85), who took literally the Neo-Confucian idea of returning to the classical truth. Yamaga Soko felt that even the Neo-Confucian teachings of the Sung dynasty were not the truth but pointed back to the original teachings of Confucius himself. Yamaga Soko saw in Confucius's teaching a strong ethical principle, and he criticized Neo-Confucian teachings such as the philosophy of Chu Hsi for making metaphysical notions more important than ethical principles. Like earlier thinkers of the Tokugawa period, Yamaga Soko worried about the inactivity of the warriors (*samurai* or *bushi*) in the prolonged peace of Tokugawa, and he proposed a code of personal ethics for warriors. His work entitled *The Way of the Warrior* is the first systematic attempt to set forth what later was called Bushido. The notions of self-discipline and loyalty in this code of life were very influential for popular ethics in subsequent centuries.

Yamaga Soko was so outspoken in his criticism of orthodox Neo-Confucianism that he was ordered into exile; but he only deepened his conviction that people should return to the true ethical teaching of Confucius, and he gave a nationalistic turn to this idea. He insisted that the Japanese people were truer to Confucius than were the Chinese because the Japanese practiced a more complete loyalty of son to father and subject to lord than had the Chinese.

The controversy between the orthodox Chu Hsi school and other schools continued. In 1790 the government issued an edict forbidding Confucian teaching other than the ideas of the Chu Hsi school. However, it was impossible to stop minds from thinking, and one after another thinkers appeared who developed their own blend of Confucian and Japanese systems of thought. Although each thinker had his own message, some similarities are found in the works of many writers of the seventeenth through the nineteenth centuries. Neo-Confucian and Confucian studies had invigorated historical and philological studies of the Chinese classics, and this carried over to a study of Japanese classics. Interest in Japanese history led to a heightened nationalism and a revival of Shinto studies. There was a serious concern for developing a total rationale for the social and political order, to be offset by a deeper pursuit for a personal philosophy of life. This philosophizing was not idle speculation but was concerned with the actual management of government and the practical affairs of daily life (including family relations and farming). Not restricted to scholars and philosophers, these teachings formed the basis of lectures by popular scholars who drew large followings of warriors, merchants, and even common people. As these teachings spread to the common people, they tended to provide a broad rationale for the social order and to reinforce hierarchical social values generally, especially in the family.

143
*Buddhism,
Neo-Confucianism,
and
Restoration
Shinto in the
Tokugawa
Period*

In several regards, the Japanese institutional forms justified by Confucian ideals differed from their counterparts in China. For example, in China the relationship between a soldier and his master was a formal tie that could be formally broken; in Japan the loyalty of a warrior to his master was absolute and lifelong and could not be broken. In China the family took precedence over other social institutions; in Japan the family was a kind of "prototype of social organization" for other institutions.[5] The Japanese family was the training ground and model for loyal participation in larger social and political units—villages, businesses, and even the state.

All these teachings and social institutions helped shape the mental framework of the Japanese people as they left the Tokugawa period and entered the modern world. Some scholars have argued that such value systems played an important part in the formation of modern Japan.[6]

RESTORATION SHINTO: THE MOVEMENT FOR A PURIFIED SHINTO

Ever since the eighth century, Shinto had been overshadowed by the more highly systematized foreign traditions popular at court and among nobility, but it had remained a vital part of the religious life of the local communities. Even during the most flourishing periods of Buddhism, there were Shinto scholars who remained true to their Shinto heritage. In medieval times Kitabatake Chikafusa (1293–1354) wrote a theological defense of the divine ancestry of the emperor and the centrality of Japan in Shinto conceptions. Indeed, the medieval schools of Shinto, though borrowing heavily from foreign traditions, had as their ultimate goal the improvement of Shinto's role in Japanese religion. There had always been some support for Shinto among the "loyalists"—individuals around the imperial court who favored the return of the emperor to actual power. It is only natural that they were opposed to rule by a military leader and his warriors. There were religious commitments on both sides of this issue. In Tokugawa times, the several lines of Shinto support were united and reinforced by a powerful movement called Restoration Shinto.

Restoration Shinto was not a simple resuscitation of Shinto, for Shinto had never died out; nor was it a sudden awakening. It was the culmination of the work of previous centuries and earlier scholars, stimulated by several peculiar conditions of Tokugawa times. The isolation of Japan from foreign influence for about two centuries had positive as well as negative results. While foreign influence was excluded, national pride and national strength grew. Another stimulus for Restoration Shinto came from Neo-Confucianism. It must be remembered that Neo-Confucianism had to divorce itself from the Buddhist temples in order to become an independent movement; thus it was more favorably disposed to Shinto than to Buddhism. In addition, Neo-Confucianism had become so thoroughly Japanized that its main goal was to support the Japanese tradition and the political system. Neo-Confucianism encouraged and supported the policy of isolating Japan from the world. Thus, it and Shinto shared a common goal of glorifying the Japanese nation. Interest in the Chinese classics stimulated interest in the Japanese classics. Eventually Shinto developed such a high degree of self-consciousness that it rejected all foreign influence, including Neo-Confucianism.

From the seventeenth through the nineteenth centuries, an illustrious line of Shinto theorists advanced the cause of Shinto as a "native" tradition—a cause that had been neglected too long in favor of the "foreign" traditions of Confucianism and Buddhism. The interest in Japanese classics was placed on firm ground when Kada Azumamaro (1669–1736) founded a school of National Learning for the purpose of studying Japan's own literature. This led the way for two of the leading scholars of Japanese language and literature, Kamo Mabuchi (1697–1769) and Motoori Norinaga (1730–1801). A systematic treatment showing Shinto to be superior to all religions was developed by Hirata Atsutane (1776–1843), who used arguments borrowed from other religions (including Christianity) to prove Shinto's superiority. These scholars helped to renew interest in ancient Japanese culture and to stimulate the development of Japanese nationalism.

The arguments of these Shinto scholars have been of great religious importance, and they have influenced the course of the nation and its cultural identity. The scholars' appeals for a return to the pure Japanese spirit were a significant factor in the momentous political change of the Meiji Restoration (to be discussed in Chapter 15). The rediscovery of Japanese literature and poetry is equally important, for the scholars paved the way for modern appreciation of Japanese classics.

Ancient Japanese writings, especially the *Kojiki* but also valuable poetry and novels, had been neglected for so long that few people could read or understand them. In fact, the ancient literature had been smothered under a mantle of Chinese and Buddhist interpretation. Mabuchi and Motoori discarded the prevailing Buddhist and Chinese clichés. They succeeded in showing that the early poetry and other writings did not conform to abstract Buddhist or Confucian ideals but reflected the "true" Japanese spirit before it had become "spoiled" by foreign influences. Implicit in their criticism was the idea that everything Japanese had been natural, spontaneous, and pure, but foreign influence had destroyed that naturalness and purity. The tone of the criticism was often irrational, even mystical, advocating a return to the original state of purity from which the Japanese had fallen.

MOTOORI NORINAGA AND RESTORATION SHINTO

Of all the Shinto writers of this period, Motoori stands out as the one whose scholarly achievements command the greatest respect. He laid a permanent foundation for studying ancient Japanese writings on the basis of sound linguistic principles, and he elaborated his viewpoint into a perceptive view of human life and artistic creativity. Motoori used systematic linguistic evidence to show that the Chinese ideas in the *Nihongi* (written in Chinese) were later additions to Japanese culture; and he focused attention on the study of the *Kojiki*, which was written in a form clearly reflecting ancient Japanese language.[7] Because the study of ancient Japanese writings had been neglected, few people could read and understand the ancient language of the *Kojiki*. Most scholars simply applied abstract Confucian and Buddhist notions to both the *Kojiki* and the *Nihongi*, as well as to other writings such as the poetry of the *Manyoshu* and the long novel *Tale of Genji*. Motoori completed a thorough analysis of the language and ideas of the *Kojiki*, comparing it with other ancient Japanese writings. He spent thirty years writing his commentary on the *Kojiki*, and the scholarly value of this monumental work is still appreciated.

Motoori also led the way to a new awareness of the artistic achievement of the *Tale of Genji* by stripping away the layers of Chinese and Buddhist ideas that had been superimposed upon it. He insisted on reading and interpreting the *Tale of Genji* in terms of its own dramatic unity rather than in terms of abstract notions borrowed from Chinese and Buddhist philosophy. Motoori preferred the freshness and honesty of the *Tale of Genji*, which paints a very lifelike picture of the events of the Japanese court in the eleventh century. The hero of this tale, Genji, is involved in many amorous intrigues, which conflict with notions of Buddhist ethics and Confucian conduct. Motoori, however, did not shrink from this apparent literary inconsistency with ethical ideals; instead, he applauded the *Tale of Genji* for showing that human emotions do not always follow the dictates of reason. He went beyond his own time in advancing the notion of the primacy of the emotions over intellect in art, developing a theory of art that is relevant for literary criticism today. He wrote:

> Since novels have as their object the teaching of the meaning of the nature of human existence, there are in their plots many points contrary to Confucian and Buddhist teaching. This is because among the varied feelings of man's reaction to things—whether good, bad, right, or wrong—there are feelings contrary to reason, however improper they may be. Man's feelings do not always follow the dictates of his mind.[8]

The idea of art as a reflection of the imperfections of human life seems quite modern; yet it was deeply imbedded in the ancient Japanese world-view, including the notion of the *kami*.[9] Motoori directly criticized the overly intellectual and rational views of Confucianism and Buddhism, favoring instead the more direct appreciation of life—with all its ambiguities—found in ancient Japanese writings and in Shinto generally. He praised the *Kojiki* for its honesty in depicting evil *kami*, for all life is a mixture of good and evil, right and wrong. Motoori believed that people should learn from accounts of evil deities and avoid the impurity or pollution that gave rise to them, thereby avoiding much evil. But he argued that it is better to accept Shinto views of the coexistence of good and evil than to follow the "false" and "deceptive" views of Confucianism and Buddhism, which paint an untrue picture of life in terms of abstract ideals.

Motoori was especially contemptuous of Buddhist teachings that humans can transcend death and therefore should not be sorrowful at death. He wrote that such teachings are deceptive because they are contrary to human sentiment and fundamental truths of life. Motoori insisted that life is sorrowful and that people must be true to their emotions by marking death with sorrow. This inherent emotional life of human beings is not limited to reflection on death but touches all aspects of life and nature. Motoori called it *mono no aware*. The term is so emotionally charged that it is difficult to translate, but it is generally regarded as being central to the world-view of Japanese art and religion. This pure, emotional response to the beauty of nature, the impermanence of life, and the sorrow of death is similar to the religious attitude toward *kami:* The *kami* are behind and within nature and one's life, and a person should revere the *kami* immediately and directly without stopping to evaluate intellectual arguments about their existence.

147
*Buddhism,
Neo-Confucianism,
and
Restoration
Shinto in the
Tokugawa
Period*

Motoori was too much a man of his time to escape completely from the "foreign" influence that he criticized. He read Confucian materials and participated in Buddhist ceremonies. But he approached these imported traditions with the same depth of emotional response that he felt toward the *kami,* for he believed that the value residing in these traditions was part of the workings of the *kami.* This idea is expressed in one of Motoori's poems:

> Shakyamuni[10] and Confucius
> Are also kami;
> Hence their Ways are branch roads
> Of the broad Way of Kami.[11]

Generally the movement known as Restoration Shinto was not limited to religion but influenced cultural and political developments as well. In terms of organized religious institutions, it sought to reinstate Shinto as the true Japanese religion, purified of its foreign borrowings. Culturally, the leaders of Restoration Shinto tried to revive interest in Japanese classics for their own sake. In terms of politics, the movement contributed to the growing support for a "restoration" of imperial rule. In late Tokugawa times these patterns of thought became linked to a general dissatisfaction with the Tokugawa government, and they gave rise to ultranationalistic tendencies. Restoration Shinto and these related forces play a significant role in the complex events of the Meiji Restoration, the subject of the next chapter.

NOTES

1. The term *shogun* has become familiar to many Westerners through the successful novel and television program by the same title—*Shogun,* written by James Clavell (New York: Dell, 1980).
2. For a glimpse of this glittering world see Howard S. Hibbett, *The Floating World in Japanese Fiction* (London: Oxford University Press, 1959).
3. Masaharu Anesaki, *History of Japanese Religion* (London: Kegan Paul, Trench, Trubner, 1930; reprint ed., Rutland, Vt.: Charles E. Tuttle Company, 1963), p. 260.

4. John Whitney Hall, "The Confucian Teacher in Tokugawa Japan," in *Confucianism in Action*, ed. David S. Nivison and Arthur F. Wright (Stanford, Calif.: Stanford University Press, 1959), p. 291. An excerpt from this article is included in H. Byron Earhart, *Religion in the Japanese Experience: Sources and Interpretations* (Belmont, Calif.: Wadsworth, 1974), pp. 66–69.

5. Mitsuo Tomikura, "Confucianism," in *Japanese Religion*, ed. Ichiro Hori (Tokyo: Kodansha International, 1972), pp. 110–11.

6. For the most complete and provocative account of one teacher, Ishida Baigan (1685–1744), and the influence of his teachings (Shingaku) on the formation of modern Japan, see Robert N. Bellah, *Tokugawa Religion: The Values of Pre-Industrial Japan* (Glencoe, Ill.: Free Press, 1957; reprint ed., Boston: Beacon Press, 1970).

7. For additional comments on the *Kojiki* and *Nihongi*, see Chapter 4.

8. Ryusaku Tsunoda et al., *Sources of Japanese Tradition* (New York: Columbia University Press, 1958), paperback ed., Vol. 2, p. 29.

9. For a lengthy quotation of Motoori's view of *kami*, see p. 8.

10. Shakyamuni is another name for Buddha.

11. "Way of Kami" is Motoori's expression for Shinto. The poem is quoted from the translation of Shigeru Matsumoto, *Motoori Norinaga, 1730–1801* (Cambridge, Mass.: Harvard University Press, 1970), p. 164.

SELECTED READINGS ━━━━━━━

Bellah, Robert N. *Tokugawa Religion: The Values of Pre-Industrial Japan*. Glencoe, Ill.: Free Press, 1957; reprint ed., Boston: Beacon Press, 1970. A sociological analysis of a highly eclectic Tokugawa movement; important for tracing popular values that helped shape modern Japan.

Earhart, H. Byron. *Religion in the Japanese Experience: Sources and Interpretations*. Belmont, Calif.: Wadsworth, 1974. See Part Fifteen for the dilemma of Shinto and Buddhism as organized religions in modern Japan (including excerpts from Tsukamoto's article).

Holtom, Daniel C. *The National Faith of Japan: A Study in Modern Shinto*. New York: Dutton, 1938; reprint ed., New York: Paragon Book Reprint Corp., 1965. See pp. 44–52 for a brief treatment of Restoration Shinto (treated as "Renaissance Shinto").

Kishimoto, Hideo, and Wakimoto, Tsuneya. "Introduction: Religion During Tokugawa." In *Japanese Religion in the Meiji Era*. Edited by

Hideo Kishimoto. Translated by John F. Howes. Tokyo: Obunsha, 1956, pp. 3–33. A critical overview of religion in the Tokugawa period.

Matsumoto, Shigeru. *Motoori Norinaga, 1730–1801*. Cambridge, Mass.: Harvard University Press, 1970. A detailed study of the foremost scholar and proponent of Restoration Shinto.

Smith, Warren W., Jr. *Confucianism in Modern Japan: A Study of Conservatism in Japanese Intellectual History*. 2d ed. Tokyo: Hokuseido Press, 1973. See pp. 6–40 for a historical summary of Neo-Confucianism in the Tokugawa period.

Tomikura, Mitsuo. "Confucianism." In *Japanese Religion*. Edited by Ichiro Hori. Translated by Yoshiya Abe and David Reid. Tokyo: Kodansha International, 1972, pp. 105–22. A concise overview of Confucianism in Japanese thought and society.

Tsukamoto, Zenryu. "Japanese and Chinese Buddhism." In *Religions and the Promise of the Twentieth Century*. Edited by Guy S. Metraux and François Crouzet. New York: New American Library, 1965, pp. 229–44. A leading Buddhist scholar's critical analysis of "formalized Buddhism" in Tokugawa times.

Tsunoda, Ryusaku, et al. *Sources of Japanese Tradition*. New York: Columbia University Press, 1958. See Chapters 16, 17, and 18 for translated documents concerning Neo-Confucianism in Japan.

CHAPTER 15

The Meiji Restoration and Nationalistic Shinto

For more than two hundred years, the Tokugawa rulers maintained peace on a feudal basis, but increasingly the effectiveness of their regime declined. Economically, severe problems of indebtedness led to widespread suffering and peasant uprisings. In addition, toward the end of the Tokugawa period there was the political threat of foreign insistence upon open trade with Japan. As the government became increasingly inefficient in meeting these problems, more and more people came to favor the restoration of the emperor. There had always been factions supporting the emperor against the Tokugawa ruler, but now the position of these factions was reinforced by several new developments. An attempt to link the Tokugawa government and the imperial family was unsuccessful. Dissatisfaction with Neo-Confucianism as a means of regulating the country was growing, and so was interest in the study of Western science. As a result of these factors, between 1867 and 1868 the Tokugawa government ended and the emperor was "restored," at least in name, to his position as head of state.

THE POLITICAL AND RELIGIOUS SIGNIFICANCE OF THE MEIJI RESTORATION

The Meiji Restoration drew its name from the reinstallment of the emperor, but in actuality it was no simple restoration or return to beginnings. On the contrary, the Meiji period (1868–1912) divides feudal Japan from modern Japan. The whole system of government was reorganized along the lines of a nation-state. The office of the *shogun* was abolished. The emperor formally headed a centralized government with a constitution and elected legislators. The feudal domains were replaced with prefectures, which administered local government as a branch of the central authority. A new capital was established at Tokyo. To finance the government, a national tax system was adopted. It was obvious that if the central government was to be sovereign, feudal armies would have to be replaced with an imperial or national army. These radical transformations in politics and economics took time, requiring the adjustment of sincere ideals to realistic possibility.

151
*The Meiji
Restoration
and
Nationalistic
Shinto*

In conjunction with the political and economic changes of the Meiji Restoration, there were significant changes in religion. The religious transition from Tokugawa times into the Meiji era may be described as the replacement of state patronage of Buddhism with state patronage of Shinto (or nationalistic Shinto). The religious transition, too, took time and involved experimentation. In general there was a negative purpose (the demotion of Buddhism) and a positive purpose (the elevation of Shinto).

The motive for demoting Buddhism is easily understood, for Buddhism had been in effect a branch of the Tokugawa feudal government. Furthermore, the financial corruption and spiritual decline of Buddhism made it an easy target for the reforming zeal of the Meiji architects. The motive for elevating Shinto is obvious, too, even though it was a difficult policy to implement. The general notion was that just as the emperor had been restored to his rightful status as (titular) head of the state, so should Shinto be restored to its rightful position as the old imperial religion—and new state religion.

In the transitional period an exaggerated zeal against the old regime and Buddhism was accompanied by an exaggerated enthusiasm for the program of the newly restored Shinto. Until the Meiji period, most Shinto shrines had been under heavy Buddhist influence. This was natural, since Shinto shrines and Buddhist temples were built side-by-side and the priests of the two traditions cooperated in the worship within both edifices. However, during the Tokugawa period, high-ranking Buddhist priests often came to control Shinto shrines. In reaction to this situation, many Meiji reformers were outspoken in their desire to "purify" Shinto from the foreign influence of Buddhism. Japan has always presented a baffling mixture of the old and the new, and the Meiji Restoration attempted its own blend, seeking to return to the pure, original Japanese government and religion, while boldly opening Japan to all kinds of new, foreign ideas and usages.

THE ATTEMPT TO RESTORE SHINTO AS
THE ONLY JAPANESE RELIGION

Restoration meant purifying Shinto shrines and the Shinto priesthood from Buddhist influence. Buddhist statues were removed from shrines, and Buddhist priests were ejected. However, the proximity of the two priesthoods is further illustrated by this very move: Many Buddhist priests simply renounced their Buddhist ordination and overnight became Shinto priests. For a while Buddhism suffered from persecution. There was a widespread cry to eliminate Buddhism and Buddhist monks. Many priceless Buddhist treasures were wantonly destroyed, while others were bought for a pittance to become the nucleus of museum collections in the West.

In general, as Buddhism was disestablished, Shinto was established. The ideal was to return to the earlier period when Shinto had played a prominent role in government. Accordingly, in 1868 Shinto was proclaimed the sole basis of the government. Not only was the emperor the head of the state (and the imperial rituals were state rituals), but there was also a Department of Shinto within the government, superior to other departments. In addition to purifying Shinto from Buddhist influence, the department began to regulate Shinto on a centralized, nationwide basis. For example, the hereditary succession of Shinto priests was abolished so that all Shinto priests could be appointed by the Department of Shinto as government officials. Shinto priests were used to propagate purified Shinto, especially in districts where Buddhist influence was strongest.

An imperial rescript or proclamation in 1870 explained the rationale for such policies. According to the rescript, the Japanese nation had been founded by the gods *(kami)* and preserved by an unbroken line of emperors who maintained "the unity of religion and state." This unity was considered indispensable for the restoration activities of the Meiji era. By 1871 there was an official policy of using Shinto parishes for registration purposes, instead of the Buddhist parishes of Tokugawa times. After the expulsion of Christianity in the midseventeenth century, the government had required every family to belong to a Buddhist temple to ensure the prohibition of Christianity. In the early Meiji period, the new government required every person to register at a local Shinto shrine, at birth and upon change of residence.

The purpose of the Shinto parish system was to unify the state, rather than to attack Buddhism or Christianity.

It is difficult to imagine the turmoil and disorder that accompanied the transition from feudal to modern times. The Meiji government, or at least one major faction, sought to reduce the chaos by returning to the ideals of Shinto. However, neither government order nor intellectual persuasion was able to transform the complex religious history of Japan into a completely Shinto affair. Some people feared (and some hoped) that Buddhism was doomed to extinction, together with the Tokugawa feudal regime. But the criticism and persecution of Buddhism had a purging effect. Although caught at its lowest ebb of spiritual resources, Japanese Buddhism rallied to fight for its own role in the creation of the new modern state. In fact, in the Meiji era Buddhism became more active than Shinto in developing a systematic critique against Christianity.

Two factors persuaded the new government to back down from its exaggerated enthusiasm for Shinto as the sole foundation of the state: first, the renewed strength of Japanese Buddhism within Japan; second, the clamor for religious freedom in Japan by foreign spokesmen. The renewed strength of Buddhism made it impossible for the Department of Shinto to handle both Shinto and Buddhist affairs. Therefore, the Department of Shinto was abolished, and between 1872 and 1875 there was a brief attempt to administer both Shinto and Buddhism within a newly created Department of Religion. But it was impractical to try to reunify Shinto and Buddhism in the joint administration of the Department of Religion. Thus in 1877 the Department of Religion was abolished, and a temporary Bureau of Shrines and Temples was set up; it lasted until the official designation of "shrine Shinto" in 1882.

The second factor making it impossible to recognize Shinto as the only religion in Japan was the insistence by foreigners that Japan allow freedom of religion and accept Christian missionaries. With the official opening of Japan to foreign intercourse in 1868, Christian missionaries (both Catholic and Protestant) entered Japan. Technically, the Tokugawa proscription of Christianity had not yet been lifted. At this time Japan, emerging from a seclusion of about two centuries, was very sensitive to foreign criticism. Government groups went abroad to observe the functioning of Western countries so that the Meiji government could be established on sound lines. Japanese officials desired to copy Western practices that they thought would be beneficial to Japan, and they actively sought to establish relations with Western nations. Western diplomats pleaded for the reintroduction of

Christianity into Japan. Against this background of Western insistence, and possibly stimulated by the more liberal minds of the Meiji era, in 1873 the ban against Christianity was lifted. Christianity was a recognized religion and Christian missionaries could legally enter Japan. At the same time the regulation for compulsory registration at Shinto shrines was dropped. From about 1875, the government attitude toward religion shifted to a new direction.

THE ESTABLISHMENT OF NONRELIGIOUS SHRINE SHINTO

In effect, officials of the new government decided that if they could not make Shinto the sole religion of the state, then they would make the state into a semi-Shinto institution. Shinto remained deeply involved in state matters, but the state declared Shinto to be nonreligious in character. To be more precise, a law of 1882 divided Shinto into shrine Shinto (sometimes called nationalistic or state Shinto by Western writers) and sect Shinto. Under the category of shrine Shinto the law included most of the Shinto shrines throughout the country, excluding only those that had developed special sect forms. (This government action did not create any new shrines; it changed the status of most local shrines.) From 1882, only adherents of shrine Shinto could call their buildings shrines *(jinja)*, for they alone were state institutions. A special Bureau of Shrines was set up in the Department of Home Affairs to deal with the administration of the shrines as state institutions.

Under the category of sect Shinto were included thirteen groups that had developed as sects of Shinto or had accepted Shinto forms in order to gain government recognition as independent sects. The thirteen sects were considered separate religions by the government. The buildings of sect Shinto could not be called shrines; they were called *kyokai*, a term usually translated as "church." Sect Shinto had the same religious status as the sects of Buddhism and Christianity. In fact all these religions (shrine Shinto being excluded by definition) were supervised by a Bureau of Religions within the Department of Education.

This policy, on the surface a separation of religion and state, was of great convenience to the Meiji government. It paid lip service to religious freedom, since technically no religion was required and no religion was prohibited. At the same time it provided a free hand for using the supposedly nonreligious shrine Shinto to unify the country through patriotic support of the state. The Constitution of 1899 guaranteed religious freedom, which was attainable as long as shrine Shinto was considered nonreligious. On the other hand, the Imperial Rescript on Education of 1890 assured that Shinto and Confucian principles would be respected in the moral education of the people in order to unify the nation.[1] The rescript enjoined loyalty to the state as a corollary of reverence for the imperial ancestors who founded it. The rescript did not advocate a new tradition, but its teaching was used in every Japanese school to instill reverence for the emperor and unquestioning loyalty to the state. "Religious" teaching as defined by the state, meaning especially Buddhist and Christian teaching, was excluded from schools. In general, shrine Shinto was supported politically and economically by the government.

Theoretically all religions were free to manage their own affairs, but in practice they were restricted or even suppressed. For example, in the early 1900s the government was attempting to unify the nation more effectively and to utilize local shrines to encourage loyalty to the emperor and patriotism toward the state. To implement this policy, the government required small local shrines to "merge" into single village shrines, so that the government could control shrine activities and inculcate patriotism more efficiently. Local people did not want to "merge" their small shrines but could not resist the government order. They reluctantly dismantled the small shrines. After World War II, many local groups reestablished the small shrines that they had been forced to abandon in the merger process.[2]

SHRINE SHINTO AS AN EXPRESSION OF NATIONALISTIC MILITARISM

Shrine Shinto has been called nationalistic Shinto by Westerners because it was used as a major support to the Japanese nationalism that preceded World War II. Most Japanese people who grew up after 1890 received a public education of nationalistic ethics. Those who questioned absolute loyalty to the state were definitely in the minority: some liberal intellectuals, a few members of the so-called New Religions, and a few Christians. The 1890 Rescript on Education had been prompted by a reaction to excessive Westernization; by 1930 another surge of antiforeign feeling was sweeping through the country. Especially after 1930, when Japan's relations with foreign countries deteriorated, it became a serious matter to question the state's authority.

In 1938 all schools were required to use an ultranationalistic textbook that emphasized the uniqueness and supremacy of Japan as a political and religious unity; in Japanese this "national entity" is called *kokutai*.[3]

Japanese nationalism, however, did not appear for the first time in the twentieth century, and its religious justification was not taken exclusively from Shinto. The term *kokutai* was used in the Tokugawa period by scholars combining Neo-Confucian and Shinto thought. As we saw in Chapter 14, Neo-Confucian and Shinto thought became closely related in the late Tokugawa period: One expression of the relationship was emphasis on *kokutai* as "an inner essence or mystical force residing in the Japanese nation as a result of Amaterasu's" divine revelation. A modern Western scholar has defined *"kokutai* thought" in Tokugawa times in this way:

> According to *kokutai* thought, Japan is a patriarchal state, in which everyone is related and the imperial house is the main or head family. The emperor is the supreme father, and loyalty to him, or patriotism, becomes the highest form of Filial Piety. Because of the command of Amaterasu, this structure is both sacred and eternal; compliance with its requirements is the obligation and deepest wish of every Japanese.[4]

The Tokugawa tradition of nationalism, including features such as absolute loyalty to the emperor, forms the background for Meiji developments of nationalism and Shinto.

The question of nationalism is a delicate one because the bad memory of World War II still survives. Many Western treatments of Shinto, written prior to and during World War II, tended to depict Shinto as the main source of Japanese nationalism and the cause of the war. Even today in the United States there remains a popular conception that the cause of the war was Shinto. According to this view, because Shinto commanded worship of an emperor-god, Japanese soldiers were bound to follow the emperor's command to extend the Japanese empire into foreign lands. However, this exaggeration is more representative of American wartime fears than of the actual situation in Japan.

Since the end of World War II, there has been a reassessment of Shinto and its relationship to nationalism and militarism. Earlier Western notions probably placed too much emphasis on the nationalistic aspects of Shinto and linked it too closely to its manipulation by the government. This misconception tended to view the essence of Shinto as the unity of state and Shinto during the past century. But to call this tradition "state Shinto" and then to think of it as indicating the nature of Shinto through its long history is obviously a mistake. It is more difficult, but more true to the facts, to try to distinguish between the perennial tie of Shinto to the Japanese identity, on the one hand, and the modern manipulation of this tie for militaristic purposes on the other hand. The widely respected Shinto scholar Muraoka, who refused to support nationalistic interpretations of Shinto before and during World War II, rejected the notion that Shinto by nature is militaristic. In a calm assessment of Shinto in the academically free postwar period he concluded that, "judging from the overall character of the legends of the *Kojiki* and *Nihongi,* it is clear that no militaristic or ultranationalistic intent" existed in the notion of a sacred country.[5]

157
*The Meiji
Restoration
and
Nationalistic
Shinto*

Another inadequacy of "state Shinto" as a blanket term is that it fails to differentiate between the intentions of the government administrators, the shrine priests, and the people at large. It is quite likely that these three groups often participated within the same governmentally controlled shrines, but each had different intentions: The government administrators might have been concerned mainly with ideological control of the populace; the shrine priests might have had in mind ritual and theological concerns; and the people may have looked for simple blessings of their homes and welfare.

One of the problems in reassessing twentieth-century Shinto is the lack of precise terms differentiating traditional Shinto from its nationalistic involvement. One scholar attempting to reappraise Shinto has proposed separating the discussion of the "Kokutai cult" from the topic of Shinto as such. Kokutai cult is defined as "Japan's emperor-state–centered cult of ultranationalism and militarism," which "included elements of Shinto mythology and ideology and . . . utilized Shinto institutions and practices" but "was not a form of Shinto." Defined in this manner, the Kokutai cult consisted of six elements compulsory for all Japanese: (1) "acceptance of the doctrine that the Emperor was 'sacred and inviolable' "; (2) veneration or worship of spirits of the imperial ancestors and imperial rescripts; (3) unquestioned acceptance of ancient myths and their chauvinistic interpretation in modern works such as the nationalistic textbook *Kokutai no Hongi;* (4) the observance of national holidays, centering in the glorification of the imperial line; (5) worship of *kami* at shrines and in the home (before the *kamidana*); (6) financial support of local shrines and festivals.[6] This interpretation highlights the complexities of the relationship of Shinto to nationalism; it also demonstrates the need for an understanding of nationalism in Japan.

Factors that gave rise to nationalism in Japan, like the causes of war, are many and complex. They include the whole context of economic, political, and social conditions in prewar Japan. One scholar who has studied nationalism in Japan claims that nationalism can be fostered by one or more of a number of elements, including geographical separateness, common racial descent (actual or supposed), a common language, and common religious beliefs. His conclusion is that, "Although few nations are influenced by all the recognized elements of nationalism, in Japan each of the elements not only is present but exists in an unusually strong form."[7] Shinto was but one factor contributing to Japan's ultranationalism. In fact, the pioneer Western scholar of Shinto nationalism, Daniel C. Holtom, has shown that Japanese Buddhism competed with Shinto in claiming to support and protect the nation: "If . . . Buddhism has never declared a holy war, it has nonetheless proclaimed all Japanese wars holy."[8] Even Japanese Christians were quick to announce their support of the state program. The ironies of history present a much stranger case. The Chinese tradition of Confucianism had become so Japanized through the centuries that the Japanese could appeal to Confucianism as their own rationale for their "benevolent rule" of Manchuria and Korea. Especially after 1933, Confucianism in Japan became an important rationale for supporting ultranationalism and militarism.[9]

During the first four decades of the twentieth century, Japan's energies were heavily concentrated on the strengthening of nationalism and militarism; and religion, especially Shinto, was used to further these aims. However, proper historical perspective is crucial if we are to understand Shinto. We must see shrine Shinto as a modern development within a tradition with a long history. We should avoid the temptation to view the whole history of Shinto in terms of its modern nationalistic phase. For, although shrine Shinto captured the limelight in the modern period, in the countryside Shinto shrines preserved much of the traditional religious life. The major activities at local shrines repeated the age-old pattern: events such as annual festivals for spring and fall associated with agriculture, the elaborate New Year's celebrations, and special village-wide festivities invoking the blessing of the *kami*. Although nationalism pervaded even these local Shinto shrines, it represented an overlay directed by the central government but did not eliminate the religious life of the shrines. As Muraoka has described the situation: "Instead of the doctrines and thought of Shrine Shinto causing the Imperialism and expansionism of the politicians and the military, it was rather Imperialism and expansionism that enhanced the doctrine of Shrine Shinto."[10]

Shinto (in its modern form of shrine Shinto) tended to dominate other religious traditions in the period from 1868 to 1945—a period in which nationalism and then ultranationalism combined with militarism were the keynotes of Japanese life. Because of shrine Shinto's dominance over Shinto as a whole and shrine Shinto's close association with the war effort, after the surrender of 1945 many Japanese people lost trust in Shinto.

Nationalistic religion was not the problem of Shinto alone. In early Japanese history as well as before World War II, Buddhism and Confucianism were equally aligned with the national welfare. In the next two chapters we will see how the increasing formalism heightened the need for a renewal of religious life.

NOTES

1. For a translation of "The Imperial Rescript on Education," see H. Byron Earhart, *Religion in the Japanese Experience: Sources and Interpretations* (Belmont, Calif.: Wadsworth, 1974), pp. 203–04.
2. See Wilbur M. Fridell, *Japanese Shrine Mergers, 1906–12: State Shinto Moves to the Grassroots* (Tokyo: Sophia University, 1973).
3. See John Owen Gauntlett for a translation of this text, *Kokutai no Hongi: Cardinal Principles of the National Entity of Japan*, ed. Robert King Hall (Cambridge, Mass.: Harvard University Press, 1949).
4. David Magarey Earl, *Emperor and Nation in Japan: Political Thinkers of the Tokugawa Period* (Seattle: University of Washington Press, 1964), pp. 236–37.
5. Tsunetsugu Muraoka, "Separation of State and Religion in Shinto: Its Historical Significance," in his *Studies in Shinto*, trans. Delmer M. Brown and James T. Araki (Tokyo: Ministry of Education, 1964), p. 242.
6. William P. Woodard, *The Allied Occupation of Japan, 1945–1952, and Japanese Religions* (Leiden: E. J. Brill, 1972), p. 11.
7. Delmer M. Brown, *Nationalism in Japan: An Introductory Historical Analysis* (Berkeley: University of California Press, 1955; reprint ed., New York: Russell & Russell, 1971), pp. 2–7, 12.
8. Daniel C. Holtom, *Modern Japan and Shinto Nationalism: A Study of Present-Day Trends in Japanese Religions*, rev. ed. (Chicago: University of Chicago Press, 1947; reprint ed., New York: Paragon Book Reprint Corp., 1963), p. 148.
9. See Warren W. Smith, Jr., *Confucianism in Modern Japan: A Study of Conservatism in Japanese Intellectual History*, 2d ed. (Tokyo:

Hokuseido Press, 1973); an excerpt from Smith (which illustrates the role of Confucianism in Japanese nationalism) is included in Earhart, *Religion in the Japanese Experience*, pp. 69–74.

10. Muraoka, "Separation of State and Religion in Shinto," p. 243.

SELECTED READINGS

Earhart, H. Byron. *Religion in the Japanese Experience: Sources and Interpretations*. Belmont, Calif.: Wadsworth, 1974. See Part Fourteen for selected documents on the close relation between religion and state, including "The Imperial Rescript on Education" and excerpts from *Kokutai no Hongi;* see also pp. 218–22 for excerpts from the article by Hori and Toda and pp. 69–74 for excerpts from Smith.

Holtom, Daniel C. *Modern Japan and Shinto Nationalism: A Study of Present-Day Trends in Japanese Religions*. Rev. ed. Chicago: University of Chicago Press, 1947. Reprint ed., New York: Paragon Book Reprint Corp., 1963. Contains historical information on nationalistic Shinto, including the nationalistic activities of Christianity and Buddhism in Japan.

Hori, Ichiro, and Toda, Yoshio. "Shinto." In *Japanese Religion in the Meiji Era*. Edited by Hideo Kishimoto. Translated by John F. Howes. Tokyo: Obunsha, 1956, pp. 35–98. A brief critical treatment of Shinto in the Meiji period.

Muraoka, Tsunetsugu. "Separation of State and Religion in Shinto: Its Historical Significance." In *Studies in Shinto*. Translated by Delmer M. Brown and James T. Araki. Tokyo: Ministry of Education, 1964, pp. 230–44. A critical and balanced assessment of the original character of Shinto, its distortion before and during World War II, and its prospects after the climactic events of 1945.

Smith, Warren W., Jr. *Confucianism in Modern Japan: A Study of Conservatism in Japanese Intellectual History*, 2d ed. Tokyo: Hokuseido Press, 1973. See pp. 41–102 for the role of Confucianism during the Meiji period.

Tsunoda, Ryusaku, et al. *Sources of Japanese Tradition*. New York: Columbia University Press, 1958. See Chapters 24–27 for the variety of liberalism and nationalism from pre-Meiji times to 1945.

CHAPTER 16

Religious Currents from 1868 to 1945

In the period from 1868 (marking the Meiji Restoration and the reopening of Japan to the West) to 1945 (marking the end of World War II), nationalism pervaded every aspect of Japanese life. After 1890 the government exerted increasing control over organized religion; prior to World War II the government laid down strict rules for the consolidation of denominations (both Buddhist and Christian) in order to control them more effectively. Shinto, especially shrine Shinto, was a main channel for this nationalism, but other religious traditions were equally affected. Indeed, one scholar feels that after 1933 Confucianism played an even greater role in supporting the national polity *(kokutai)*. Confucianism defined the central theme of *Kokutai no Hongi,* the nationalistic textbook that was required reading in all schools after 1938.[1] In Chapter 15, Buddhism and Christianity were also cited as being heavily influenced by the nationalistic movement. However, it would be a mistake to see the religious history of this period only in terms of nationalism. A brief description of Buddhism, Christianity, and the New Religions reveals important religious undercurrents in addition to the major current of nationalism. These undercurrents are important not only for understanding the prewar period, but especially for understanding the critical spiritual mood of postwar Japan.

BUDDHISM: THE STRUGGLE FOR RENEWAL, ESPECIALLY WITHIN BUDDHIST SCHOLARSHIP

With the Meiji Restoration, Buddhism was faced with an unexpected crisis. Several centuries of patronage by the Tokugawa government (1600–1867) had led Buddhist priests and temples to take for granted their superior positions of wealth and leisure. They became so firmly entrenched that financial corruption and spiritual lassitude went unchecked. Then in a flash the Tokugawa government fell and an important source of their income vanished. It was bad enough that the Meiji Restoration did not stop with a mere reform of Buddhism but instead chose to disestablish Buddhism and establish Shinto in its place. Even worse, perhaps, was the severe criticism and persecution of Buddhism stimulated by the zeal to restore Shinto. It is true that some of the destruction of Buddhist temples during the transitional period can be attributed to the misplaced enthusiasm that accompanies any radical social change. On the other hand, much of the criticism against Buddhism—financial and moral corruption—was justified.

At first the Buddhist priests could comprehend neither the sociopolitical transformation nor the criticism against Buddhism. As a whole, Buddhism tried to maintain in the Meiji period the same role and position it had known during the Tokugawa period: religiously, preoccupation with ancestral rites; politically, subservience to the state. Buddhist priests were so preoccupied with funerals and masses that they came to be referred to jokingly as the "undertakers of Japan"; they strove to be at least second to Shinto as the supporters of the state. However, implicit in the Meiji criticism of Buddhism was a call for a spiritual as well as a moral renewal of Buddhism. To a certain extent Japanese Buddhism is still wrestling with the problem of spritual renewal.

Japanese Buddhism's vitality in the early Meiji period was illustrated by the fact that the government was forced to recognize it as a religion of the people. Nor did Buddhism lack devout and far-sighted priests. Some priests, rather than lamenting the persecution of Buddhism, recognized Buddhism's disestablishment as a blessing in disguise. They had the courage to acknowledge the criticisms leveled against Buddhism and advocated its spiritual rebirth. An outstanding example of the attempt to reform Japanese Buddhism is Kiyozawa Manshi (1863–1903), who openly criticized Buddhism's traditional pattern of hereditary family membership in temples. He advocated a renewal of personal Buddhist faith and a reorganization of Buddhism as a "brotherhood" based on small groups of believers. Although he was not successful, his ideas provided inspiration for postwar reform of Buddhist institutions.

In actuality, Japanese Buddhism was threatened from several sides simultaneously. Shinto strove to abolish or suppress it as a decadent and foreign religion. Christianity attacked it on doctrinal grounds. In addition, Buddhism like Confucianism was threatened with extinction by the onslaught of Western science and philosophy. Buddhism's competition with Shinto can be seen in the familiar pattern of nationalistic religion. Buddhism's encounter with Western learning and Christianity, however, must be seen as a remarkable innovation in Japanese religious history.

Buddhist priests accepted the challenge of Western learning by sending priest-scholars to Europe. As early as 1876 Nanjo Bunyu went to England to study Sanskrit texts with F. Max Müller. This marked an important meeting of East and West, for Müller was the founder of the "science of religion" in Europe and Nanjo was the first Japanese Buddhist to adopt Western methods of historical and philological scholarship. From this time forward, the Buddhist priest-scholars who studied in the best European universities (and published in French, German, or English) strengthened their native erudition with the critical methods of European scholarship (especially those of history and philology).

On the Japanese side this scholarly cooperation had two positive results. The reforming desire of devout Buddhists was rewarded with a direct knowledge of early Indian Buddhism. Formerly their knowledge of Buddhism had been filtered through Chinese Buddhism. A second positive result was a growing confidence in Western methods of critical scholarship and Western philosophy. The Buddhist scholars were competent in relating comparable philosophical movements in the European and Buddhist traditions. Also they were fully capable of using one philosophy to criticize another. During this upsurge of scholarly activity, monumental publishing ventures were undertaken, among which were the reprinting of the Buddhist canon (in Chinese), compilation of documents from Japanese Buddhism, and publication of erudite encyclopedias and reference works on all aspects of Buddhism.

On the whole, Buddhist priests have been much more in touch with Western culture than Shinto priests have been. With the establishment of Western-style universities in the Meiji era, Buddhist priests came to be trained in departments of Indian and Buddhist philosophy where the classical languages of Buddhism (Pali and

Sanskrit as well as Tibetan) and modern European languages were emphasized. Buddhist appropriation of Western learning and cooperation with Western scholars represented one of the most remarkable possibilities for the renewal of Buddhism in the prewar period.

This possibility for renewal, however, only further complicated an already complex Japanese Buddhism, which was split between traditional piety and modern intellectualism. Popular Buddhism continued in the same patterns as in Tokugawa times, while some Buddhist priests and intellectuals tended to think in terms of appropriated Western concepts. At about this time the systematic or "scientific" study of religion was founded in Japan. This established the academic study of religion apart from traditional fields such as Shinto studies, Buddhist studies, and Chinese studies. Anesaki Masaharu was the first occupant of the chair of the science of religion at Tokyo University in 1905. Some Shinto scholars, notably Kato Genchi, furthered the Japanese study of the science of religion by pioneering Shinto studies in the light of comparative research. These new currents of thought did not affect the people at large, but they did raise problems for many intellectuals, especially the scholars and students who had accepted Christianity.

CHRISTIANITY: STRENGTH AND WEAKNESS SINCE 1868

The story of Christianity in Japan from 1868 to 1945 shows some similarities with the Christian century of Roman Catholic missions from about 1550 to 1650. In both periods early phases of Christian success linked with Japanese acceptance of Western culture were followed by phases of Christianity's decline due to Japanese reaction against the West. Apart from these general similarities, there were some remarkable dissimilarities in the two periods. For example, in the later period, Protestant as well as Roman Catholic missionaries came to Japan.

Christian missionaries arrived in Japan in the late 1850s, soon after the signing of treaties with Western powers. However, they were unable to achieve results until 1873, when the Tokugawa ban on Christianity was lifted. Between 1868 and 1872 there had been several arrests of Christians, especially Catholics.

After 1873, Christianity tended to gain followers. However, the fortune of Christianity in Japan seems to have been shaped by three major factors, which made it difficult to gain individual converts but at the same time made Christianity an important contributor to the formation of the new Japanese government. The first factor is that the official attitude of Christianity toward other traditions has usually been to favor conversion rather than syncretism. The blending of Christianity with other traditions has occasionally taken place, but usually on an unofficial basis and over a long period of time. Thus the Japanese had to make a radical leap from their own tradition in order to accept Christianity. (By contrast, both Buddhism and Confucianism were more open and syncretistic in their contact with Japanese culture and religion.) The second factor is that the Japanese people were not only self-conscious but proud of their long, unique heritage. To be Japanese usually meant to participate in this heritage—semireligious activities such as respect for (or veneration of) the emperor—and also in Shinto and Japanese Buddhism. From 1868 to 1945 there was an active discussion as to whether one could be both a devout Christian and a loyal Japanese. The third factor was that Japanese officials looked to the West for models of government and science. This meant an initial acceptance of Christianity as the spiritual culture of the West, until the Japanese realized that they could be Westernized (and industrialized) without becoming Christian.

Social turmoil after 1868 turned many defeated warriors of the feudal lords to Christianity. Having lost their effort to maintain the Tokugawa government and state Buddhism, they saw Christianity as a means of ordering Meiji society and government. Some scholars have thought that the religious fervor and courageous loyalty of these early Christians was as much a carryover from their Confucian warrior training as it was a product of their Christian conversion. At any rate, the Christian faith spread to the middle classes of the cities, so that in the 1870s evangelism was being carried out by Japanese Christians. These sincere Japanese Christians were eager to avoid denominationalism, favored financial self-support by Japanese churches, and tried to eliminate Western customs hindering the development of a truly Japanese Christianity.

They quickly attained almost complete financial independence, but the problems of denominationalism and difficulties in developing a distinctively Japanese Christianity have persisted to the present. For example, the famous Japanese Christian Uchimura (1861–1930) is noted for his statement about his love for the "two J's": "I love two J's and no third; one is Jesus, and the other is Japan."[2] However, his example of blending the Christian and Japanese traditions was a rare exception. For many Japanese Christians the imitation of countless foreign national customs and denominational practices in Japan seemed superfluous. Nevertheless, Christmas became quite popular

Advertisement at a Tokyo store for the "Christmas cake" that has become popular throughout Japan. Santa Claus, represented as a Caucasian man in a red and white outfit, is aided by a smiling Japanese girl. They encourage shoppers to "please order early." (Tokyo, 1979)

for many Japanese people, apart from its specific Christian significance. It is still celebrated as a children's festival and is nearly as commercialized as it is in the West.[3]

Christianity gained many of its followers from the young people who attended Christian schools. Christian missionaries made a great contribution to Japanese education, particularly in girls' schools and in the teaching of foreign languages such as English. Young people were encouraged to attend these schools and thus came into contact with Christianity, which was taught openly or privately. In fact until the late 1880s, the tendency for uncritical acceptance of anything Western, including Christianity, alarmed both the government and the priests of Shinto and Buddhism. In the late 1880s, however, Japan's humiliation by Western powers through unequal treaties stimulated reactionary support for Japanese independence from foreign missions. The 1890 Imperial Rescript on Education cleverly removed religious instruction from education on the pretext of religious freedom. In reality, it was a result of the new government policy to counteract Western (and Christian) influence by supporting shrine Shinto and the emperor.

The early Japanese Christians who studied abroad in Europe and the United States were greatly influenced by modern education, movements for women's rights, socialism, and liberal politics. These men played very important roles in shaping the more humane aspects of Meiji government. However, even though Christianity provided the rationale for these social and political reforms, social issues and socialism came increasingly to be conceived apart from Christianity.

Although Japan became committed to Western models in education and industrialization, she could do so without accepting Christianity. Furthermore, well before 1900, several innovations caused strife within Japanese Christianity. Denominationalism became a tragic fact. Theological disagreement between the new liberals and older conservatives further fragmented Japanese Christianity. In addition, the evolutionistic and atheistic philosophies of the West presented live options for many intellectuals. As the quality of government schools equaled and then surpassed that of Christian schools (run by missionaries and Japanese Christians), more Japanese found they could accept Western culture without accepting Western religion. Japanese philosophers, for example, are at home with all periods and schools of Western philosophy. Although there were some devout Japanese Christians, Christianity did not become a major religion in Japan.

After 1890, the youth came under the influence of nationalistic education, and the mood of the country gradually changed from nationalism to ultranationalism. Victories in the Sino-Japanese War (1894–95) and the Russo-Japanese War (1904–05) greatly increased nationalistic fervor. From this time through 1945 Japan's primary focus was strengthening Japan against the Western powers. People were no longer attracted to Christianity just because it was a foreign religion.

Most Japanese Christians supported all aspects of nationalism and militarism. For example, they supported both the Sino-Japanese and Russo-Japanese wars not only by praying for victory but also by sending aid for the combat troops. By the time of the Russo-Japanese War, some Christian intellectuals had become pacifists, but they were the exceptions. Later, in the 1930s, Japanese ministers were sent to Manchuria at the request of the Japanese soldiers who were Christians.

Statistics of religious affiliation are particularly difficult to determine in Japan, but by the turn of the century there were about 75,000 church members and by the late 1930s about 300,000 Christians. Because the total population was about 80 million at this time, the percentage of Christians—both Protestant and Roman Catholic—was lower than it had been at the high point of Roman Catholicism in the early seventeenth century. Of course, one can argue that in the sixteenth and seventeenth centuries mass conversions of feudal domains took place, whereas in the nineteenth and twentieth centuries conversions were individual and more sincere. Nevertheless, before World War II, the total number of church members constituted less than 1 percent of the total population. This number is small even when compared with the individual New Religions of the same period.

THE NEW RELIGIONS: NEW VARIATIONS FROM OLD TRADITIONS

The term "New Religions" *(shinko shukyo)* has been given to a number of religious movements that first appeared in late Tokugawa times, gained strength after the Meiji Restoration, and became a dominant force after World War II. The term *shinko shukyo,* literally "newly arisen religions," was first used by journalists to imply that the new-comers were upstarts. Leaders of the New Religions prefer the more neutral term *shin shukyo,* literally "new religions." However, the term "New Religions" is misleading because these movements are neither completely new nor are they necessarily complete religions in the Western sense. Every New Religion contains elements from one or more of the preexisting traditions: folk religion, Shinto, Buddhism, Confucianism, religious Taoism, and even Christianity. Therefore, these religious movements are as much renovators as innovators, as much renewed religious traditions as new traditions. The later religious movements are often seen as splinters or branches of the main Japanese traditions. The new movements are not necessarily "complete" religions because often they did not break age-old religious patterns such as having Buddhist priests perform funeral and memorial rites. In other words, the New Religions do not necessarily claim the exclusive attention of their adherents, nor do they necessarily meet all of a person's religious needs. They may be seen as religious cults or religious societies rather than as independent religions with exclusive claims. Only the Jodo Shin sect and Nichiren sect among Japanese traditions (and some New Religions deriving from Nichiren Buddhism) expressed an exclusive claim to absolute truth.

In order to understand the emergence of the New Religions, it is necessary to recognize the context of Japanese religion and society from which they sprang. By late Tokugawa times, when the first New Religions appeared, organized religion in Japan had become highly formalistic and stagnant. From late Tokugawa times through the post-Meiji era, social and economic conditions were very depressed for poor farmers and city laborers. Although one factor leading to the Meiji Restoration was peasant revolts, the money economy and tax system of the Meiji era only increased the tendency for small farmers to become helpless tenants. Farmers who became city laborers suffered from the low wages and poor working conditions of the early capitalistic system. The New Religions drew many of their leaders and members from the depressed classes, people who had suffered together and now shared their religious experiences. Economic and social crises helped to stimulate a spiritual renewal in the older traditions by forming special religious movements.

The New Religions got their start in the early nineteenth century but were not allowed complete freedom of organization and practice until 1945. Both the Tokugawa government and the later government maintained a strict control over religious sects. During the late Tokugawa period, the new religious movements were forced to continue within the traditional forms of Shinto or Buddhism. They continued with varying phases of recognition or suppression until 1882, when state Shinto was separated as a government institution from sect Shinto. Eventually, thirteen religious movements were recognized and supervised as religious subdivisions of Shinto. Several of the thirteen sects preserved special Shinto traditions and were actually sect developments of Shinto. Other sects were organized around elements of folk religion and blendings of Buddhism, Confucianism, and religious Taoism. Their origins are so diverse and their later doctrinal systems so complex that it is difficult to make general statements about them.[4]

One of the distinguishing features of all the New Religions is that a living person usually served as either organizer or founder. In most cases the impetus for organizing a religion came from the charismatic quality of the founder, who was considered semidivine or divine; his or her utterances became revealed scripture. Even the sect developments of Shinto selected special *kami* from the *Nihongi* and *Kojiki* as objects of worship. The New Religions offered specific objects of faith and appealing forms of worship. They usually promised the solution of all problems through faith and worship. Some of the founders were led to their crucial religious experience (or revelation) by a personal crisis that was solved by the new faith. Often the New Religions practiced faith healing but also promised solutions to personal crises such as financial and marital difficulties.

It may be argued that no religious movement at any time or place is completely new. The New Religions of Japan certainly demonstrate continuity with earlier Japanese traditions. The six persistent themes of Japanese religious history can be found in the New Religions.[5] On the other hand, these movements display a certain amount of originality and uniqueness. An outstanding feature is that they made a direct appeal to individual faith, whereas organized religion in Japan had formerly depended upon family membership along hereditary or geographical lines. Each new movement picked up a spark from one of the old traditions and fanned it into a dynamic spiritual force. For example, in the twentieth century, Nichiren Buddhism was revived by a number of sects (such as Soka Gakkai) that placed their trust in the *Lotus Sutra* and in Nichiren practices. Once a New Religion gained followers, it tended to be crystallized in the form of organized scriptures, doctrine, worship, and priesthood.

The New Religions have received much criticism as unrefined, superstitious, and interested mainly in acquiring money. However, their vitality is proven by the number of followers they attracted. Even in prewar Japan, before they received their biggest stimulus, many sects could claim from several hundred thousand to several million members.[6] In postwar Japan it is remarkable that Soka Gakkai could gain millions of members in a few decades, but the total number of Protestant and Catholic Christians did not exceed a half-million members after almost a century of mission work. The New Religions represent the greatest possibility for religious renewal up to the present day. In the next chapter we will look briefly at two of them.

NOTES

1. See Warren W. Smith, Jr., *Confucianism in Modern Japan: A Study of Conservatism in Japanese Intellectual History,* 2d ed. (Tokyo: Hokuseido Press, 1973), pp. 156ff. See also John Owen Gauntlett, trans., *Kokutai no Hongi: Cardinal Principles of the National Entity of Japan,* ed. Robert King Hall (Cambridge, Mass.: Harvard University Press, 1949).

2. "Two J's" in Ryusaku Tsunoda et al., *Sources of Japanese Tradition* (New York: Columbia University Press, 1958), Chapter 29. This translation is included in H. Byron Earhart, *Religion in the Japanese Experience: Sources and Interpretations* (Belmont, Calif.: Wadsworth, 1974), p. 114.

3. See David W. Plath, "The Japanese Popular Christmas: Coping with Modernity," *Journal of American Folklore,* Vol. 76 (1963), 309–17. This article is abridged in Earhart, *Religion in the Japanese Experience,* pp. 265–70.

4. See Daniel C. Holtom, *The National Faith of Japan: A Study of Modern Shinto* (New York: Dutton, 1938; reprint ed., New York: Paragon Book Reprint Corp., 1965), pp. 189–286, for a description of the thirteen "Shinto sects" in prewar times.
5. For an analysis of the New Religions in terms of these six persistent themes, see H. Byron Earhart, "The Significance of the 'New Religions' for Understanding Japanese Religion," *KBS Bulletin on Japanese Culture*, Vol. 101 (April–May 1970), 1–9. This article is abridged in Earhart, *Religion in the Japanese Experience*, pp. 249–54.
6. See Holtom, *The National Faith of Japan*, p. 285, for membership figures of the thirteen "Shinto sects" in 1937.

SELECTED READINGS

Earhart, H. Byron. *Religion in the Japanese Experience: Sources and Interpretations*. Belmont, Calif.: Wadsworth, 1974. See pp. 84–97 for excerpts from Holtom; see pp. 249–54 for the significance of the New Religions.

Holtom, Daniel C. *The National Faith of Japan: A Study of Modern Shinto*. New York: Dutton, 1938. Reprint ed., New York: Paragon Book Reprint Corp., 1965. See pp. 189–286 for a prewar sketch of the thirteen divisions of sect Shinto.

Murakami, Shigeyoshi. *Japanese Religion in the Modern Century*. Translated by H. Byron Earhart. Tokyo: University of Tokyo Press, 1980. A critical overview of Japanese religion and the problem of freedom of religion after 1868.

Oguchi, Iichi, and Takagi, Hiroo. "Religion and Social Development." In *Japanese Religion in the Meiji Era*. Edited by Hideo Kishimoto. Translated by John F. Howes. Tokyo: Obunsha, 1956, pp. 311–57.

Scheiner, Irwin. *Christian Converts and Social Protest in Meiji Japan*. Berkeley: University of California Press, 1970. Discusses the warriors who, after the Meiji Restoration, shifted from Confucianism to Christianity as a personal and social philosophy.

CHAPTER 17

Two New Religions: Tenrikyo and Soka Gakkai

Of all the New Religions that have arisen in Japan since the early nineteenth century, Tenrikyo and Soka Gakkai are two of the most important. They may highlight some striking similarities and differences among New Religions. Both are new movements, founded and organized outside the established religions. Tenrikyo has been more closely associated with Shinto; Soka Gakkai comes out of the Nichiren Buddhist tradition. Both movements arose during the active period of the New Religions, in the past century and a half, but at different extremes of this period. Tenrikyo was a pioneer New Religion, the first to succeed on a large scale, and served as a model for later movements. Soka Gakkai arose about a century later in the prewar period and flourished only after World War II, yet its rapid success has made it the envy of other groups. Although both were deliberately founded, the religious dynamics of their founding differ. Tenrikyo is oriented around its founder, who is seen as a living *kami* who creates her own sacred scriptures and rites. Soka Gakkai reveres as absolutely powerful Nichiren and the *Lotus Sutra*, which its founder rediscovered, but does not place nearly so much trust in the founder as such. Tenrikyo arose in the countryside and has maintained its strength there while moving into the cities; Soka Gakkai arose in the city and has been strongest among urban people while making some inroads in the countryside.

THE MANY NEW RELIGIONS: DIFFERENCES
AND SIMILARITIES

173
*Two New
Religions:
Tenrikyo and
Soka Gakkai*

Our brief look at Tenrikyo and Soka Gakkai will reveal a number of important features of New Religions, but it is well to point out some characteristics of the many New Religions that differ from these two major movements. Some New Religions were not founded so decisively by one person but tended to coalesce around distinctive regional traditions; this is the case with several movements originally included among the thirteen members of sect Shinto. Not all the New Religions can be traced clearly to either Shinto or Buddhism; a number of them are highly syncretistic. Healing is important for several New Religions, much more important than for Tenrikyo and Soka Gakkai. Some are more closely related to the Western tradition, through spiritualism and a spiritualistic interpretation of Western science. Although mission activity is practiced by both Tenrikyo and Soka Gakkai, many groups are active only in Japan. And, of course, not all the New Religions are so large as Tenrikyo and Soka Gakkai. What we discover in Tenrikyo and Soka Gakkai, then, is a sampling from the hundreds of active New Religions, but a sampling that is too limited to provide the basis for generalizing about all the New Religions.

TENRIKYO: A LIVING *KAMI* AND A JOYOUS LIFE

The religious nature of Tenrikyo is reflected in the dramatic events surrounding its founding. The founder of Tenrikyo, Mrs. Nakayama Miki (1798–1887, usually referred to by her given name of Miki), led a rather uneventful life as the wife of a farmer until 1838. Miki's son had been ill, and several times she had called in a popular exorcist to cure him. In premodern Japan, illness was usually seen as due to the presence of evil spirits, which were driven out by exorcists. In this case the exorcist (a *yamabushi*) used a woman as a medium; after he put the medium into a trance she would identify the evil spirit to be exorcised. But this time when the exorcist was called to heal Miki's son, the exorcist's regular medium was absent, so Miki herself served as the medium.

Miki's trance experience was unusual. Instead of the customary brief possession and "diagnosis" of illness, Miki received a divine revelation in the form of permanent possession by a *kami* who claimed to be the true original *kami*. The name of this divinity, Tenri O no Mikoto, is usually translated into English as "God the Parent" by Tenri authorities. (*Tenri* means "heavenly wisdom" and *O no Mikoto* is equivalent to "royal divinity.") This divinity spoke a rather new message through the mouth of Miki: The *kami* had loaned Miki her body, but now he was reclaiming it and demanding that Miki spend the rest of her life spreading his message. Her family reluctantly yielded to the demand. This 1838 event marks the traditional founding of Tenrikyo, the religion of heavenly wisdom. From this point Miki is viewed as a kind of living *kami*.

Quickly Miki's fame as a living *kami* spread, and people came to ask her for spiritual help, particularly for protection against smallpox and for safe childbirth. Gradually there developed a group of people who had received such help from Miki. A carpenter (whose wife had been healed by Miki after childbirth) first built a small worship hall and eventually helped bring the teachings of Miki into a more highly organized form. As Miki attracted a larger following and began to hold religious services, she came to the attention of the authorities and was subject to harassment and even arrest. In late Tokugawa times, religious organizations were closely supervised, and unrecognized religious movements were subject to prosecution. Nevertheless, Miki persevered in her mission of proclaiming faith in Tenri O no Mikoto, and her family spread the message to the surrounding area, as far as Osaka. The earliest worship phrase, *Namu Tenri O no Mikoto*, is comparable to the Pure Land phrase *Namu Amida Butsu* and to the Nichiren phrase *Namu Myoho Renge Kyo*. (*Namu* translates roughly as "praise be" or "I put my faith in.") Eventually, as her following became larger and as Miki devoted more time to her group (especially after the death of her husband), there emerged all the trappings of an organized religion.

Central to the ethos of this movement was the founder as a living *kami*; her life was a kind of divine model. What she wrote was considered revelation and came to be the scripture of Tenrikyo. The songs she composed became hymns, and the dance she created was transformed into Tenrikyo liturgy. The gestures she used in the dance became standard ritual gestures. Her scripture indicated a nearby spot as the place where the world and human beings were created (by Izanagi and Izanami); this spot, considered the center of the world, became the site for the main shrine of Tenrikyo. The shrine was built in accordance with Miki's revelation. Thus there is a square opening in the roof and a wooden column underneath. The corporate worship and elaborate liturgies that Miki established continue to be performed around this column under the open roof. Although these features have assumed a mysterious symbolism within later Tenrikyo, they obviously signify a channel for continued communication between Heaven and humans.

As Tenrikyo gradually developed into a larger organization around the central figure of Miki, it also developed a kind of ethical philosophy of life based on her teachings. Miki taught that "At the very beginning of the world, God the Parent created mankind out of his earnest desire to make them live a *yokigurashi*, a joyous life. Mankind, however, ignoring the will of God the Parent Who created them to live a life of *yokigurashi* in the truest sense of the word, has come to abuse their minds which were granted to them as their own, and becoming self-willed, come to regard life as a gloomy world."[1] Because men and women have become self-centered and selfish, they are surrounded with gloom. But once an individual recovers his or her oneness with God the Parent he or she once again participates in the joyous creation of the world. The means to this joyous life is faith in God the Parent and "sweeping away" one's evils through the worship services instituted by Miki. From a historical viewpoint we might say that this religious reform is based on a return to Japanese peasant values: gratitude to the sacredness of the cosmos and ethical obligation to place social good before individual profit.

Miki herself worked hard at manual labor and the menial tasks of farming, and her family successors continue this practice, though on a more occasional and formal basis. For the average member of Tenrikyo, much emphasis is placed on voluntary labor for the erection of Tenrikyo buildings, and it is customary for these people to spend long periods at the Tenri headquarters in unpaid labor. Many Western visitors to Tenri headquarters are so impressed with the infectious happiness and energetic enthusiasm of these voluntary laborers that they compare the atmosphere of Tenrikyo to the vitality of Christianity in its first century of development.

When Miki died in early 1887, Tenrikyo had already emerged as a rather well organized religion, so it suffered no critical shock due to the loss of this charismatic leader. The founding site (later called the city of Tenri) became a kind of Mecca for pilgrimage, with the model of Miki's life and teaching as the compass for the individual believer. The first religious shrines had been erected and the liturgical lines laid down. Succession in the leadership was taken over by male heads, or patriarchs, of Mrs. Nakayama's family. At the turn of the century, Tenrikyo was so highly organized that it had divisions for training ministers, propagation, and missions, and later these divisions approached the complexity of their counterparts in American denominations.

As Tenrikyo became more highly organized, first it was forced to accept supervision from other recognized religious bodies, and in 1908 it was granted relatively independent status as an official sect of Shinto. By assuming the subordinate role of a Shinto sect, Tenrikyo was thereby able to operate more freely. Only after World War II did it attain real independence. Tenrikyo now boasts a large publishing house, issuing works not only in Japanese but in other Asian and Western languages. Tenri University is a leading private university with an excellent library. The highly efficient central headquarters at the modern city of Tenri is backed up by a large nationwide network of local branches and a number of overseas branches.

The success story of Tenrikyo is a good example for understanding the dynamic power of the New Religions and their impact on the religious scene. Tenrikyo is firmly rooted in traditional Japanese religion, as evidenced in the revelation to Miki through a kind of shamanistic possession. Centering on the charismatic leadership of Miki and relying on established religion only for government recognition, Tenrikyo developed its own scriptural, liturgical, ecclesiastical, and social forms. Thereby Tenrikyo was the first movement to proceed from individual revelation to large-scale religious organization. According to a Tenrikyo publication, by 1899 "the whole number of the churches was 1,493; that of the missionaries, 18,150; and that of the believers, about 2,000,000."[2]

There is no doubt that Tenrikyo's success encouraged other groups to form and to look upon Tenrikyo's development as a model for their development. But if Tenrikyo has the distinction of being the pioneer or model New Religion, it is also the first New Religion to become fully organized, or "established." Tenrikyo started with every member a convert drawn into a rather loose group, but eventually second-, third-, and even fourth-generation members were participating in a highly elaborate ecclesiastical framework. The fate of many would-be New Religions is rather brief because they are unable to move from charismatic leadership and the initial group to become a fully institutionalized organization. Tenrikyo made the transition with relative ease, translating the charisma of Miki into institutional lines of authority and liturgy. Compared with other New Religions, Tenrikyo has had rather few groups splitting away from it.[3] Like all larger religious organizations, it has received some criticism for increasing formalism and for pressuring believers financially to support the bureaucracy. Such is the dilemma of all organized religion: how to preserve the founding inspiration and the initial vitality within the framework of permanent institutions.

SOKA GAKKAI: FAITH IN THE *LOTUS SUTRA* AND A HAPPY LIFE

Makiguchi Tsunesaburo (1871–1944), the founder of Soka Gakkai, was a teacher from Hokkaido who developed a new theory of education or theory of value. Makiguchi contrasted the usual philosophical triad of truth, beauty, and goodness with his triad of beauty, benefit (or gain), and goodness. He held that truth is objective and absolute, whereas values are subjective and relative; in other words, truth has to be discovered, but values have to be created. (The literal meaning of *Soka Gakkai* is "Value Creation Society.") This theory, too complicated for simple summary, was developed out of Makiguchi's work in education, but it took on added significance when he became an active believer in the Nichiren Shoshu branch of Buddhism. This meant, roughly, that the absolute truth was identified with Nichiren and the *Lotus Sutra*; the values to be created were identified as aspects of the happy life available through this absolute faith.

During the 1930s, Makiguchi and Toda Josei (1900–58), a teacher in the school where Makiguchi was principal, made the first efforts to propagate the new message. They had attracted only several thousand members by 1941 when World War II began. During World War II the movement was suppressed because Makiguchi and Toda refused to comply with wartime directives ordering unified religious support for the military; this would have compromised the absolute truth of Nichiren and the *Lotus Sutra* with other Buddhist groups and Shinto. The two leaders were imprisoned. Makiguchi died while in prison, but Toda was released in 1945 shortly before the end of the war. The original movement was so completely destroyed that it is safe to say that Toda is the second founder.

In 1951 Toda decided to devote all of his time to transform Soka Gakkai from a membership of several thousand families to his goal of 750,000 families before he died; the goal was achieved in 1957. This phenomenal success was due in part to Toda's organizational ability, for he mobilized a large youth division that enthusiastically converted great numbers. Also he was helped by the close ties he renewed with Nichiren Shoshu. After Toda's death in 1958, his protégé Ikeda Daisaku (1928–), who had been in the forefront of the youth division, became Soka Gakkai's third president (in 1960).

Toda's aggressive conversion policies and the violent tactics of the youth division had given Soka Gakkai a bad reputation, which Ikeda attempted to improve. Ikeda favored expansion of membership by peaceful persuasion, and he oversaw the development of cultural and political activities within Soka Gakkai. Ikeda has consolidated this movement into a sophisticated and highly efficient modern organization. Ikeda, although a protégé of Toda, is more attractive as a charismatic leader. He has traveled extensively through major countries of the world and is equally at home with Japanese and non-Japanese dignitaries. There is a constant flow of his publications on Buddhism, as well as on social and international issues, in Western-language editions. In 1979, he left the presidency of Soka Gakkai for the position of honorary president, but he appears to have retained much influence.

To understand the traditional religious background of this dynamic modern movement, we must review the inspiration of Nichiren and its later fate. Nichiren emphasized absolute, exclusive faith in the *Lotus Sutra* and recitation of faith in the *Lotus Sutra* through the phrase *Namu Myoho Renge Kyo* (or *Nammyoho Renge Kyo,* the form preferred by Soka Gakkai). After Nichiren's death, his followers split into groups that in time turned into hard denominational lines. By the late Tokugawa period, people devoted to Nichiren as a model of religious faith and to the *Lotus Sutra* as a source of religious guidance were increasingly frustrated with Nichiren denominations. Some formed voluntary organizations called *ko,* which eventually developed into New Religions. Other New Religions (such as Soka Gakkai and Rissho Koseikai) also emphasize faith in the *Lotus Sutra* but emerged directly from the general current of faith in Nichiren and the *Lotus Sutra,* without the intermediate development of voluntary organizations *(ko).*

Soka Gakkai is more recent than the early Nichiren-derived New Religions but is by far the largest, most dynamic, and most efficiently organized. Its ethos is defined by the solution of all personal and societal problems through absolute faith in the *Lotus Sutra.* Soka Gakkai holds to absoluteness not only in the commitment of the believer, but also in the absolute truth of its message. Therefore, it follows that all other religions are false. Likewise, all personal and cultural values must be dependent on this absolute truth. One positive aspect of this absolute faith in an absolute truth is its promise to solve all personal and cultural problems. One negative aspect is seen in the frequent accusation that, especially during the aggressive conversion campaign of the 1950s, absolute faith in the *Lotus Sutra* led believers to use *any* means to convert people.

The dynamics of Soka Gakkai can best be seen by the way in which a new member is taken into the organization. The grassroots strength of Soka Gakkai derives from small discussion groups of from twenty to thirty people who meet informally in members' homes to share testimonials, discuss personal problems, and study Soka Gakkai doctrine. Nonmembers usually make their first contact with Soka Gakkai when a member who happens to be a friend, relative, or coworker persuades them to attend a meeting. After several meetings, the nonmember may seek to solve his or her problems in the context of such a group with faith in Nichiren and the *Lotus Sutra*; but in order to become a member of Soka Gakkai, he or she must formally be admitted into Nichiren Shoshu. This necessitates removing all traces of other religions from his or her home—throwing out or burning the Shinto and Buddhist elements and images that traditionally were an integral part of most homes (Christian elements, if present, also are forbidden). Only then can the individual go to a Nichiren Shoshu temple for the official conversion rites, at which time he or she is given a wooden tablet with the title of the *Lotus Sutra* carved in it. The tablet is patterned after the one Nichiren made and is a sacred object to be placed in the now-empty family altar. Twice every day, morning and night, the member expresses faith in the *Lotus Sutra* by chanting the title of this sutra (*Nammyoho Renge Kyo*) and recites passages from it before the sacred object. From this time the member will participate in the discussion groups and the other activities of Soka Gakkai. The new member must also become active in converting others and is expected to make a pilgrimage to the head temple of Nichiren Shoshu, Taiseki-ji near Mount Fuji. Several million members make the trip annually.

The organizational structure of this lay movement is amazingly effective and tight-knit. There are several interlocking and overlapping subgroups. On the lowest level, there is an inviolable link between a member and the person who converted him or her, completely apart from geographic or organizational ties. The member also belongs to the small "unit" of ten or twelve families; from five to ten units constitute one "group"; a number of groups make up a "district." The next structural element is the "chapter," including from one to two thousand families; several chapters form a "general chapter"; next comes "headquarters," followed by "joint headquarters," which is directly controlled by the leadership of Soka Gakkai. After 1955, Soka Gakkai also introduced the "block" system of geographical units. Every family belongs to the smallest geographical block, and subsequent larger blocks include all Soka Gakkai families. Not only does every family belong to both a "unit" and a "block," but every individual also belongs to the men's, women's, or youth division.[4] It is also possible for one to take competitive examinations on Soka Gakkai doctrine and achieve the academic rank of instructor, assistant professor, or full professor.

The movement publishes its own religious materials in Western and Asian languages, has conducted highly successful fund-raising campaigns, and has completed phenomenal building programs in Tokyo and at Taiseki-ji. Its Soka University, which opened in 1971, may be seen as the apex of its organizational and building programs. But most of Soka Gakkai's notoriety comes from its participation in politics.

In 1964 Soka Gakkai developed the Komeito (Clean Government Party) as a full-fledged party with a large number of local and national candidates; it has been highly successful in electing candidates. Due to the nature of the Japanese political system, many political offices are filled by voting in the top several candidates out of a large field. Soka Gakkai has been able to judge accurately how many votes will be needed to elect a candidate and then, based on how many votes they can command in that area, put up only as many candidates as they can elect. Komeito, the only religiously based party in Japanese history, has already become a major national force. Komeito and Soka Gakkai have been accused of attempting to gain religious control over the state—a charge they deny. However, after an incident in 1969 and 1970 when both were charged with suppressing publication of a book critical of Soka Gakkai, there was an investigation in the National Diet.[5] Afterward, Soka Gakkai officially separated itself from Komeito. Since then, Komeito has tended to decline somewhat in strength, and the future development and direction of this political movement are uncertain. But Soka Gakkai has been so efficient in mobilizing a large number of people that it raises a still-unanswered question: What is the motivation behind and the goal of this movement? This question is also of concern overseas because Soka Gakkai (under the name of Nichiren Shoshu) has become a sizeable movement in American and European cities.

THE SIGNIFICANCE OF THE NEW RELIGIONS:
OLD WINE IN NEW BOTTLES

The lesson of Soka Gakkai throws a great deal of light on the New Religions in general. For example, we remember that Tenrikyo moved from charismatic leadership of a living *kami* to a large-scale organization. Soka Gakkai also has had charismatic leadership, but its primary focus has been on the *Lotus Sutra;* this demonstrates the ability to revive a traditional sacred treasure and develop a large-scale religious organization around it. This is like putting old wine in new bottles: The old wine is Nichiren and his interpretation of the *Lotus Sutra;* the new bottle is the lay organization of Soka Gakkai. The "old bottles" of organized religion have tended to break apart under the pressures of modern life, especially in cities where secularism and alienation are high. The dilemma of balancing "old" and "new" in such a modern situation is whether traditional religion can still speak meaningfully to human lives.

Soka Gakkai has been subjected to more adverse criticism by Western journalists and scholars than any other New Religion, the most serious charge being that it is "fascist," using the cloak of religion to gain control of large masses of people for ulterior purposes. Soka Gakkai, of course, has denied the charge, claiming it is truly democratic, with power flowing from the member to the higher groups, the aim being to enrich the lives of all people (creating value based on the absolute truth). One need not be an advocate of Soka Gakkai to question the more sensational charges that it is a fascist movement about to gain religious control over the whole country. No single religious group in the past has ever been able to completely control Japan, and it is unlikely that this will happen in the future.

To recognize the ambiguous character of Soka Gakkai's organizational structure and use of power is to acknowledge the ambiguity of all socio-religious institutions and all forms of power. A closer look at the matter of national values and social control in Japan may help us assess the charges against Soka Gakkai. A serious question in all modern cultures—where small communities and folk life tend to give way to large cities, dehumanized work, and impersonally organized religions—is whether people will be controlled by (1) nationalism, (2) ideology (apart from national identity), (3) mass media and consumerism, (4) religious commitment. As is the case in other modern countries, Japan's emergence in the modern world was a complex process defying any simple explanation. Some factors, however, are worthy of special mention.

From the Meiji Restoration of 1868 to the end of World War II in 1945, Japan was controlled primarily by nationalism, with religious support from all organized religion, and a primary goal was the development of heavy industry. In fact, Japan's strong national identity probably brought immunity to the type of ideological control that overtook China in the twentieth century. (In Japan, communism has had appeal for some intellectuals and workers but has never been a dominant political factor.) Since 1945, nationalism has been present in Japan, particularly as evidenced by increasing military expenditures, but nationalism seems to be secondary to the popular desire to acquire consumer goods. Education is a good indicator of national values, and whereas nationalism in school texts has been toned down considerably since 1945, the thrust toward consumerism is much more pronounced than in prewar times. (Japan has one of the highest rates of television-set ownership per capita in the world, and advertising is highly developed.) Modern countries tend to acculturate the young in school systems where nationalism, political ideology, technical or technological competence (training for a job), and the desirability of consumer goods are all taught. These factors are related and contain implicit religious values: As we know in the West, the "Protestant ethic" of hard work has been closely related to the capitalistic system. In Japan, too, economic strength may be the new channel in which nationalism flows, and it may be fed by religious pride for the Japanese tradition. Explicit religious values, however, are weak in this modern setting; and Soka Gakkai has its finger on something important, for many modern people sense a lack of "value" in their lives. Explicit religious values in Japan seem hopelessly outranked by economic and national concerns; indeed, Soka Gakkai claims to be a religious alternative to the dominant materialism of contemporary Japan.

It is not the task of scholars to persuade people to join Soka Gakkai or any other religious organization; this is an existential decision for each individual. But the common predicament for all modern people is life within secular surroundings: Can men and women find meaning and joy in life by completely secular means? Many modern Japanese have answered "no" to this question. Individually, they have embraced one of the many New Religions; in so doing, they have affirmed traditional Japanese religious beliefs and practices but have shown their preference for organizing and expressing them in new ways.

NOTES

1. *A Short History of Tenrikyo* (Tenri, Japan: Tenrikyo Kyokai Honbu, 1956), pp. 79–80.
2. Ibid., p. 158.
3. For an "inside" account of one split from Tenrikyo, see Yoshie Sugihara and David W. Plath, *Sensei and His People: The Building of*

a *Japanese Commune* (Berkeley: University of California Press, 1969).

4.   See the "Organizational Chart" in *The Nichiren Shoshu Sokagakkai* (Tokyo: Seikyo Press, 1966), p. 19. A high official of Soka Gakkai has informed me that this 1966 publication and the organizational chart no longer reflect the actual conditions of the movement.
5.   This episode is described in Hirotatsu Fujiwara, *I Denounce Soka Gakkai,* trans. Worth C. Grant (Tokyo: Nishin Hodo, 1970).

SELECTED READINGS

Arai, Ken. "New Religious Movements." In *Japanese Religion*. Edited by Ichiro Hori. Translated by Yoshiya Abe and David Reid. Tokyo: Kodansha International, 1972, pp. 89–104. A concise overview of the definition and major features of the New Religions.

Earhart, H. Byron. *Religion in the Japanese Experience: Sources and Interpretations*. Belmont, Calif.: Wadsworth, 1974. See Part Fifteen for selected documents on the New Religions, including excerpts from the article by Earhart and the Tenrikyo and Soka Gakkai publications listed below.

———. "The Significance of the New Religions for Understanding Japanese Religion." *KBS Bulletin on Japanese Culture*, Vol. 101 (April–May 1970), 1–9. A general discussion of the New Religions in terms of six persistent themes in Japanese religion.

Murata, Kiyoaki. *Japan's New Buddhism: An Objective Account of Soka Gakkai*. New York: Walker/Weatherhill, 1969. A general introduction based mainly on the publications of Soka Gakkai.

The Nichiren Shoshu Sokagakkai. Tokyo: Seikyo Press, 1966. A publication by this organization about its philosophy of life, activities, and goals.

A Short History of Tenrikyo. Tenri, Japan: Tenrikyo Kyokai Honbu, 1956. Published by Tenrikyo headquarters, it includes chapters on the life of the founder, the history of the movement, and its activities.

Straelen, Henry van. *The Religion of Divine Wisdom: Japan's Most Powerful Movement*. Kyoto: Veritas Shoin, 1957 (and later editions). The first complete account of Tenrikyo by a Western scholar.

CHAPTER 18

Religion in Postwar Japan

When World War II ended in 1945, a dramatically new age dawned in Japan. For the first time the nation had been defeated, her soil occupied. These events precipitated a reversal of the nationalistic mood that prevailed from 1868 to 1945. Japanese religion still has not fully recovered from the disorientation caused by the defeat. Not only religion but all areas of Japanese life changed remarkably since World War II. In this chapter we will survey the situation of Shinto, Buddhism, Christianity, and New Religions in the postwar period; in the next chapter we will comment on recent changes in Japanese life and see how they help us to understand the religious situation generally.

SHINTO: DISESTABLISHMENT AND POPULAR DISFAVOR

The most obvious religious effect of the defeat was the official disestablishment of shrine Shinto by order of the Allied occupation forces. The emperor announced defeat over the radio. Later he made the announcement that he was not a god but was only human.[1] The occupation forces did not intend to change Shinto insofar as it was the religion of the people but insisted that neither Shinto nor any other religion should be the tool of militaristic nationalism. This clearly indicated the end of Shinto's "nonreligious" status and special role in government. In effect, Shinto shrines throughout the country once more were treated as religious institutions, along with Buddhist temples and Christian churches. Shinto priests ceased being government officials, and government subsidies to shrines stopped. As Muraoka has interpreted this postwar change of events, "the removal of all state prerogatives was a heavy blow for shrine Shinto," but "this was a just and inevitable retribution."[2] Even more important was the removal of religious nationalism from school textbooks and the mass media.

It is hard to comprehend what happened in the minds of the Japanese people at the time of defeat and thereafter. Some Westerners, on the basis of the fanatic resistance of Japanese soldiers during the war, predicted that every Japanese town would put up a last-ditch defense. Yet after the emperor's broadcast announcing surrender, there was almost no resistance. Even in defeat the emperor's authority commanded obedient respect.

Shinto had profited the most from government support between 1868 and 1945, so of course it suffered the most from the removal of support. Although Shinto suffered from financial loss, even greater was the loss of the people's sympathy. When people lamented the war's destruction, they tended to blame Shinto as the tradition most closely allied to the war machine. Another setback was the disorganization of Shinto. Government control of Shinto before World War II was disliked even by the sincere Shinto priests, but at least it welded Shinto into a national religious force. After the war there was complete religious freedom for the first time. Any religious group was able to organize and qualify for tax exemption as a religious body. Ironically, this even meant greater freedom for local Shinto shrines. As was mentioned in Chapter 15, in the early 1900s some local groups had been forced by the government to abandon small shrines and "merge" with centralized village shrines. After World War II, many local groups were free to reestablish the shrines they had abandoned. These reestablished shrines preserve some of the close relationship to village groups and regional customs that have been the heritage of Shinto for centuries. Most of the postwar Shinto shrines reorganized as the Association of Shinto Shrines, but the prewar groups of sect Shinto declared their independence from Shinto control. Both the Shinto shrines and the Buddhist temples were divested of much of their land holdings, removing a main source of income.

A delicate problem of the postwar period has been the exact relationship of the emperor to the state and to Shinto. There has been disagreement about what it means for the emperor to be the symbolic head of the state. On the one hand are those few who would like to abolish the emperor even as a symbol; on the other hand are those few who would like to give the emperor a more important role in government. In the middle are the majority, who seem to be indifferent or respectful (but not worshipful) toward this national symbol. The rituals of the emperor are considered his private cult, but there is the troublesome matter of the considerable expense for the ceremonies. Also, Shinto priests feel that the emperor still should function as the chief priest of Shinto and the nation. A further complication is the problem of state financing for certain shrines, such as Ise, which have traditionally received state funds.

Yasukuni Shrine in Tokyo, which since Meiji times developed into a national shrine for the war dead, has been a problem since 1945. Some people have favored more state support for the shrine, even financial support, seeing the shrine as a harmless patriotic monument, somewhat like the Tomb of the Unknown Soldier in America. Others have feared that explicit state support for Yasukuni Shrine would be the first step toward reviving the unity of state and religion that gave rise to ultranationalism and militarism before and during World War II.

BUDDHISM: THE CONTINUING NEED FOR RENEWAL

Although Buddhism had supported the war effort, it did not suffer so much as Shinto from the stigma of defeat. Nevertheless, it was hard pressed due to the loss of temple lands. Furthermore, Buddhism felt the disorganization that resulted from complete religious freedom. Even after 1868 the lines between main temples and subtemples had been strictly maintained, and before World War II the government required all Buddhist temples to maintain strictly defined denominational ties. The Allied occupation removed such government restrictions. After 1945, temple affiliations became more flexible; and at a time when landed revenues were lost, Buddhist sects suffered when branch temples became financially independent. These are some of the practical problems, but basically Buddhism had not responded to the earlier voices calling for spiritual renewal. Buddhist priests and temples continued to function in funeral and memorial services for most Japanese, but often without inspiring great religious feeling.

Some renewal of Buddhism has taken place through increasing participation by lay people, and there has been some attempt to change Buddhism from the traditional affiliation by families to a more personal commitment. (One Pure Land denomination used the slogan "From a Household Religion to a Personal Religion.")[3] The need for Buddhism to deal with changing family patterns, especially the trend toward nuclear families, is documented by a recent sociological study, which reports that in one metropolitan residential area of white-collar workers, "only about 30% of the nuclear families as against 90% of the extended families have Buddhist altars in their homes."[4] However, attempts to change the pattern of hereditary family membership in Buddhist temples ("household Buddhism") have been the exception rather than the rule, and generally temples have continued their major concern for funerals and rites for the dead.

The major postwar innovations for temple Buddhism (not unlike those for shrine Shinto) are priests taking outside jobs (such as part-time teaching jobs) and the utilization of temple buildings for financial gain by means of kindergarten classes and tourism. Some intellectuals, especially the internationally known scholars of Buddhism, have actively propagated the message of Buddhism as a pan-Asian or even a worldwide religion, but they have made little impact on the lives of Japanese Buddhists. In the postwar period, the greatest interest in Buddhism has been in the Buddhist-inspired New Religions.

CHRISTIANITY: THE PROBLEMS OF DENOMINATIONALISM

After World War II, widespread dissatisfaction with Shinto and general indifference toward Buddhism might have provided a great opportunity for Christianity to gain converts. Such was not the case. Christianity continued through the war years, somewhat suppressed by the government but led by Japanese ministers without the aid of foreign missionaries. Christian churches suffered a greater loss from wartime bombing than Shinto and Buddhism because most Christian churches were in large cities. The reentrance of foreign missionaries after the war did not cause a radical change in religious affiliation. Christianity was still at a distinct disadvantage because of denominational splintering, theological disagreement, and the perennial problem of developing a truly Japanese Christianity. To this day, Christianity is viewed by most Japanese as a foreign religion. Furthermore, the crisis of defeat forced both Shinto and Buddhism to reconsider their basic foundations, giving them greater strength in meeting Christianity intellectually.

No longer was there a simple choice between native and foreign philosophies of life. Even long before the war, Japanese intellectuals had become acquainted with Western agnostic and atheistic philosophies, and the extreme crisis of the postwar years pushed some to the materialistic philosophy of Marxism. (In fact, in Japan Christianity and Marxism possess some similarities. Both tend to appeal to intellectuals on the basis of a universal message seeking to transform the Japanese social order.[5] Especially in the postwar period, some Christians and Marxists have cooperated in opposing right-wing movements such as the attempt to restore pre–World War II nationalism.) Immediately after the war there was a serious food shortage, followed by the combined problems of reconstruction and inflation. These conditions did not make the ethical monotheism of Christianity any more attractive to the Japanese than it had been before the war. In postwar Japan it is estimated that Christians represent less than 1 percent of a total population of about 100 million. Most of those who made a decision of faith as individuals turned to the New Religions.

THE POSTWAR BOOM OF NEW RELIGIONS

Whereas Buddhism and Confucianism dominated the Tokugawa period, and Shinto dominated the period from 1868 to 1945, since World War II the New Religions have captured the limelight, for several reasons. First, they more than any other religious tradition escaped the stigma of association with the nation's defeat. Although the leaders of some New Religions supported the war effort, several of the groups came into conflict with the government's control of religion both before and during the war. Those that had been persecuted during the war emerged almost victorious amid the general sense of defeat. Thus the religions that sprang up after the war rejected the past and looked forward with hope to the future. (Depending on how they are counted, there have been several hundreds of New Religions since the war.)

Second, the new movements profited the most from religious freedom after World War II. They were able to attain complete independence for the first time, and the "old" religions of Shinto and Buddhism were forced to compete with them on their level because of the loss of revenue from land and government support.

Several other reasons can be advanced for the phenomenal success of the new groups in postwar Japan. The newer movements, because they were new, possessed no commitment to outmoded forms and spoke immediately to the religious needs of the nation. In postwar times, the population shifted from being 70 percent rural and 30 percent urban and became 70 percent urban and 30 percent rural. Great mobility tended to dissolve traditional ties to Shinto and Buddhism and make conversion to a New Religion all the more likely.[6] Moreover, the New Religions had a thoroughly Japanese character, which enabled them to give a Japanese answer to spiritual questions. The new movements reflect all the persistent themes in Japanese religious history. This helps to explain how the postwar membership of some of them could equal or better the total number of Christians in Japan. Another point of strength was the tendency for the New Religions to be openly syncretistic, often taking the best features from Buddhism, Shinto, and even Christianity. A theme emphasized by some of the new movements is the unity of all religion. They not only make universalistic statements about religion but send missionaries abroad to spread their faith.

There is considerable speculation about the future role of the New Religions in Japan. Some people fear their growth and increasing power. On the other hand, scholars close to the scene have begun to suggest that the postwar peak of the New Religions is already past and a leveling-off is under way. Indeed, the New Religions themselves have become institutionalized. They now constitute organized religions like the Buddhist and Shinto groups. They have even formed their own Association of New Religions. Most of the new groups have great financial resources and impressive headquarters in Tokyo or at religious centers elsewhere.

At the same time, it is worth noting that some of the recent movements are not complete religious organizations. Members of many New Religions are still buried in Buddhist ceremonies by Buddhist priests. Thus it would be a mistake to think that Buddhism and Shinto are defunct. Japanese history shows many cases where a slumbering tradition was revitalized, and it is quite likely that, as time passes, the differences between new and old religions will diminish. The newer movements may become more highly organized and institutionalized, and Buddhism and Shinto may adopt some of their successful activities (such as discussion groups) and organizational forms (such as lay participation).

NOTES

1. See Daniel C. Holtom, *Modern Japan and Shinto Nationalism: A Study of Present-Day Trends in Japanese Religions*, rev. ed. (Chicago: University of Chicago Press, 1947; reprint ed., New York: Paragon Book Reprint Corp., 1963), pp. 215–18, for a translation of the "Directive for the Disestablishment of State Shinto"; see pp. 219–20 for a translation of the "Imperial Rescript on the Recon-

struction of New Japan," including the so-called renunciation of divinity. These translations can also be found in H. Byron Earhart, *Religion in the Japanese Experience: Sources and Interpretations* (Belmont, Calif.: Wadsworth, 1974), pp. 27–34.

2. Tsunetsugu Muraoka, "Separation of State and Religion in Shinto: Its Historical Significance," in his *Studies in Shinto*, trans. Delmer M. Brown and James T. Araki (Tokyo: Ministry of Education, 1964), pp. 239–40.

3. Kiyomi Morioka, "The Changing Family and Buddhism in Postwar Japan," in his *Religion in Changing Japanese Society* (Tokyo: University of Tokyo Press, 1975), p. 11.

4. Ibid., p. 106.

5. See Norihisa Suzuki, "Christianity," in *Japanese Religion*, ed. Ichiro Hori (Tokyo: Kodansha International, 1972), p. 73.

6. See Fujio Ikado, "Trend and Problems of New Religions: Religion in Urban Society," in *The Sociology of Japanese Religion*, ed. Kiyomi Morioka and William H. Newell (Leiden: E. J. Brill, 1968), pp. 101–17.

SELECTED READINGS

Creemers, Wilhelmus H. M. *Shrine Shinto After World War II*. Leiden: E. J. Brill, 1968. A detailed study of the status and organization of Shinto, especially the impact of reorganization after World War II.

Dore, Ronald P. *City Life in Japan: A Study of a Tokyo Ward*. Berkeley: University of California Press, 1958. See pp. 291–373 for a description of religious life in postwar Tokyo, based on survey research and interviews.

Earhart, H. Byron. *Religion in the Japanese Experience: Sources and Interpretations*. Belmont, Calif.: Wadsworth, 1974. See pp. 222–31 for excerpts from Dore and pp. 27–34 for excerpts from Holtom.

Holtom, Daniel C. *Modern Japan and Shinto Nationalism: A Study of Present-Day Trends in Japanese Religions*. Rev. ed. Chicago: University of Chicago Press, 1947. Reprint ed., New York: Paragon Book Reprint Corp., 1963. See Chapters 7 and 8 for comments on Shinto just after World War II and the appendixes for the directive disestablishing Shinto and the emperor's own "renunciation of divinity."

Kiyota, Minoru. "Buddhism in Postwar Japan: A Critical Survey." *Monumenta Nipponica*, Vol. 24, Nos. 1–2 (1969), 113–36. A critical analysis of postwar Buddhism, contrasted with the success of the New Religions.

Morioka, Kiyomi. "The Changing Family and Buddhism in Postwar Japan." In *Religion in Changing Japanese Society.* Tokyo: University of Tokyo Press, 1975, pp. 99–113. A sociological analysis of the attempt of Pure Land sects to transform their social organization, in response to social change such as the trend toward nuclear families.

Muraoka, Tsunetsugu. "Separation of State and Religion in Shinto: Its Historical Significance." In *Studies in Shinto.* Translated by Delmer M. Brown and James T. Araki. Tokyo: Ministry of Education, 1964, pp. 230–44. A valuable reassessment of Shinto by a famous scholar of Shinto studies shortly after World War II.

Woodard, William P. *The Allied Occupation of Japan, 1945–1952, and Japanese Religions.* Leiden: E. J. Brill, 1972. A detailed analysis of religious developments and Allied policy toward religion in the occupation period.

CHAPTER 19

Religious Life in Contemporary Japan

In the previous chapter, we surveyed the general situation of *institutional* religion in postwar Japan as manifest in the attempt of various religious organizations to recover from the physical and spiritual ravages of World War II. But this survey of institutional strength is only one aspect of the contemporary religious scene; it excludes the personal dimension of religion. A question that Westerners often ask is whether the Japanese are religious. This question refers to personal religious commitment and can be answered either affirmatively or negatively. By looking briefly at various interpretations of this question, we can gain a better vantage point for understanding religious life in Japan today.

ARE THE JAPANESE RELIGIOUS?

When Westerners ask whether the Japanese are religious, they may be wondering whether the Japanese are religious in the same way that Americans and Europeans are religious. And this, in turn, is asking if the Japanese belong exclusively to one religious organization as a Protestant, Catholic, or Jewish person would. For most Japanese, the answer is "no," for usually they participate in several religious traditions. Because, in theory, all the families living in the vicinity of a local Shinto shrine may be considered "parishioners" of that shrine, and because most families have some ties to a parish Buddhist temple, a family may be counted as members of both Shinto and Buddhism. Thus the number of people "belonging" to any of the religions in Japan may be almost twice as large as the nation's total population. In the modern period, several exceptions to the general practice of simultaneous participation in several religions are Japanese members of New Religions and Japanese Christians who choose not to participate in other religious traditions.

Another implicit aspect of the question about the religiosity of the Japanese is how they identify themselves religiously. An American might say, "I am Christian" or "I am Jewish." Unless a Japanese person is a Christian, he or she is not likely to identify exclusively with one religion. A non-Christian is not likely to say, "I am Shinto" or "I am Buddhist." In fact, some Japanese express surprise when Westerners ask what their religion is. Usually Japanese do not ask other Japanese what their religion is, and depending on the context and the degree of acquaintance, the question can be considered impolite. (By contrast, in Japan a question about one's age—for both women and men—usually is not considered impolite, unless it is addressed to a young woman of marriageable age.) If a Japanese person is put in a situation where the direct question "What is your religion?" must be answered, he or she may respond, "I have no religion." This does not necessarily mean that the person is against or indifferent to religion; it may simply mean that he or she does not identify exclusively with one religion the way a Christian or Jew might. Even if the Japanese person responds, "I am a Buddhist," the answer does not necessarily mean that the person is committed to exclusive affiliation with (and regular attendance at) one Buddhist institution. More likely it means that the person's *family* observes Buddhist rituals for the family ancestors.

A contrast of Japanese with Muslims may highlight some hallmarks of religious identification that do *not* apply to Japanese people. For example, Muslim students on American campuses usually identify themselves religiously as Muslims. Not only will they state, "I am a Muslim," but they will specify the meaning of this statement with a creedal statement about belief in Allah, and they will implement the belief by weekly prayers on Friday; also they observe dietary restrictions against eating pork and drinking alcoholic beverages. It is in this sense that the Japanese are *not* religious: Usually they do not identify with a particular creed, do not attend weekly religious services, and do not observe religiously based dietary restrictions. (Nor do they observe any religiously based customs of dress, such as are seen in some religions.) On large American campuses it is now common to see special buildings for Muslim students to observe religious prayers. But even if the number of Japanese students in Western countries greatly increased, we would not expect to see special buildings for religious use by Japanese students, for Japanese religion does not usually lend itself to these kinds of creedal and institutional forms.

Generally Japanese religion is not expressed in creeds (which are more characteristic of monotheistic religions), and it is not organized into exclusive denominations. Therefore, as we have seen, a simple counting of members is misleading. Also, standard questionnaires on religion, used in Europe and America, are not always relevant in Japan. Questions about whether the Japanese believe in God cannot be answered clearly "yes" or "no" or given a numerical percentage. Rather, one must honestly reply that the Japanese do not emphasize belief in God in the way that monotheistic religions do. If we want to understand Japanese religion, we should try to view it in terms of Japanese notions such as *kami*.

It may be worth mentioning that posing the right questions about religion is also a problem for Japanese trying to understand Western religion. Recently when I was in Japan studying a New Religion and gave the members a chance to ask me about American religion, one of the first questions was, "Is it true that Americans don't venerate their ancestors, and if so, why?" This was a difficult question, but the person was eventually satisfied when I explained that in America ancestors do not constitute the central social and religious fact that they do in Japan. In other words, the central religious importance that the Japanese place on ancestors, Americans tend to place on God.

Are the Japanese religious? We might as well ask whether they are social, political, and economical. The answer to all of these questions is "yes." The catch, of course, is that the Japanese are religious, social, political, and economical in their own way. Some *general* features of Japanese life are common to all other cultures. For example, Japanese religion, like the religions of all other cultures, consists of symbols, beliefs, and practices that provide an orientation to reality and a means of celebrating participation in that reality—all of which is treasured and handed down to the next generation. Similarly, social, political, and economic aspects of Japanese culture share *general* features with other cultures.

If we say that society has to do with the organization and interaction of human relationships (such as kinship and territorial units), that politics has to do with national identity and the securing and administering of power, that economics has to do with the creation and distribution of wealth—then of course the Japanese are social, political, and economical. In each instance, however, the Japanese have developed distinctive cultural traditions. In the religious realm, they have emphasized notions such as *kami* and nature. In the social realm, kinship (family) and group identity have special significance for Japanese. In the political realm, traditional notions of power and authority have led to strong loyalty to political parties and a form of parliamentary government that are distinctively Japanese. In the economic realm, the Japanese have forged their own pattern of cooperation for labor, business, and government. In other words, all aspects of Japanese culture—the religious, social, economic, political—share some general features with all cultures while maintaining distinctively Japanese characteristics. The heart of the matter, then, is not *whether* the Japanese are religious but *in what way* are the Japanese religious. We should never conclude that the Japanese (or any other people) are *not* religious because their beliefs and practices differ from those of our culture.

PERSISTENT THEMES IN CONTEMPORARY JAPANESE RELIGION

Two different ways to view contemporary Japanese religion are to emphasize continuity with the past and discontinuity with the past. In this section we will focus on continuity, in the next section on discontinuity. Perhaps the most convenient way to highlight continuity of contemporary Japanese religion with the past is to investigate the present status of the persistent themes identified in Chapter 2: the closeness of human beings, gods, and nature; the religious character of the family; the significance of purification, rituals, and charms; the prominence of local festivals and individual cults; the pervasiveness of religion in everyday life; and the nature bond between religion and the nation.

Human beings, the gods, and nature are still interrelated. Although in 1945 the emperor renounced his divinity, and although the notion of *kami* is not taken so literally today, nevertheless the presence of *kami* remains important. New Religions still honor founders and their descendants as living *kami*. The fact that family ancestors still constitute the most widely venerated objects of ritual ceremonies is further testimony to the ease with which men and women bridge the gap to the realm of the *kami*. Nature may be seriously polluted, but it is still revered and extolled, particularly in graphic art and literature.

The family has changed considerably in recent years but is still considered the basic religious unit. This is evident from the fact that statistics of religious membership are still given in households (rather

*The reflective sticker above the Toyota emblem on the trunk of a car is a "traffic safety"
charm from the Omiya Hachiman Shrine. (Tokyo, 1979)*

than as individual members). The extended family is not so important
as it once was, and the nuclear family has become more important.
This change has meant fewer observances before Shinto altars *(kamidana)* and Buddhist altars *(butsudan)* in homes. But family ancestors
remain important in the lives and minds of the Japanese people. Contemporary Japanese still have a sense of identity with and obligation
toward their family ancestors and usually do not fail to observe memorial services for their immediate ancestors.

Although the proliferation of purifications, rituals, and charms that
Japan once knew has greatly diminished, many are still found in
present-day Japan. Most traditional charms, although not used as
extensively as before, can be obtained with no trouble. At many temples and shrines one can buy time-honored amulets to ensure safe
childbirth and avoid sickness. The most widespread example is probably the paper charm for traffic safety, conspicuously displayed in
taxis, buses, and private cars. This protective device has even been
"modernized" in the form of a yellow reflector that is attached with
adhesive to the back of an automobile. Another modern variation on
the theme of charms is a good-luck charm to ensure success in school
exams, purchased either for oneself or for a family member.

Local festivals have become abbreviated or curtailed, but festivals
in cities and regions have prospered. Festivals in small villages have
suffered because of the loss of manpower, money, and interest. City
and regional festivals that attract tourists have flourished. This general trend has its exceptions, however. For example, the widespread
festival on November 15 for children aged 3, 5, and 7 (called Shichi-

go-san) was formerly celebrated by parents dressing their children in elaborate traditional clothing and taking them to a nearby Shinto shrine. Recently, ease of transportation has made it possible to take children to more distant shrines, and the innovations are as interesting as the continued custom. On November 15, 1979, I visited a mountain shrine an hour south of Tokyo. The cable car from the foot of the mountain to the shrine was free for families participating in the Shichi-go-san festival, and many young girls wore Western formal dresses (such as long velvet dresses) instead of the more costly *kimono*.

Individual cults reflect the same pattern: Some centers are languishing, while others are bustling and wealthy. The visitor to Japan who has extra time at the new Narita airport outside Tokyo may verify the popularity of cults by visiting the nearby Narita-san, a temple complex dedicated to Fudo.

As social and economic conditions have changed, probably the persistent theme that has changed most is the role of religion in everyday life. In the past, religious observances were closely tied to the cultivation of rice by hand; now that most rice is transplanted by machine, such festivals are rarely seen. Radical changes in occupations and crafts have also meant a sharp drop in religious activities related to occupations. However, Japanese religion is still very much related to the problems of daily life. As previously noted, probably the most popular charm in all Japan is the one for traffic safety. And in a recent nationwide questionnaire distributed to members of a New Religion, for "motive of joining" many replied with answers such as sickness and family difficulties. The New Religions have been active in bringing problems such as financial and marital difficulties into the context of religious counseling, especially in small discussion groups. In other words, as the circumstances of daily life have changed, so have the means of relating religion to daily life.

The natural bond between Japanese religion and the Japanese nation lives on today, although not so much in explicit terms as in implicit understandings. The Japanese generally do not consider the divine founding of Japan to be a historical event, but their notion of Japanese culture and the Japanese people as a unique historical entity is implicitly religious. Similarly, some would interpret the high degree of cooperation between labor, business, and government in Japan as a sacrifice of individual benefit for the good of the nation as a whole— very close to a religious commitment. Usually this tie is implicit, but in some cases the tie becomes explicit, as when a Shinto priest "purifies" or dedicates a new airplane for an airline. And conservative religious groups still view filial piety and loyalty to the state as integral parts of worshiping the *kami* and *bodhisattvas*.

As the culture has changed, so has the way in which religion is related to it. Viewed in terms of continuity, however, the persistent themes of Japanese religion are still abundantly present in contemporary Japanese life.

APPROACHES TO RELIGIOUS CHANGE

In the remainder of this chapter, we will examine the major changes religion has undergone in recent years. This subject is complicated not merely by the complexity of events but also by the variety of approaches one can take to the subject of social change generally and religious change specifically. It is well to point out some approaches that are not so profitable for interpreting cultural change in Japan. There has often been a tendency to juxtapose too sharply the traditional and the modern, as if the two categories were mutually exclusive—as if one stepped across the boundary of traditional Japan and "entered" modern Japan. Phrased a little differently, this approach assumes that the traditional is an element that is discarded when the modern element is accepted. One Japanese scholar has criticized this artificial division of Japanese culture into "pieces of two kinds" and suggests that "the 'traditional' is one aspect (not element) of the same social body which also has 'modern' features."[1] To the extent that this insight is valid for Japanese culture, it probably holds true for most societies, which are mixtures of traditional and modern aspects. We will better understand change in Japanese culture if we see it as a combination of old and new, not as a replacement of the old with the new.

Another temptation we should resist is the notion that transformations in Japanese culture are simply due to Western influence—"Westernization." It is true that Western influence, especially American influence, has been very important during the past century and a half. But we should not forget that Japan's shift from an agricultural-rural society to an urban-industrial society started long before Western contact. And Japan's present industrial and commercial organization has been so innovative and effective that Western leaders are now interested in learning lessons from Japan.[2]

It would be just as misleading to call this process "Japanization" as it would be to put labels such as "Westernization" or "Americanization" on the earlier interaction between Japan and the West. The

changes Japan has undergone are the result of a combination of
Japanese institutions and selected Western borrowings that were modified according to Japanese specifications. In other words, the changes should be seen as a combination of Japanese and Western models, not as a replacement of Japanese models with Western models.

The question of religion and change, also, is a matter that can be approached from widely diverging viewpoints. One view is that religion is part of traditional life; and when people become "modern," they reject the traditional in favor of the "rational," thus causing religion to decline or even disappear. A second view is that religion is an integral part of the world-view and behavior of a culture, so that when the culture undergoes basic change, religion also changes significantly.

This complex theoretical problem is not limited to Japanese religion, but our discussion must be limited to the Japanese situation. The first view is not without merit, for it is clear that in some discernible ways (which we will examine shortly), the role of Japanese religion is less than it once was. But this view is severely limited because it tends to consider the traditional as an element that is replaced by the modern. This makes the first viewpoint less useful than the second viewpoint: The first tends to look at decline and disappearance, whereas the second is able to look at change in terms of both loss and reformulation. Although we cannot solve the larger theoretical issue here, the basic point to remember is that the questions we ask determine the answers we get.[3] If we ask, "How has religion declined in modern Japan?" we will tend to learn only about the decline. If, on the other hand, we ask, "How has religion continued or persisted into the present?" we will tend to learn how religion has been modified and handed down today. This second view is the approach taken in this chapter, in consistency with the viewpoint throughout this book, of tracing continuity and change in Japanese religious history.

It is well to remember that life is always changing, so the change that we observe in contemporary Japan is not basically different from changes that have occurred throughout Japanese history. All aspects of Japanese life have changed from time to time, although the change that has occurred in the past century or so, especially after World War II, has been more sudden and sweeping. Some of the changes were dramatic legal changes, such as the new legal situation after World War II: freedom of religion, greater rights for women, more "democratic" rights generally. Others, such as the shift from a rural-agricultural lifestyle to an urban-industrial lifestyle, had been taking place for a long time but became more pronounced. For several centuries, people had been leaving the countryside for the city, but in the postwar period the population reversed the former 70 percent rural and 30 percent urban balance to 70 percent urban and 30 percent rural. Even the "farm" population is only peripherally involved in farming; few young and middle-age men consider themselves full-time farmers. Most farm families have full-time and part-time jobs off the farm, and farming itself has become highly mechanized, with the majority of work done by women and older men.

These are the kinds of long-term, basic changes that are so important for considering in connection with religious changes. For as the economic pattern shifts, social institutions such as the family are modified, and the religious activities of the family are altered. Especially in the villages of the countryside such economic and social changes have had a devastating effect on religion. Often with so many young people migrating to the cities there are not enough young people to carry out a festival. With economic life following a factory schedule rather than the seasonal rhythms of nature, even the remaining "farm" people can hardly take time off from their side jobs to participate in an agricultural festival. This is one sense in which religion has declined or, we might say, has a lesser role in contemporary Japan: Fewer people participate in local festivals; less time is spent in these festivals; the timing of them is adjusted to fit economic schedules; and the rituals themselves may be abbreviated or even disappear.

TRANSFORMATIONS OF RELIGIOUS LIFE IN CONTEMPORARY JAPAN

The "decline" of traditional village religion can be illustrated by some of the results of a recent restudy of the village of Kurusu (on the island of Shikoku), studied first in 1951 and then twenty-four years later. The 1951 date of the initial study is in the postwar period, by which time many "traditional" customs had already been greatly modified or curtailed. Twenty-four years later, in 1975, the pattern of change was much more noticeable. The dominance of the six-day work week is seen in the fact that shrine festivals and memorial services are held mainly on Sundays. The obvious reason, of course, is that this is the only time the villagers have free; village and family rituals are no longer major junctures of an annual cycle. To put it bluntly, "color television has long outshone the gilt and jollity of village festivals."[4]

Americans sometimes joke that television sets are the central altar in American homes and that family activities and attention center on television viewing. There is reason to believe that in Japan television viewing as a leisure activity is replacing former religious practices in the Japanese family. In 1951 every Kurusu home but one had a Shinto-style home altar *(kamidana)* and observed daily offerings. In 1975 the altars had not been removed, but few made offerings at the altars except at New Year's. *Kamidana* were included in two new homes that had been built recently, but the old men who built the homes were not sure their children would maintain rituals at the altars.

Buddhist rituals for family ancestors, too, have been adjusted to fit modern convenience. Although the day for a funeral is still determined by the old ceremonial calendar (with "lucky" and "unlucky" days for funerals), the memorials for ancestors are often held not on the annual anniversary of death but on a Sunday that is close to the anniversary. This obviously works a hardship on the Buddhist priest, who must rush from house to house on the Sundays that fall close to the annual ceremony for the dead *(bon)*. The three Buddhist priests in the Kurusu area, however, have secular part-time jobs to supplement their religious occupation as priests.

In traditional times, and even as late as 1951, a funeral was conducted mainly by the Buddhist priest and the hamlet association in cooperation with the bereaved family. There was a procession in which the corpse was carried from the home to a nearby cremation ground. Members of the hamlet association lit the funeral pyre and kept it burning all night long in order to reduce the body to ashes, which the family would collect the next morning. By 1975 professionalism had taken over. In 1960 an electric crematorium with an oil furnace back-up had been built in a nearby town, and an undertaker assumed many of the functions of the hamlet association, transporting the body in a hearse to the crematorium. Before 1960, the coffin was in the shape of a cask and the body was seated in a flexed position; but since neither the automobile hearse nor the door of the crematorium furnace could accommodate such a tall coffin, corpses have had to be laid out prone in long narrow boxes called "sleeping coffins."[5]

Events in the village of Kurusu are signs of the "decline" of religion in Japan. However, while religion is declining, it is also growing or increasing. Two examples will be used to illustrate the growth of religion in contemporary Japan—a new festival in Kobe and activities in the New Religions generally. The Kobe festival may be considered the antithesis of developments in Kurusu.

The "bird boat" in a harbor festival of the Shiogama-Matsushima area. A sacred palanquin (omikoshi) *can be seen in the center of the boat. (about 1963)*

Whereas local festivals and religious activities are declining and disappearing, some older festivals in cities are becoming more elaborate and a few new ones are being developed. Kobe, a city of more than a million people just south of Osaka, is well known in the modern period as a major seaport. Kobe has an international flavor; many non-Japanese live there, and the Kobe festival reflects this cosmopolitanism. The Kobe festival was created in 1971 by combining the port festival, which had been held thirty-eight times between 1933 and 1970, and the Kobe carnival, held four times between 1967 and 1970. The inspiration for both festivals had been foreign. The port festival was patterned after the Rose Festival of Portland, Oregon; the model for the Kobe carnival was the carnival of Rio de Janeiro.

The specifically religious elements of the Kobe festival are overshadowed by the kinds of activities associated with American parades. Shinto priests still pray for the prosperity of the harbor, and the mayor presents offerings to the sea, but these activities are not so important as the parade, which features Japanese queens and princesses from the foreign community residing in Kobe. Like other Japanese cities, Kobe is divided into wards, and each ward has its separate celebrations (especially prayers for traffic safety), more traditional in character.

Japanese scholars who have studied the Kobe festival have called it "a festival with anonymous *kami*," because from the beginning its religious character was underemphasized. The people who plan and carry out the festival actually state that the festival is "without religious ceremonies" and "without divinities." We might be tempted to

Young men preparing to shoulder a sacred palanquin (omikoshi) *in a small local festival in the city of Sendai. (about 1963)*

view it as a kind of secular festival, lacking most of the traditional religious elements. However, the scholars analyzing the festival are quick to point out that it is not the case that traditional "elements were merely withdrawn; instead, new values were attached to the festival in a positive way." These new values are a clear sense of community consciousness (in a city that more than doubled its size in the postwar recovery period), the symbol of Kobe as a sort of sacred space replacing traditional *kami,* and internationalism.

If the Kobe festival appears to the non-Japanese reader to be a confused mixture of traditional features and borrowed elements, a similar sense of confusion is found among Japanese participants. Some Japanese liked it because it was full of pleasure, gaiety, and relaxation; they overlooked the surviving religious elements. Some Japanese disliked it, criticizing it as an "imitation of foreign festivals" and claiming that "without the *kami* it is nothing at all like a real festival." Anyone who has seen a more traditional Japanese festival must sympathize with those who criticize the Kobe festival as *"kami*-less," not simply because of its nonreligious character, but also because it tends to be gaudy and commercialized. However, such urbanized festivals must be understood in historical perspective. As early as the fifteenth century "the focus of interest shifted to the para-festival activities"[6] such as parades and public entertainment. Therefore, it would be a mistake to view the Kobe festival as an instance of "Westernization." It is not just an occasion of borrowing non-Japanese elements; it may be seen as an extension of urban festivals dating back five centuries.

A second example of how religion has grown or increased in contemporary Japan is the activities of the New Religions. In the traditional setting, participation in religious life was narrowly limited to
the family, village, and regional centers, with perhaps an occasional
pilgrimage to a distant shrine or temple. As we have seen, various
factors have weakened family and village institutions and celebrations. A conspicuous change that has taken place in the last century,
especially in the postwar period, is the proliferation of religious activities on the part of the New Religions. We have already examined
two New Religions—Tenrikyo and Soka Gakkai—which illustrate a
typical, dramatic expansion of religious life, both in the nature and in
the extent of participation.

In the traditional religious practice of most Buddhist temples and
Shinto shrines, people participated mainly by virtue of birth in a
residential area and membership in a specific family. A person took
part in the rites of a local Shinto shrine because being born in the
"parish" of that shrine made him or her a parishioner: The *kami* of the
local shrine was a tutelary deity, and the person was under the protection of the *kami*. A person participated in the rites of a Buddhist
temple because it was the hereditary family temple of the man's family (women joined the temple of their husbands). A family was tied to
a local Buddhist temple especially through funerals and rites for the
spirits of the family dead. This pattern of residential and hereditary
participation contrasts sharply with membership in a New Religion.

To be a member of a New Religion requires a conscious choice, at
least for the first generation of believers. Groups formed without
regard to kinship and territorial considerations, on the basis of a voluntary decision, are called voluntary organizations. The difference
between traditional religious groups and voluntary organizations
goes further than a decision to join. In former times there was no nationwide network of believers, and even religious institutions such as
temples were only loosely linked. New Religions, however, provide
a commonality of belief, practice, and social cohesion that is shared
by Japanese throughout the Japanese islands and in some cases by
Japanese and non-Japanese in other countries. Although the number
of foreign members is rather small, it is emphasized in the literature
of the various groups because it demonstrates that the Japanese member is part of an international organization.

The sense of identity felt by a member of a New Religion is quite
different from that felt by a member of a traditional family and village.
The heart of a New Religion is not one organization but clusters of
small groups, often meeting in homes. The small discussion groups

One New Religion, Byakko Shinko-kai, stressing international peace, has erected pillars advocating universal peace in Japanese and English. This pillar in front of an old Buddhist building on Mount Oyama gives some idea of the mixture of national tradition and international currents found in contemporary Japan. (1979)

are the recruiting base for the New Religions. An acquaintance, friend, or relative extends the invitation and leads in the new member. Usually a person joins after his or her personal problem has been resolved through the religious faith and practice of the group. The discussion group is more intimate than the traditional village and more democratic than the traditional family. Members of discussion groups meet regularly to share daily experiences, worship, and simple refreshments. From time to time, members travel to regional meetings or to national headquarters and sacred centers, where huge, colorful festivals are held. The fact that individuals from distant regions can travel to their New Religion's national headquarters and share social and religious experiences is a remarkable change from the relative isolation of traditional festivals. It represents a dramatic expansion of religious organization.

The example of Kurusu has demonstrated religious decline. The Kobe festival and the social organization of the New Religions are signs of religious growth or expansion. These are but three instances of the changes that religion has undergone and continues to undergo in contemporary Japan. They show not only the "more" and "less" of religion in present-day Japan, but also what is new. For example, in the village of Kurusu it is a relatively new pattern for most celebrations to be on Sunday, and small matters, such as the new shape of the coffin, should not be overlooked. The Kobe festival was deliberately designed as a "new kind of festival." And the very term *"New Religion"* indicates that it is a new form of socio-religious organization. Other brief examples will illustrate new emphases in contemporary practices.

There had long been special prayers for the repose of the spirits of infants in the case of stillbirth or miscarriage. With the dramatic increase in artificial abortions (which are legal) during the past few decades, many women have sought religious relief after an abortion. Some temples have specialized in so-called abortion masses, and their grounds are literally filled with plaques or small stone statues bought as part of the service. At the other end of the life cycle, the combination of greater longevity and smaller families has made aging grandparents less welcome in their children's homes. One religious response has been the rise to popularity of a temple near Nara, where busloads of grandparents go to pray for a quick and painless death. These last two instances are somewhat unusual; however, they point up the fact that religion in Japan is not dead but is ever changing.

Organizationally, too, new possibilities are arising. Just as we saw the new wave of internationalism in the Kobe festival, so democracy is another major thrust of postwar Japan. The Otani branch of Pure Land Buddhism, once considered one of the most "feudal" institutions of contemporary Japan, has been wracked by internal change. Partly because of early social reformers, who insisted that the personal faith of *individuals* was the basis for Pure Land Buddhism (rather than ancestral memorial rites for *households*), and partly because of postwar democratic trends, a concerted drive has been made to remove absolute power from a hereditary abbot and place it in the hands of a lay board of devout members. The result has been rather ugly litigation in the civil courts, but whatever the outcome, this bold new move may lay down the precedent for more democratic representation by lay members in the established Buddhist denominations and prepare the way for reorganizing Buddhism on the basis of individual faith.

Another change is the shift from religious to nonreligious patterns. For example, in Kurusu, professional undertakers have assumed part of the traditional role of Buddhist priests. In Kobe, there was the attempt to create a "new kind of festival" based on secular models rather than religious foundations. The same religious-to-secular change can be seen in more subtle and distant shifts. For example, youth groups and participation in festivals in traditional villages have greatly diminished, but in the city a young man's "initiation" into a business organization in some ways corresponds to the more explicitly religious initiation in the countryside. Companies and offices often observe morning routines (or rituals?) of exercises, statements of company slogans, and even singing of company songs. The obvious purpose of such activities is to stress loyalty to the company and encourage hard work. They are not explicitly religious, but they are in some ways analogous to the local village rites for achieving identity.

The foregoing are but a few illustrations of how in contemporary Japan religion has declined, increased, developed new forms, and given way to other forms of specialization. The contemporary scene is much too complicated to be summed up in these few examples, but perhaps they will give the reader some idea of the changes that are still occurring.

NOTES

1. Chie Nakane, *Japanese Society* (Berkeley: University of California Press, 1970), p. ix.
2. See Ezra F. Vogel, *Japan as Number One: Lessons for America* (Cambridge, Mass.: Harvard University Press, 1979; reprint ed., New York: Harper & Row, 1980).
3. For a volume of essays discussing the notion of "secularization" and how it might be applied to Japanese religion, see *Proceedings of Tokyo Meeting of the International Conference on Sociology of Religion, 1978*; reprinted in *Japanese Journal of Religious Studies,* Vol. 6, Nos. 1–2 (March–June 1979), 1–386, especially Noriyoshi Tamaru, "The Problem of Secularization," pp. 89–114.
4. R. P. Dore, in Robert J. Smith, *Kurusu: The Price of Progress in a Japanese Village, 1951–1975* (Stanford, Calif.: Stanford University Press, 1978), pp. xi–xii.
5. Ibid., pp. 212–24.
6. Nobutaka Inoue et al., "A Festival with Anonymous Kami," in *Proceedings of Tokyo Meeting of the International Conference on Sociology of Religion, 1978*; reprinted in *Japanese Journal of Religious Studies,* Vol. 6, Nos. 1–2 (March–June 1979), 163–85.

SELECTED READINGS

Dore, Ronald P. *City Life in Japan: A Study of a Tokyo Ward.* Berkeley: University of California Press, 1958. See pp. 291–373 for the most comprehensive and perceptive interpretation of religion in the immediate postwar period.

Inoue, Nobutaka, et al. "A Festival with Anonymous Kami." In *Proceedings of Tokyo Meeting of the International Conference on Sociology of Religion, 1978*. Reprinted in *Japanese Journal of Religious Studies*, Vol. 6, Nos. 1–2 (March–June 1979), 163–85. Analysis and interpretation of the Kobe festival as a new kind of festival in urbanized society.

Proceedings of Tokyo Meeting of the International Conference on Sociology of Religion, 1978. Reprinted in *Japanese Journal of Religious Studies*, Vol. 6, Nos. 1–2 (March–June 1979), 1–386. A volume of essays discussing the notion of "secularization" as it arose in European and American sociology, and its application to Japanese religion, with special essays interpreting the nature of religion in modern Japan.

Smith, Robert J. *Kurusu: The Price of Progress in a Japanese Village, 1951–1975*. Stanford, Calif.: Stanford University Press, 1978. A restudy of the village of Kurusu after twenty-four years; the excellent materials on religion interpret religious change in the larger context of social and economic change in the village and nation as a whole.

CHAPTER 20

Conclusion: The Challenge for Japanese Religion

We have viewed Japanese religion through three major historical periods, but the story does not end here. Throughout this span of several thousand years, Japanese religion has developed a distinctive tradition, yet it has undergone significant change. It is difficult for historians to predict the future, but the best basis for discussing the future prospects of Japanese religion is in terms of the recent transformations and their implications for continuity and innovation.

Contemporary Japan presents a complex challenge to religion. Both Shinto and Buddhism developed in an agricultural nation and were closely related to an agricultural lifestyle (as well as to income from land). As the nation became increasingly industrialized and urbanized, both religions suffered. The heart of Shinto, defined by agricultural rhythms, is threatened in an industrial-urban setting. Buddhism is hard hit by social mobility, which has upset its parish system. There is great disparity in the financial condition of individual shrines and temples. Those that depended mainly on government subsidy or income from land have fallen on hard times. On the other hand, some temples and shrines flourish because of other sources of income. Some receive money by virtue of being the centers of popular cults. The older historical landmarks and those in scenic resort areas draw money from sightseers and vacationers. One might expect that Buddhism and Shinto will reorganize on the basis of a more dynamic faith, imitating the recent success of the New Religions. However, several decades after 1945, it is still too soon to see what the religious leaders are willing and able to do.

Shinto and Buddhist leaders are investigating these problems, however. Shinto scholars especially are probing the meaning of Japanese culture in an attempt to maintain the Shinto heritage in the modern world. Buddhist scholars have become more active in the worldwide Buddhist movement. The New Religions are Japanese at heart, but some are making an earnest bid to become world religions. Religious Taoism and Confucianism are inconspicuous survivals within other traditions, popular beliefs, and (for Confucianism) social values. Folk religion is still important, but its influence has been severely attenuated by industrialization and urbanization. A general dilemma is the movement away from religion and toward secular interests.

By the Tokugawa period, growing cities and expanding commercialism were shifting attention to the glitter of city life. In the twentieth century, industrialism and urbanization experienced unprecedented growth, and secularism became much more pervasive. Religious devotion remained strong in the countryside, but indifference to organized religion became a fact of city life. To a certain extent, the New Religions have capitalized on this indifference, but they are unable to change the nature of city life. For example, leisure is a problem in any modern city, and the Japanese man in the street is likely to spend most of his idle time in a *pachinko* parlor, a kind of slot-machine gallery. People with nothing useful to do have little interest in religion. On the other hand, many intellectuals and writers have gone beyond indifference to religion to express a pessimistic view of the meaninglessness of life. Japan regards her novelists as cultural heroes, and some of Japan's most respected novelists have committed suicide.[1] If religion represents a positive affirmation of life and the world, secularism at most views life as an opportunity for hedonism. In the shadow cast by secularism is the "negative ideal" of suicide to defeat meaninglessness. Perhaps this extreme form of secularism represents the most serious challenge to religion, for it rejects any traditional religious answer.

The religious problem in Japan is not so different from the problem in the West. To be resolved is the question of how cultural, spiritual, and religious values can be articulated and perpetuated in the modern world.[2] Japan must find a way to maintain her cultural and religious heritage while contributing to a world culture. What is at stake is not simply a matter of making Japanese religion conform to new social and economic conditions. At the heart of the problem is a human and spiritual question that asks what it means for a Japanese person to live in the present world. This involves the question of how men and women relate to their national history and to the world at large. It implies the question of how they define themselves in relation to the natural world and to other people. The answering of these questions is the task of the Japanese people. This task presupposes a reassessment of Japanese religion.[3]

As we watch the drama of Japanese religion unfold, we perceive the richness of this tradition as well as the serious problems facing it. We see that the Japanese people are proud of their tradition, and we sympathize with their attempt to use traditional resources to face contemporary problems. We sympathize with them, for in the final analysis all modern people are facing a common problem: the problem of relating one's own religious traditions to contemporary questions. As we study Japanese religion and other religious traditions, we realize, however, that the challenge of modernity presents an opportunity for creativity. This study gives us the chance to see ourselves not just as members of the Western tradition, but as participants within the worldwide history of religious experience. People of different cultures invariably have somewhat different perceptions of human experience, the world at large, and the nature of reality. We are not Japanese, and therefore our cultural perceptions will never coincide completely with Japanese perceptions. But we do not have to become Japanese in order to appreciate the richness of their tradition and recognize our common humanity as we face the perennial question of how to live a meaningful life.

NOTES

1. See Howard S. Hibbett, "Akutagawa Ryunosuke and the Negative Ideal," in *Personality in Japanese History*, ed. Albert M. Craig and Donald H. Shiveley (Berkeley: University of California Press, 1970), pp. 425–51, esp. p. 449.
2. Masaharu Anesaki was well aware of these issues even before World War II. See his views in his *History of Japanese Religion* (London: Kegan Paul, Trench, Trubner, 1930; reprint ed., Rutland, Vt.: Charles E. Tuttle Company, 1963), pp. 375–409; and in his article "An Oriental Evaluation of Modern Civilization," in *Recent Gains in American Civilization*, ed. Kirby Page (New York: Harcourt Brace Jovanovich, 1928), pp. 329–57. The article is abridged in H. Byron Earhart, *Religion in the Japanese Experience: Sources and Interpretations* (Belmont, Calif.: Wadsworth, 1974), pp. 258–61.

3.   See Robert N. Bellah, ed., *Religion and Progress in Modern Asia*
     (New York: Free Press, 1965), for a discussion of this problem of
     religion and modernity in terms of the notion of progress. Note
     especially the remarks of Clifford Geertz, pp. 166–67.

SELECTED READINGS

Anesaki, Masaharu. "An Oriental Evaluation of Modern Civiliza-
    tion." In *Recent Gains in American Civilization*. Edited by Kirby
    Page. New York: Harcourt Brace Jovanovich, 1928, pp. 329–57.
    Reprinted in Anesaki's *Katam Karaniyam: Lectures, Essays and
    Studies*. Boston: Marshall Jones Company, 1936, pp. 32–51. An
    early discussion of the role of religion in modern civilization by
    the father of the science of religion in Japan.
Bellah, Robert N., ed. *Religion and Progress in Modern Asia*. New York:
    Free Press, 1965. A discussion of the problem of religion and
    modernity in terms of "progress."
Earhart, H. Byron. *Religion in the Japanese Experience: Sources and Inter-
    pretations*. Belmont, Calif.: Wadsworth, 1974. See Part Seventeen
    for selected documents on the history and future of Japanese
    religion, including excerpts from Anesaki; see also pp. 222–35
    for the problem of religious indifference and secularism.
Kitagawa, Joseph M. *Religion in Japanese History*. New York: Columbia
    University Press, 1966. See pp. 331–40 for an assessment of the
    future of Japanese religion.

Annotated Bibliography on Japanese Religion: Selected Works

This bibliography is divided into the following sections:

Special Bibliographies on Japanese History and Religion
Special Reference Works on Japanese History and Religion
Periodicals for Japanese History and Religion
Histories and Works on Japanese Culture
Histories and General Works on Japanese Religion
Shinto
Buddhism
Confucianism
Religious Taoism
Folk Religion
Christianity
New Religions

The symbol † precedes works that, because of their introductory, concise, or comprehensive character, are recommended for first reading. The symbol * precedes works that were available in paperback editions at the time the bibliography was compiled.

214
*Japanese
Religion:
Unity and
Diversity*

SPECIAL BIBLIOGRAPHIES ON JAPANESE
HISTORY AND RELIGION

†Association for Asian Studies. *Cumulative Bibliography of Asian Studies,
1941–1965.* Author Bibliography, 4 vols.; Subject Bibliography, 4
vols. Boston: G. K. Hall & Company, 1969–70. This work is continued in *Cumulative Bibliography of Asian Studies, 1966–70.* Author
Bibliography, 3 vols.; Subject Bibliography, 3 vols. Boston: G. K.
Hall & Company, 1972–73. The most convenient and comprehensive listing of materials on Asian subjects. For Japanese materials,
see the heading "Japan" in the Subject Bibliography; for religion,
see the subheading "Philosophy and Religion." Materials after
1970 will be found in the annual *Bibliography of Asian Studies* published by the Association for Asian Studies.

Bando, Shojun, et al. *A Bibliography on Japanese Buddhism.* Tokyo: Cultural Interchange Institute for Buddhist Press, 1958. Exhaustive
rather than selective; includes obscure Western-language articles
and books, classified mainly by sect lines.

Beautrix, Pierre. *Bibliographie du Bouddhisme Zen.* Brussels: Institut
belge des hautes études bouddhiques, 1969. Arranged topically, it
includes English publications and features an author index for
746 items.

Dobson, W. A. C. H. "The Religions of China (Excepting Buddhism)." In *A Reader's Guide to the Great Religions.* 2d ed. Edited
by Charles J. Adams. New York: Free Press, 1977, pp. 90–105. A
brief bibliographic essay organized historically and topically.

*Earhart, H. Byron. *The New Religions of Japan: A Bibliography of
Western-Language Materials.* Tokyo: Sophia University, 1970. 2d ed.
forthcoming from Michigan Papers in Japanese Studies. Provides
a general introduction to the New Religions and a general bibliography, followed by listings for individual New Religions;
includes author and topical indexes.

Fu, Charles Wei-hsun, and Chan, Wing-tsit. *Guide to Chinese Philosophy.* Boston: G. K. Hall & Company, 1978. A comprehensive,
annotated bibliography organized in terms of Chinese traditions
or "schools" and philosophical problems.

Fujino, Yukio, comp. *Modern Japanese Literature in Western Translations:
A Bibliography.* Tokyo: International House of Japan Library, 1972.
A convenient listing of post-1868 literature in Western-language
translations; arranged by author but also featuring an index to
translators and a title index for each Western language.

215
*Annotated
Bibliography
on Japanese
Religion:
Selected Works*

†Hall, John Whitney. *Japanese History: New Dimensions of Approach and Understanding.* 2d ed. Washington, D.C.: American Historical Association, 1966. The best bibliographical guide to Japanese history, with balanced treatment of the major problems.

*Herbert, Jean. *Bibliographie du Shinto et des sectes Shintoistes.* Leiden: E. J. Brill, 1968. Includes Japanese and Western-language materials arranged by author, with a subject index in French and Japanese.

*Holzman, Donald, et al. *Japanese Religion and Philosophy: A Guide to Japanese Reference and Research Materials.* Ann Arbor: University of Michigan Press, 1959. Reprint ed., Westport, Conn.: Greenwood Press, 1975. For those interested in Japanese-language materials; although somewhat dated, it annotates (in English) almost one thousand Japanese works on various traditions.

Ikado, Fujio, and McGovern, James R., comps. *A Bibliography of Christianity in Japan: Protestantism in English Sources (1859–1959).* Tokyo: Committee on Asian Cultural Studies, International Christian University, 1966. Books, pamphlets, and articles arranged alphabetically by author, with separate indexes by title, author, and subject.

Japan P.E.N. Club. *Japanese Literature in European Languages: A Bibliography.* 2d ed. Tokyo: Japan P.E.N. Club, 1961. Supplement, 1964, and periodical supplements in *The Japan P.E.N. News.* A convenient listing of both classical and modern works in Western-language translations (mostly English); arranged by literary categories.

Kato, Genchi, et al. *A Bibliography of Shinto in Western Languages from the Oldest Times till 1952.* Tokyo: Meiji Jingu Shamusho, 1953. Exhaustive rather than selective; arranged alphabetically by author, with subject index.

†Kitagawa, Joseph M. "The Religions of Japan." In *A Reader's Guide to the Great Religions.* 2d ed. Edited by Charles J. Adams. New York: Free Press, 1977, pp. 247–82. The best single bibliographical work on Japanese religions; arranged historically, with valuable commentary.

†Kublin, Hyman. *What Shall I Read on Japan: An Introductory Guide.* 11th ed. New York: Japan Society, 1973. A pamphlet featuring annotated listings for fifteen topics.

Reynolds, Frank E. "Buddhism." In *A Reader's Guide to the Great Religions.* 2d ed. Edited by Charles J. Adams. New York: Free Press, 1977, pp. 156–222. A comprehensive bibliographic essay on Buddhism, organized by region and topics.

*Silberman, Bernard. *Japan and Korea: A Critical Bibliography.* Tucson: University of Arizona Press, 1962. A general bibliography on Japan; arranged topically, with helpful introductions. (For recent materials, see *The Journal of Asian Studies.*)

*†Varley, H. Paul. *A Syllabus of Japanese Civilization.* 2d ed. New York: Columbia University Press, 1972. A handy historical and topical guide, with suggested readings; useful for teachers and students.

Vessie, Patricia Armstrong. *Zen Buddhism: A Bibliography of Books and Articles in English, 1892–1975.* Ann Arbor, Mich.: University Microfilms International, 1976. Books and articles (762) arranged by subject.

Yu, David. "Present-Day Taoist Studies." *Religious Studies Review,* Vol. 3, No. 4 (October 1977), 220–39. A comprehensive bibliography on Taoism, preceded by an essay explaining the different aspects of Taoism and the resources for studying them.

SPECIAL REFERENCE WORKS ON JAPANESE HISTORY AND RELIGION

†*Basic Terms of Shinto* ("Compiled by Shinto Committee for the IXth International Congress for the History of Religions"). Tokyo: Jinja Honcho (Association of Shinto Shrines), Kokugakuin University, and Institute for Japanese Culture and Classics, 1958. An authoritative and convenient vocabulary of some important Shinto terms.

Goedertier, Joseph M. *A Dictionary of Japanese History.* New York: Walker/Weatherhill, 1968. A convenient handbook of Japanese terms arranged alphabetically; contains a subject index.

†Itasaka, Gen, and Dekker, Maurits, eds. *Encyclopedia of Japan.* 8 vols. Tokyo: Kodansha International, forthcoming. Promises to be the most convenient single reference work on all aspects of Japan.

†*Japanese-English Buddhist Dictionary.* Tokyo: Daito Shuppansha, 1965. A reliable work based on a standard Japanese dictionary, with the terms translated into Roman letters and alphabetized; includes separate indexes for Chinese characters, Sanskrit, Pali, and Romanized Chinese.

†Masuda, Koh, ed. *Kenkyusha's New Japanese-English Dictionary.* 4th ed. Tokyo: Kenkyusha, 1974. A standard work; because the Japanese words are transliterated into Roman letters and alphabetized, it can be used even by those who do not read Japanese.

Yanagita, Kunio, comp. *Japanese Folklore Dictionary*. Translated by Masanori Takatsuka. Edited by George K. Brady. "Kentucky microcards, Series A, No. 18." Lexington: University of Kentucky Press, 1958. The microcards are awkward to use, but this standard reference work contains valuable material for anyone who does not read Japanese; arranged alphabetically by Japanese terms.

217
*Annotated
Bibliography
on Japanese
Religion:
Selected Works*

PERIODICALS FOR JAPANESE HISTORY AND RELIGION

Asian Folklore Studies. Tokyo, 1963–. (Formerly *Folklore Studies*, Peiking, 1942–52; Tokyo, 1953–62.) Covering Far Eastern folklore in general, it includes articles and monographs on Japanese subjects in German and English.

Bulletin de la Maison Franco-Japonaise. Tokyo, 1927–. In French; detailed monographs of a technical nature.

The Eastern Buddhist. Kyoto, 1921–37; New Series, 1965–. Articles by Buddhists on popular and scholarly topics.

Harvard Journal of Asiatic Studies. Cambridge, Mass., 1936–. Scholarly translations and articles on all aspects of Asia.

Japan Christian Quarterly. Tokyo, 1926–. Articles mainly on Protestantism and its missions in Japan.

†*Japanese Journal of Religious Studies*. Tokyo, 1974–. (Formerly *Contemporary Religions in Japan*, 1960–74.) The earlier journal focused on postwar religious developments; its successor contains both theoretical and descriptive articles.

Japanese Religions. Kyoto, 1959–. Popular articles on aspects of contemporary Japanese religions; frequently features dialogues between Christianity and Japanese religious groups.

The Journal of Asian Studies. Ann Arbor, Mich., 1956–. (Formerly *Far Eastern Quarterly*, 1941–56). The leading scholarly journal in English on Asian topics.

†*Journal of Japanese Studies*. Seattle, 1974–. A periodical developed recently by scholars of Japanese studies, with specialized articles on Japanese history and culture.

Mitteilungen der Deutschen Gesellschaft Für Natur- und Völkerkunde Ostasiens. Tokyo, 1873–. Includes monographs on specialized topics in German.

†*Monumenta Nipponica*. Tokyo, 1938–. Scholarly articles, translations, and reviews in English on all aspects of Japanese history and culture.

Philosophy East and West. Honolulu, 1951–. Descriptive and comparative articles on Asian thought systems, especially Buddhism.
Transactions of the Asiatic Society of Japan. Tokyo, 1872–. The oldest
general periodical of its kind; with a recent topical index.

HISTORIES AND WORKS ON JAPANESE CULTURE

For additional references, see Hall, Kublin, Silberman, and Varley in
"Special Bibliographies on Japanese History and Religion."

*Anderson, Joseph L., and Richie, Donald. *The Japanese Film: Art and
Industry.* New York: Grove Press, 1960. A complete history of the
film industry from 1896 to 1959, with analysis of the distinctive
characteristics of Japanese film such as content, technique, and
directors; includes numerous film clips.
*Beardsley, Richard K.; Hall, John W.; and Ward, Robert E. *Village
Japan.* Chicago: University of Chicago Press, 1959. An intensive
study of a small rice-growing community through seven years of
joint field work, with separate chapters on aspects of community
life. See Chapter 14 for religion.
Beauchamp, Edward R., ed. *Learning to Be Japanese: Selected Readings
on Japanese Society and Education.* Hamden, Conn.: Linnet Books,
1978. Reprinted articles and chapters on the history and nature
of Japanese education and related issues such as student
movements, political questions, and textbook controversies; features a comprehensive bibliography on Japanese education.
*Befu, Harumi. "Gift-Giving in a Modernizing Japan." In *Japanese Cul-
ture and Behavior: Selected Readings.* Edited by Takie Sugiyama
Lebra and William P. Lebra. Honolulu: University Press of
Hawaii, 1974, pp. 208–21. Originally published in *Monumenta
Nipponica*, Vol. 23, Nos. 3–4 (1968), 445–46. An anthropological
view of the social and ritual significance of the important Japanese custom of gift giving.
*———. *Japan: An Anthropological Introduction.* San Francisco: Chan-
dler Publishing Company, 1971. A general introduction to aspects of Japanese culture, with suggested readings and many
photographs.
*Benedict, Ruth. *The Chrysanthemum and the Sword.* Boston: Houghton
Mifflin, 1946 (and later editions). An attempt to examine distinctively Japanese assumptions about life on the basis of written
documents; superseded by recent field work such as Beardsley, et

al. (See Lebra and Lebra, *Japanese Culture and Behavior,* esp. pp. 194–98, for a critique of Benedict and *on.*)

Brown, Delmer M. *Nationalism in Japan: An Introductory Historical Analysis.* Berkeley: University of California Press, 1955. Reprint ed., New York: Russell & Russell, 1971. A historical study of the complex development of nationalism in Japan.

Chamberlain, Basil Hall. *Things Japanese: Being Notes on Various Subjects Connected with Japan for the Use of Travellers and Others.* 5th ed. rev. London: John Murray, 1905. A kind of handbook by one of the early Western authorities on Japan; the alphabetically arranged articles (although rather dated) are still of considerable interest.

Craig, Albert M., and Shively, Donald H., eds. *Personality in Japanese History.* Berkeley: University of California Press, 1970. A book of essays attempting to evaluate Japanese personality through case studies of major political and literary figures of the past few centuries.

*de Bary, William Theodore, et al. *Sources of Chinese Tradition.* New York: Columbia University Press, 1960. A companion volume to Tsunoda et al., *Sources of Japanese Tradition,* this is a convenient resource for the Chinese background of Japanese culture and religion.

†Doi, Takeo. *The Anatomy of Dependence.* Translated by John Bester. Tokyo: Kodansha International, 1973. A fascinating book that interprets Japanese behavior in terms of distinctively Japanese psychological categories.

*†Dore, R. P. *City Life in Japan: A Study of a Tokyo Ward.* Berkeley: University of California Press, 1958. A detailed sociological analysis of life in one area of postwar Tokyo, valuable for its firsthand description of all facets of city life.

*†———. *Shinohata: A Portrait of a Japanese Village.* London: Allen Lane, 1978. Reprint ed., New York: Pantheon Books, 1980. A firsthand account of all aspects of life in a village, noting changes between 1955 and 1975; includes photographs and many interviews with villagers.

*Dunn, Charles J. *Everyday Life in Traditional Japan.* New York: Putnam, 1969; Rutland, Vt.: Charles E. Tuttle Company, 1972. An interesting description of daily life before 1900, with separate chapters on various occupations; profusely illustrated with traditional drawings.

*Duus, Peter. *Feudalism in Japan.* 2d ed. New York: Knopf, 1976. A general historical treatment of feudalism in Japan as compared with feudalism in Europe.

Earl, David Magarey. *Emperor and Nation in Japan: Political Thinkers of the Tokugawa Period.* Seattle: University of Washington Press, 1964. A detailed analysis of the development of nationalism and the rise of the status of the emperor in Tokugawa times.

*Editorial Department of Teikoku-Shoin Co. *Teikoku's Complete Atlas of Japan.* Teikoku-Shoin, Japan, 1964. A handy set of national and regional maps with topographical and some economic and social information; although somewhat dated, it is a convenient small atlas.

Elisseeff, Vadime. *Japan.* Translated from the French by James Hogarth. Geneva: Nagel Publishers, 1973. A convenient overview of archaeology in Japan and archaeological excavation of early Japan, with many color illustrations.

†Fairbank, John K.; Reischauer, Edwin O.; and Craig, Albert M. *East Asia: The Modern Transformation.* Boston: Houghton Mifflin, 1965. The chapters on Japan form a highly respected and widely used text on modern Japanese history. (See Reischauer and Fairbank for the first volume of this two-volume work.)

*Feis, Herbert. *The Road to Pearl Harbor: The Coming of the War Between the United States and Japan.* New York: Atheneum, 1962. A scholarly interpretation of the diplomatic negotiations leading up to the war.

Haitani, Kanji. *The Japanese Economic System: An Institutional Overview.* Lexington, Mass.: Lexington Books, 1976. A good, brief introduction to the social background and economic institutions of big business in Japan.

†Hall, John Whitney. *Japan: From Prehistory to Modern Times.* New York: Delacorte Press, 1970. A standard one-volume treatment emphasizing the premodern period.

*———. "A Monarch for Modern Japan." In *Political Development in Modern Japan.* Edited by Robert E. Ward. Princeton, N.J.: Princeton University Press, 1968, pp. 11–64. A historical interpretation of the role of the emperor in traditional Japan and the use of the emperor as a symbol of supreme authority from about 1868 to 1945.

———, and Beardsley, Richard K., eds. *Twelve Doors to Japan.* New York: McGraw-Hill, 1965. Twelve general chapters on topics such as geography, history, personality, art, education, political system, economic development, and law.

Hall, Robert King. *Shushin: The Ethics of a Defeated Nation.* New York: Columbia University, 1949. A critical analysis of the nationalistic and ultranationalistic ethics textbooks of prewar and wartime

Japan that were abolished by the Allied occupation; contains lengthy translations from the textbooks concerning loyalty to emperor, ancestors, Shinto, and nation.

Harich-Schneider, Eta. *A History of Japanese Music.* London: Oxford University Press, 1973. A lengthy, technical survey of Japanese music from prehistoric times to the present century; includes three small long-play records of musical selections.

Havens, Thomas R. H. *Valley of Darkness: The Japanese People and World War Two.* New York: Norton, 1978. An interesting account of the effect of World War II on the Japanese people, including many translated wartime documents—letters, diaries, and newspapers.

*Henderson, Harold G. *An Introduction to Haiku: An Anthology of Poems and Poets from Basho to Shiki.* Garden City, N.Y.: Doubleday, 1958. A sensitive introduction to haiku; a good first book for becoming acquainted with Japanese culture and art.

Hsu, Francis L. K. *Iemoto: The Heart of Japan.* Cambridge, Mass.: Schenkman Publishing Company, 1975. An interpretation of Japanese society, its "economic miracle," and social solidarity, generally in terms of the familial character *(iemoto)* of secondary groupings.

*Inoguchi, Rikihei, and Nakajima, Tadashi, with Pineau, Roger. *The Divine Wind: Japan's Kamikaze Force in World War II.* New York: Bantam Books, 1960. One of the better "war stories," told by two Japanese aviators involved in the war effort and part of the suicidal *kamikaze* force.

*Ishida, Takeshi. *Japanese Society.* New York: Random House, 1971. A general introduction to aspects of Japanese society.

*Jansen, Marius B., ed. *Changing Japanese Attitudes Toward Modernization.* Princeton, N.J.: Princeton University Press, 1965. Articles by leading scholars on specific problems of modernization; this is the first of five volumes on modern Japan published by Princeton University Press. (See also Shively.)

——— . *Japan and Its World: Two Centuries of Change.* Princeton, N.J.: Princeton University Press, 1980. An overview of the dramatic changes in Japan (and in relations between Japan and Western nations), from virtual isolation two centuries ago to "Japan's Search for Role in the Twentieth Century."

†Japan National Tourist Organization, comp. *Japan: The New Official Guide.* Tokyo: Japan Travel Bureau, 1975. A remarkable guidebook to Japan, its detailed maps and historical information on every locale make it a must for travelers. The 1975 edition has

much information on industry and commerce. Earlier editions, especially the ninth revision of *Japan: The Official Guide* (1962), usually available in used-book stores in Japan, contain more information on cultural and historical landmarks.

Japanese National Commission for UNESCO, comp. *Japan: Its People and Culture.* 3d ed. Tokyo: University of Tokyo Press (Ministry of Education), 1973. A convenient one-volume handbook of information on Japan; for religion see pp. 179–96.

†Kamei, Katsuichiro, et al. *The Heibonsha Survey of Japanese Art.* 31 vols. New York: Weatherhill/Heibonsha, 1972–79. English translation of a Japanese-language series of general introductions to the various media and periods of Japanese art; features readable texts and lavish illustrations; volume 31 is an index to the series. (For two volumes on religion, see Watanabe in the "Shinto" section of this bibliography and Sawa in the "Buddhism" section.)

*Keene, Donald, ed. *Anthology of Japanese Literature from the Earliest Era to the Mid-Nineteenth Century.* New York: Grove Press, 1955. Selected translations from all forms of literature, arranged by historical period.

*†———. *Japanese Literature: An Introduction for Western Readers.* New York: Grove Press, 1955. A concise survey of poetry, theater, and novels.

———. *Living Japan.* Garden City, N.Y.: Doubleday, 1959. A popular, impressionistic introduction to Japan through many photographs and general discussions.

Kidder, J. Edward, Jr. *The Birth of Japanese Art.* New York: Praeger Publishers, 1965. A discussion of the art of prehistoric and early Japan, with some color plates and several hundred black and white illustrations.

*Kimball, Arthur G. *Crisis in Identity and Contemporary Japanese Novels.* Rutland, Vt.: Charles E. Tuttle Company, 1973. A short, interesting interpretation of postwar Japanese novels in terms of "identity crisis"; includes a convenient syllabus for a reading course on postwar Japanese novels.

Kokudo, Chiriin (Geographical Survey Institute), ed. *The National Atlas of Japan.* Tokyo: Japan Map Center, 1977. The most complete atlas of Japan in English; features hundreds of maps with extensive information on physical, social, economic, cultural, and administrative aspects.

*Kornhauser, David. *Urban Japan: Its Foundations and Growth.* London: Longman, 1976. A brief, up-to-date, and well-written general introduction to the urban and rural landscapes and their relation-

223
*Annotated
Bibliography
on Japanese
Religion:
Selected Works*

ship to historical and commercial-industrial developments; the illustrations effectively give a sense of the Japanese landscape.

*Lebra, Joyce, et al. *Women in Changing Japan*. Stanford, Calif.: Stanford University Press, 1976. Separate chapters describe women in eleven occupational fields, providing valuable interviews of women engaged in these occupations; "women and suicide" is also treated.

*Lebra, Takie Sugiyama. *Japanese Patterns of Behavior*. Honolulu: University Press of Hawaii, 1976. An analysis of both normal and deviant behavior, showing that "the Japanese are extremely sensitive to and concerned about social interaction and relationships."

*———, and Lebra, William P., eds. *Japanese Culture and Behavior: Selected Readings*. Honolulu: University Press of Hawaii, 1974. Interesting articles on various aspects of Japanese behavior by anthropologists, sociologists, and psychologists.

Lockwood, William W. *The Economic Development of Japan: Growth and Structural Change*. Expanded ed. Princeton, N.J.: Princeton University Press, 1968. A standard, comprehensive survey of Japanese economic development, starting with the nineteenth-century Japanese historical setting and tracing subsequent economic growth.

Malm, William P. *Japanese Music and Musical Instruments*. Rutland, Vt.: Charles E. Tuttle Company, 1959. A comprehensive overview of Japanese music and musical instruments, treating both history and performance; features many illustrations and some musical transcriptions.

†Maraini, Fosco. *Japan: Patterns of Continuity*. Tokyo: Kodansha International, 1971. A perceptive appreciation of Japanese culture past and present, profusely illustrated with striking color photographs.

———. *Meeting with Japan*. Translated by Eric Mosbacher. New York: Viking Press, 1959. A kind of travel book, whose impressions are complemented by many good photographs.

*Miller, Roy Andrew. *The Japanese Language in Contemporary Japan: Some Socio-linguistic Observations*. Washington, D.C.: American Enterprise Institute for Public Policy Research; Stanford, Calif.: Hoover Institution on War, Revolution, and Peace, 1977. A general treatment of the nature of Japanese language and its relationship to Japanese social and cultural identity.

*Miner, Earl. *An Introduction to Japanese Court Poetry*. Stanford, Calif.: Stanford University Press, 1968. Based on the longer, standard work *Japanese Court Poetry* (by Miner and Robert H. Brower), this general treatment provides translations of major court poets from A.D. 550 to 1500 and an overview of themes such as nature and love as well as religious influence.

Mishima, Yukio. *The Sea of Fertility*. A tetralogy consisting of *Spring Snow* (1972), translated by Michael Gallagher; *Runaway Horses* (1973), translated by Michael Gallagher; *The Temple of Dawn* (1973), translated by E. Dale Saunders and Cecilia Segawa Seigle; and *The Decay of the Angel* (1975), translated by Edward G. Seidensticker. Publication dates are for the original English-language editions published in New York by Knopf; subsequently reprinted in a paperback edition in New York by Pocket Books. These four novels, in effect Mishima's brilliant last testament before his suicide in 1971, dramatize the plight of modern man; the extensive references to religion, especially Buddhist philosophy, occasionally temper Mishima's nihilism with a kind of existentialist quest.

Mitchell, Richard H. *Thought Control in Prewar Japan*. Ithaca, N.Y.: Cornell University Press, 1976. A detailed analysis of the laws and actual prosecution for eliminating revolutionaries from 1868 to 1941; valuable for documenting measures used to develop a highly unified national consciousness in this period.

*†Morris, Ivan. *The Nobility of Failure: Tragic Heroes in the History of Japan*. New York: Holt, Rinehart and Winston, 1975; New York: New American Library, 1976. A perceptive historical and literary analysis of the "tragic hero," from mythological figures and medieval warriors to the "kamikaze" suicide feats of World War II.

*————. *The World of the Shining Prince: Court Life in Ancient Japan*. New York: Knopf, 1964; New York: Penguin Books, 1979. A valuable insight into the values and aesthetics of court life.

*Munsterberg, Hugo. *The Arts of Japan: An Illustrated History*. Rutland, Vt.: Charles E. Tuttle Company, 1957. A handy one-volume treatment of various art forms (including folk art), with many illustrations.

*Najita, Tetsuo. *Japan*. Modern Nations in Historical Perspective Series. Englewood Cliffs, N.J.: Prentice-Hall, 1974. An analysis of the formation of modern Japan, contrasting "bureaucratic" and "idealistic" tendencies as the key to social and political dynamics.

*Nakamura, Hajime. *A History of the Development of Japanese Thought from 592 to 1868*. 2 vols. Tokyo: Kokusai Bunka Shinkokai (Society for International Cultural Relations), 1967. A historical survey, emphasizing the distinctiveness of Japanese thought.

*†Nakane, Chie. *Japanese Society*. Berkeley: University of California Press, 1970. A provocative analysis of Japanese society emphasizing its "vertical structure."

Onoda, Hiroo. *No Surrender: My Thirty-Year War*. Translated by Charles S. Terry. Tokyo: Kodansha International, 1974. The biography of a Japanese soldier who continued guerrilla warfare on a Philippine island from 1944 to 1974 provides rare insight into the psychology of wartime Japan.

*Paine, Robert Treat, and Soper, Alexander. *The Art and Architecture of Japan*. Rev. ed. Baltimore: Penguin Books, 1975. A scholarly historical analysis divided into painting and sculpture, and architecture, with numerous plates.

Plath, David W. *Long Engagements: Maturity in Modern Japan*. Stanford, Calif.: Stanford University Press, 1980. A fascinating account of aging or "maturity" told through the life histories of four contemporary Japanese, compared with characters in Japanese novels.

*Putzar, Edward. *Japanese Literature: A Historical Outline*. Tucson: University of Arizona Press, 1973. A volume of translated essays by Japanese scholars surveying Japanese literature by historical period; includes a convenient list of translations and studies of Japanese literature.

*†Reischauer, Edwin O. *Japan: The Story of a Nation*. Rev. ed. New York: Knopf, 1974. A popular presentation by a leading Japanologist; a good first book on Japan.

†_____, and Fairbank, John K. *East Asia: The Great Tradition*. Boston: Houghton Mifflin, 1958. The chapters on Japan form a highly respected and widely used text on premodern Japanese history. (See Fairbank and Reischauer for the second volume of this two-volume work.)

Reynolds, David K. *Morita Psychotherapy*. Berkeley: University of California Press, 1976. Introduction to the distinctively Japanese form of psychotherapy developed by Morita Shoma, which includes some Buddhist influence.

*Sansom, Sir George. *A History of Japan*. 3 vols. Stanford, Calif.: Stanford University Press, 1958–63. A standard Western work, especially valuable for cultural history, covering the span from earliest times until 1867.

_____. *Japan: A Short Cultural History*. Rev. ed. New York: Appleton-Century-Crofts, 1943. A brief historical treatment of Japanese culture.

*Shikibu, Murasaki. *The Tale of Genji*. 2 vols. Translated by Edward G. Seidensticker. New York: Knopf, 1976. Reprint ed., Rutland, Vt.:

Charles E. Tuttle Company, 1978. A new translation of a Japanese classic, it reveals the court pageantry and religious life of medieval Japan.

*Shively, Donald H., ed. *Tradition and Modernization in Japanese Culture.* Princeton, N.J.: Princeton University Press, 1971. Articles by leading scholars on specific problems of modernization in Japanese culture; this is the fifth of five volumes on modern Japan published by Princeton University Press. (See also Jansen.)

†Smith, Robert J. *Kurusu: The Price of Progress in a Japanese Village, 1951–1975.* Stanford, Calif.: Stanford University Press, 1978. A detailed anthropological description of life in the village of Kurusu, valuable for its interpretation of social, economic, and religious life in villages.

————, and Beardsley, Richard K., eds. *Japanese Culture: Its Development and Characteristics.* Viking Fund Publications in Anthropology, Vol. 34. Chicago: Aldine Publishing Company, 1962. Articles on the origin and nature of Japanese culture by Japanese and Western scholars.

*†Takeyama, Michio. *Harp of Burma.* Translated by Howard Hibbett. Rutland, Vt.: Charles E. Tuttle Company, 1966. A 1946 novel about Japanese prisoners of war in Burma at the end of World War II; originally written for high school students, it was widely read as a forceful dramatic rendering of the problems facing Japan after World War II.

*Thompson, Laurence G. *Chinese Religion: An Introduction.* 3d ed. Belmont, Calif.: Wadsworth, 1979. A brief introduction, helpful for understanding the Chinese background of Japanese religion; includes a bibliography.

*Trewartha, Glenn T. *Japan: A Geography.* Madison: University of Wisconsin Press, 1965. The most complete regional geography of Japan in English, but the economic and social information is considerably out-of-date.

*Tsuneishi, Warren M. *Japanese Political Style: An Introduction to the Government and Politics of Modern Japan.* New York: Harper & Row, 1966. A convenient introduction emphasizing the peculiarities of the "Japanese political style."

*†Tsunoda, Ryusaku, et al. *Sources of Japanese Tradition.* New York: Columbia University Press, 1958. A valuable collection of translated documents and comments on Japanese literature, thought, and religion. (See de Bary for the companion *Sources of Chinese Tradition.*)

227
*Annotated
Bibliography
on Japanese
Religion:
Selected Works*

————, and Goodrich, L. C., eds. *Japan in the Chinese Dynastic Histories*. South Pasadena, Calif.: P. D. & I. Perkins, 1951. Contains valuable Chinese perceptions of early Japan.

Ueda, Makoto. *Literary and Art Theories in Japan*. Cleveland, Ohio: Press of Western Reserve University, 1967. An overview of aesthetic theories in Japan, with translations of the writing of important Japanese writers on art theory.

————. *Modern Japanese Writers and the Nature of Literature*. Stanford, Calif.: Stanford University Press, 1976. A scholarly study of eight major modern Japanese novelists, analyzing their writings especially in terms of their theory of literature; includes a useful bibliography of critical works and translated literature.

*†Varley, H. Paul. *Japanese Culture: A Short History*. Expanded ed. New York: Praeger Publishers, 1977. A concise historical survey of Japanese culture, with numerous photographs.

*————, with Morris, Ivan and Nobuko. *Samurai*. New York: Dell, 1972. A general treatment of the origins of the *samurai* (warrior) class and its role in Japanese history.

*†Vogel, Ezra F. *Japan as Number One: Lessons for America*. Cambridge, Mass.: Harvard University Press, 1979. Reprint ed., New York: Harper & Row, 1980. A provocative work interpreting the "success story" of modern Japanese business and society in terms of the lessons that America can learn from Japan.

*————. *Japan's New Middle Class: The Salary Man and His Family in a Tokyo Suburb*. 2d ed. Berkeley: University of California Press, 1971. The result of extensive field work, it provides insight into contemporary family life.

*Ward, Robert E. *Japan's Political System*. 2d ed. Englewood Cliffs, N.J.: Prentice-Hall, 1978. An interpretation of Japan's political system in terms of the historical-cultural setting as well as the political dynamics and organs of government.

HISTORIES AND GENERAL WORKS ON JAPANESE RELIGION

For additional references, see the bibliographies for Buddhism, Christianity, New Religions, Shinto, and Taoism in "Special Bibliographies on Japanese History and Religion."

Abe, Yoshiya. "Religious Freedom Under the Meiji Constitution." *Contemporary Religions in Japan*, Vol. 9, No. 4 (December 1968),

268–338. This book-length work, continued in the four subsequent issues of this journal, is a balanced treatment of the
extent of religious freedom under the Meiji Constitution, discussing the background issues and factions for and against actual
religious freedom.

†Anesaki, Masaharu. *History of Japanese Religion.* London: Kegan Paul,
Trench, Trubner, 1930. Reprint ed., Rutland, Vt.: Charles E. Tuttle
Company, 1963. A standard one-volume history, somewhat
outdated.

———. "An Oriental Evaluation of Modern Civilization." In *Recent
Gains in American Civilization.* Edited by Kirby Page. New York:
Harcourt Brace Jovanovich, 1928, pp. 329–57. Reprinted in
Anesaki's *Katam Karaniyam: Lectures, Essays and Studies.* Boston:
Marshall Jones Company, 1936, pp. 32–51. A stimulating discus-
sion of the role of religion in modern civilization.

———. *Religious Life of the Japanese People.* Revised by Hideo
Kishimoto. Tokyo: Kokusai Bunka Shinkokai (Society for International Cultural Relations), 1961. A convenient overview of
Japanese religion, with valuable remarks on the turmoil of the
prewar and postwar religious situation; contains illustrations.

Armstrong, Robert Cornell. *Just Before the Dawn: The Life and Work of
Ninomiya Sontoku.* New York: Macmillan, 1912. An early popular
presentation of the life and teachings of Ninomiya Sontoku
(1787–1856), the farmer-philosopher or "peasant sage of Japan."

Basabe, Fernando M.; Anzai, Shin; and Lanzaco, Federico. *Religious
Attitudes of Japanese Men: A Sociological Survey.* Tokyo and Rutland,
Vt.: Sophia University and Charles E. Tuttle Company, 1968. An
attempt to survey belief and lack of belief by the questionnaire
method; includes questionnaires, results, and conclusions.

———; Anzai, Shin; and Nebreda, Alphonso M. *Japanese Youth Con-
fronts Religion: A Sociological Survey.* Tokyo and Rutland, Vt.:
Sophia University and Charles E. Tuttle Company, 1967. An attempt to survey religious attitudes by the questionnaire method;
includes questionnaires, results, and conclusions. (The two preceding books by Basabe et al. are summarized in a popular
paperback edition: Basabe, Fernando M. *Japanese Religious Attitudes.* Maryknoll, N.Y.: Orbis Books, 1972.)

Bellah, Robert N., ed. *Religion and Progress in Modern Asia.* New York:
Free Press, 1965. A discussion of the problem of religion and
modernity in terms of "progress."

*———. *Tokugawa Religion: The Values of Pre-Industrial Japan.* Glencoe,
Ill.: Free Press, 1957. Reprint ed., Boston: Beacon Press, 1970. A

229
*Annotated
Bibliography
on Japanese
Religion:
Selected Works*

sociological analysis of a highly eclectic Tokugawa movement; important for tracing popular values that helped shape modern Japan. See the continuation of this thesis in "Reflection on the Protestant Ethic Analogy in Asia," in Bellah's *Beyond Belief: Essays on Religion in a Post-Traditional World* (and other articles in this volume), New York: Harper & Row, 1970, pp. 53–63.

Blacker, Carmen. "Religion in Japan." In *Historia Religionum: Handbook for the History of Religions.* Vol. 2, *Religions of the Present.* Edited by C. J. Bleeker and George Widengren. Leiden: E. J. Brill, 1971, pp. 516–49. A good, brief treatment of the history and nature of Japanese religion and a short treatment of the study of religion in Japan.

*Bloom, Alfred. "Japan: Religion of a Sacred People in a Sacred Land." In *Religion and Man.* Edited by W. Richard Comstock. New York: Harper & Row, 1971, pp. 336–94. A concise summary of Shinto and Buddhism.

Bonet, Vincente M., ed. *Religion in the Japanese Textbooks.* 3 vols. Tokyo: Enderle Book Company, 1973–74. A critical review of the treatment of religion in all textbooks approved for junior and senior high schools by the Ministry of Education.

Clement, Ernest. "Calendar (Japanese)." In *Encyclopaedia of Religion and Ethics.* Edited by James Hastings. Vol. 3. Edinburgh: T. and T. Clark, 1908–26, pp. 114–17. A general picture of the Japanese calendar. (Many of the articles concerning Japanese religion in this encyclopedia are outdated.)

Davis, Winston Bradley. *Toward Modernity: A Developmental Typology of Popular Religious Affiliations in Japan.* Cornell East Asia Papers, 12. Ithaca, N.Y.: Cornell China-Japan Program, 1977. A detailed and sophisticated sociological analysis of Japanese religion, focusing on "the religious affiliations of the so-called common man."

Earhart, H. Byron. "The Ideal of Nature in Japanese Religion and Its Possible Significance for Environmental Concerns." *Contemporary Religions in Japan,* Vol. 11, Nos. 1–2 (March–June 1970), 1–26. The ideal of nature in Japanese religion is interpreted as a possible resource for environmental problems in Japan and in the West.

*† ———. *Religion in the Japanese Experience: Sources and Interpretations.* Belmont, Calif.: Wadsworth, 1974. A convenient sourcebook of brief documents revealing the history and dynamics of Japanese religion.

——— . *A Religious Study of the Mount Haguro Sect of Shugendo: An Example of Japanese Mountain Religion.* Tokyo: Sophia University,

1970. A detailed study of one Shugendo sect that incorporates influence from most Japanese religious traditions.

————. "Toward a Unified Interpretation of Japanese Religion." In *The History of Religions: Essays on the Problem of Understanding.* Edited by Joseph M. Kitagawa. Chicago: University of Chicago Press, 1967, pp. 195–225. A discussion of Western scholarship on Japanese religion in terms of the problem of understanding Japanese religion.

Erskine, William Hugh. *Japanese Festival and Calendar Lore.* Tokyo: Kyo Bun Kwan, 1933. A popular treatment of many religious aspects of the calendar, with brief descriptions of every national festival (listed by months); contains useful information on the various "cycles" governing astrological beliefs, such as lucky and unlucky days and directions, and features a complete index of Japanese calendar terms.

Frager, Robert, and Rohlen, Thomas P. "The Future of a Tradition: Japanese Spirit in the 1980s." In *Japan: The Paradox of Progress.* Edited by Lewis Austin. New Haven, Conn.: Yale University Press, 1976, pp. 255–78. An intriguing analysis of the perseverance of traditional spiritual values within many contemporary social groups, from educational institutions and companies to New Religions.

Gauntlett, John Owen, trans. *Kokutai no Hongi: Cardinal Principles of the National Entity of Japan.* Edited by Robert King Hall. Cambridge, Mass.: Harvard University Press, 1949. A translation of the nationalistic textbook used in public schools after 1938.

Haraguchi, Torao, et al. *The Status System and Social Organization of Satsuma: A Translation of the "Shumon Tefuda Aratame Jomoku."* Honolulu: University Press of Hawaii, 1976. A translation and introduction of the seventeenth-century regulations for mandatory religious registration in one area of Japan; at first a measure to proscribe Christianity, it became a means of social and political control.

†Hori, Ichiro, ed. *Japanese Religion.* Translated by Yoshiya Abe and David Reid. Tokyo: Kodansha International, 1972. A convenient one-volume treatment of Japanese religion by Japanese scholars, with concise essays on the various Japanese religious traditions and organizations; also provides addresses and statistics.

*Ikado, Fujio. *The Religious Background of Japanese Culture: The Japanese Search for Identity.* Translated by Haruko Kinase-Legget. N.p.: Nihon Kokusai Kyoiku Kyokai, 1968. A Japanese sociologist of religion's analysis of secularization, changing religious patterns, and implicit religious values in modern Japan.

Inoue, Nobutaka, et al. "A Festival with Anonymous Kami." *Japanese Journal of Religious Studies,* Vol. 6, Nos. 1–2 (March–June 1979), 163–85. Analysis and interpretation of the Kobe festival as a new kind of festival in urbanized society.

Japan. Ministry of Education. *Religions in Japan.* 2d ed. Tokyo: Government of Japan, 1963. A government publication valuable for its official statistics on organized religious bodies.

Kanamori, Tokujiro, et al. *Religion and State in Japan: A Discussion of Religion and State in Relation to the Constitution.* Bulletin No. 7. Tokyo: International Institute for the Study of Religions, 1959. Contains four articles by leading Japanese scholars discussing the historical background, and continuing problems, in interpreting religious freedom in the postwar Constitution.

Kidder, J. E., Jr. *Japan Before Buddhism.* Rev. ed. London: Thames and Hudson, 1966. The best single book on prehistoric Japan, with discussions of the religious implications of the diverse archaeological evidence.

Kishimoto, Hideo. "The Meaning of Religion to the Japanese People." In *Religious Studies in Japan.* Tokyo: Maruzen, 1959, pp. 22–28. A good contrast of Japanese religion with religion in Western civilization.

———, and Wakimoto, Tsuneya. "Introduction: Religion During Tokugawa." In *Japanese Religion in the Meiji Era.* Edited by Hideo Kishimoto. Translated by John F. Howes. Tokyo: Obunsha, 1956, pp. 3–33. This overview of religion in the Tokugawa period illustrates a critical approach to Japanese religion.

Kitagawa, Joseph M. "Prehistoric Background of Japanese Religion." *History of Religions,* Vol. 2 (Winter 1963), 292–328. A good summary of Japanese and Western scholarship on the earliest Japanese religion.

†———. *Religion in Japanese History.* New York: Columbia University Press, 1966. The most complete, up-to-date account of Japanese religion in a single volume.

———. "Religions of Japan." In *The Great Asian Religions.* Compiled by Wing-tsit Chan et al. London: Macmillan, 1969, pp. 231–305. Translated documents concerning Japanese religion from early mythology to the New Religions.

———. "Shinto" and "Mahayana Buddhism (Japan)." In *Historical Atlas of the Religions of the World.* Edited by Ismai'il Ragi al Faruqi and David E. Sopher. New York: Macmillan, 1974, pp. 127–32, 195–99. Contains maps showing distribution of population by religion and locations of important religious centers.

*LaFleur, William R. "Death and Japanese Thought: The Truth and Beauty of Impermanence." In *Death and Eastern Thought.* Edited by Frederick H. Holck. Nashville: Abingdon Press, 1974, pp. 226–56. An overview of Japanese attitudes toward death, especially those of *samurai* and Zen masters.

———. "Saigyo and the Buddhist Value of Nature." *History of Religions,* Vol. 13, No. 2 (November 1973), 93–128; Vol. 13, No. 3 (February 1974), 227–48. A detailed analysis of the appreciation of nature in early Japanese Buddhism (and Shinto), especially as seen in the poetry of the twelfth-century poet Saigyo.

Lay, Arthur Hyde. "Japanese Funeral Rites." *Transactions of the Asiatic Society of Japan,* Vol. 19 (1891), 507–44. A general survey of funeral rites from the archaeological evidence in prehistoric times through various transformations up to recent times; includes both Buddhist and Shinto practices.

*Lebra, William P. *Okinawan Religion: Belief, Ritual, and Social Structure.* Honolulu: University Press of Hawaii, 1966. A convenient overview of indigenous religion in Okinawa, useful for comparison and contrast with indigenous religion in the Japanese tradition.

Ludwig, Theodore M. "The Way of Tea: A Religio-Aesthetic Mode of Life." *History of Religions,* Vol. 14, No. 1 (August 1974), 28–50. A treatment of the art of the "tea way" as representing "a total religio-aesthetic way of life."

†Morioka, Kiyomi. *Religion in Changing Japanese Society.* Tokyo: University of Tokyo Press, 1975. A collection of short essays on the interaction of social factors and religion and the changing character of religion in the postwar period.

———, and Newell, William H., eds. *The Sociology of Japanese Religion.* Leiden: E. J. Brill, 1968 (*Journal of Asian and African Studies,* Vol. 3, Nos. 1–2 [January–April 1968], 1–138). Short, scholarly articles featuring sociological analysis of folk religion, Buddhism, Christianity, and the New Religions.

Munro, Neil Gordon. *Ainu Creed and Cult.* London: Routledge & Kegan Paul, 1962. A descriptive work based on field work earlier in this century, it includes numerous photographs.

†Murakami, Shigeyoshi. *Japanese Religion in the Modern Century.* Translated by H. Byron Earhart. Tokyo: University of Tokyo Press, 1980. A critical analysis of government suppression of religion

before 1945 and the conditions of freedom of religion since 1945; includes broad coverage of the New Religions.

*Nakamura, Hajime. *Ways of Thinking of Eastern Peoples: India, China, Tibet, Japan*. Revised English translation edited by Philip P. Wiener. Honolulu: East-West Center Press, 1964. An attempt to describe the peculiarity of the Japanese people through the thought patterns that define their culture.

Nishida, Kitaro. *Nishida Kitaro's Fundamental Problems of Philosophy: The World of Action and the Dialectical World*. Translated with an Introduction by David A. Dilworth. Tokyo: Sophia University, 1970. Two of Nishida's later (1934–35) works, representing the mature "Nishida philosophy" of the pure experience understood in terms of his own Zen experience and in terms of Western philosophy.

—————. *A Study of Good*. Translated by V. H. Viglielmo. Tokyo: Ministry of Education, 1960. Nishida, considered the foremost Japanese philosopher of this century, in his first (1911) publication wrote what some consider to be the first original Japanese philosophical work to incorporate both Western and Japanese traditions.

Nishitani, Keiji. "The Religious Situation in Present-Day Japan." *Contemporary Religions in Japan*, Vol. 1, No. 1 (March 1960), 7–24. A famous philosopher's analysis of contemporary Japanese religion, especially religious indifference and nihilism.

Norbeck, Edward. *Religion and Society in Modern Japan: Continuity and Change*. Houston: Tourmaline Press, 1970. A treatment of modern Japanese religion as a functional response to social and economic change.

Oguchi, Iichi, and Takagi, Hiroo. "Religion and Social Development." In *Japanese Religion in the Meiji Era*. Edited by Hideo Kishimoto. Translated by John F. Howes. Tokyo: Obunsha, 1956, pp. 311–57. Interprets the background of Meiji religion, as determined by social and economic factors.

†Ooms, Herman. "A Structural Analysis of Japanese Ancestral Rites and Beliefs." In *Ancestors*. Edited by William H. Newell. The Hague: Mouton Publishers, 1976, pp. 61–90. The most systematic interpretation of the Japanese rites and beliefs related to ancestors; especially helpful for gaining a quick overview of the nature of such customs.

Otsuka, Yasuo. "Chinese Traditional Medicine in Japan." In *Asian Medical Systems: A Comparative Study*. Edited by Charles Leslie.

Berkeley: University of California Press, 1976, pp. 322–40. A historical overview of Chinese traditional medicine (the use of acupuncture, moxibustion, and traditional substances) as accepted in Japan.

Pilgrim, Richard. "Zeami and the Way of No." *History of Religions,* Vol. 12, No. 2 (November 1972), 136–48. An interpretation of the spiritual and mental discipline in the No drama as leading to religious realization.

Piovesana, Gino K. *Recent Japanese Philosophical Thought, 1862–1962: A Survey.* Tokyo: Enderle Bookstore, 1963. A survey of the broad range of Western philosophy among Japanese philosophers.

Plath, David W. "Where the Family of God Is the Family: The Role of the Dead in Japanese Households." *American Anthropologist,* Vol. 66, No. 2 (April 1964), 300–17. Criticism of the older notion of ancestor worship and suggestion of its replacement with the three categories of the departed, ancestors, and outsiders.

†*Proceedings of Tokyo Meeting of the International Conference on Sociology of Religion, 1978.* Reprinted "as subsequently corrected and edited" in *Japanese Journal of Religious Studies,* Vol. 6, Nos. 1–2 (March–June 1979), 1–386. A valuable collection of essays interpreting "secularization," modern religious activities, and New Religions.

Religious Studies in Japan. Edited by Japanese Association for Religious Studies. Tokyo: Maruzen, 1959. Excellent short articles by the leading Japanese authorities on various subjects.

Sansom, Sir George. "Early Japanese Law and Administration." *Transactions of the Asiatic Society of Japan,* Second Series, Vol. 9 (1932), 67–109; Vol. 11 (1935), 117–49. Includes a description of the governmental department of religion in ancient Japan.

Union of the New Religious Organization in Japan, Research Office, ed. "Reminiscences of Religion in Postwar Japan." *Contemporary Religions in Japan,* Vol. 6, No. 2 (June 1965), 111–203. This book-length work, continued in five subsequent issues of this journal, provides a valuable inside view of the changed conditions and rapid developments among all religious organizations in postwar Japan.

Woodard, William P. *The Allied Occupation of Japan, 1945–1952, and Japanese Religions.* Leiden: E. J. Brill, 1972. A detailed analysis of religious developments and the Allied policy toward religion in the occupation period.

———. "Study on Religious Juridical Persons Law: Text of the Law No. 126 of 1951." *Contemporary Japan,* Vol. 25, No. 3 (September 1958), 418–70; Vol. 25, No. 4 (March 1959), 635–57; Vol. 26, No. 1

(August 1959), 96–115; Vol. 26, No. 2 (December 1959), 239–312.

235
*Annotated
Bibliography
on Japanese
Religion:
Selected Works*
Text and discussion of the new law governing religious bodies in
postwar Japan.

SHINTO

For additional references, see Herbert, Kato, and Kitagawa in "Special Bibliographies on Japanese History and Religion."

Aoki, Michiko Yamaguchi. *Ancient Myths and Early History of Japan: A
Cultural Foundation.* New York: Exposition Press, 1974. A discussion of ancient Japanese myths in the light of archaeology and
local traditions.

———, trans. *Izumo Fudoki.* Tokyo: Sophia University, 1971. Translation and critical introduction to an eighth-century document recording local legends and religious practices.

*Aston, W. G., trans. *Nihongi: Chronicles of Japan from the Earliest Times
to A.D. 697.* Originally published in *Transactions of the Japan Society,*
Supplement 1. London, 1896. Reprint ed., two volumes in one
with original pagination, London: Allen & Unwin, 1956. Reprint
ed., Tokyo: Charles E. Tuttle Company, 1978. Covers the same
period as the *Kojiki* but adds other tales, adopts a Chinese style
of writing, and continues the chronology to A.D. 697.

Bock, Felicia Gressitt, trans. *Engi-Shiki: Procedures of the Engi Era,
Books I–V.* Tokyo: Sophia University, 1970. A translation of
eighth-century government regulations concerning Shinto
shrines, their administration, and rituals; includes introductory
chapters on early Shinto.

———, trans. *Engi-Shiki: Procedures of the Engi Era, Books, VI–X.*
Tokyo: Sophia University, 1972. Continuation of the preceding work.

*Bownas, G. "Shinto." In *The Concise Encyclopedia of Living Faiths.*
Edited by R. C. Zaehner. Boston: Beacon Press, 1967, pp. 348–64.
A good, brief discussion of early Shinto in terms of purification
from pollution.

Buchanan, Daniel C. "Inari: Its Origin, Development and Nature."
Transactions of the Asiatic Society of Japan. Second Series, Vol. 12
(1935), 1–191. Somewhat dated but one of the few studies of a
Shinto cult—its origins, beliefs, and practices.

———. "Some Mikuji of Fushimi Inari Jinja." *Monumenta Nipponica,*
Vol. 2, No. 2 (July 1939), 518–35. A general article on "fortunes"

(*mikuji*) with an illustration of a *mikuji* and translation of ten
fortunes.

Chamberlain, Basil Hall, trans. "*Ko-ji-ki,* or Records of Ancient Matters." *Transactions of the Asiatic Society of Japan,* Vol. 10, Supplement (1882). Reprinted as separate volume, New Edition (with
"Additional notes by William George Aston"), Kobe: J. L.
Thompson & Company, 1932. Reprint ed., Tokyo: Asiatic Society
of Japan, 1973. The oldest written chronicle in Japan, combining
mythology and court chronology to about the end of the fifth
century A.D. (For a more recent translation see Philipi.)

Creemers, Wilhelmus H. M. *Shrine Shinto After World War II.* Leiden:
E. J. Brill, 1968. A detailed study of the status and organization
of Shinto, especially the impact of reorganization after World
War II.

Ellwood, Robert S. *The Feast of Kingship: Accession Ceremonies in Ancient Japan.* Tokyo: Sophia University, 1973. A detailed study of
Shinto rituals for the emperor's accession; also includes the general Shinto background of the rituals.

Fridell, Wilbur M. *Japanese Shrine Mergers, 1906–12: State Shinto Moves
to the Grassroots.* Tokyo: Sophia University, 1973. A detailed analysis of state Shinto in terms of shrine mergers—the general policies, their implementation, and overall results.

Hepner, Charles William. *The Kurozumi Sect of Shinto.* Tokyo: Meiji
Japan Society, 1935. Reprint ed., New York: Garland Publishing,
1978. An early study of the life and teachings of the founder of a
Shinto sect and its organization.

*Hirai, Naofusa. *Japanese Shinto.* Bulletin No. 18. Tokyo: International
Society for Educational Information, 1966. A general introduction
to Shinto.

Holtom, Daniel C. "The Meaning of Kami." *Monumenta Nipponica,*
Vol. 3 (1940), 1–27, 32–53; Vol. 4 (1941), 25–68. An attempt to
interpret the Japanese term *kami* through the Melanesian term
mana.

————. *Modern Japan and Shinto Nationalism: A Study of Present-Day
Trends in Japanese Religions.* Rev. ed. Chicago: University of
Chicago Press, 1947. Reprint ed., New York: Paragon Book Re-
print Corp., 1963. A good historical treatment of nationalistic
Shinto, including chapters on the accommodation of Christianity
and Buddhism to Japanese nationalism.

†————. *The National Faith of Japan: A Study in Modern Shinto.* New
York: Dutton, 1938. Reprint ed., New York: Paragon Book Reprint

Corp., 1965. Important for its historical information on Shinto; the section on sect Shinto is a good overview.

237
*Annotated
Bibliography
on Japanese
Religion:
Selected Works*

†Hori, Ichiro, and Toda, Yoshio. "Shinto." In *Japanese Religion in the Meiji Era*. Edited by Hideo Kishimoto. Translated by John F. Howes. Tokyo: Obunsha, 1956, pp. 35–98. A balanced treatment of Shinto in the Meiji period.

Institute for Japanese Culture and Classics, Kokugakuin University. *Proceedings, The Second International Conference for Shinto Studies.* Tokyo: Kokugakuin University, 1968. Collected papers by Japanese and Western scholars from a conference dealing with continuity and change in Shinto.

Kageyama, Haruki. *The Arts of Shinto.* Translated by Christine Guth. New York: Weatherhill/Shibundo, 1973. Treats the arts of Shinto in terms of their religious context; includes more than one hundred excellent plates illustrating Shinto arts.

Kato, Genchi. "The Theological System of Urabe no Kanetomo." *Transactions of the Japan Society of London,* Vol. 28 (1931), 143–50. A good treatment of the Shinto theologian Kanetomo, emphasizing his significance for later Shinto thinkers.

———, and Hoshino, Hikoshiro, trans. *Kogoshui: Gleanings from Ancient Stories.* 2d ed., rev. Tokyo: Meiji Japan Society, 1925. Written about A.D. 807, it records a rivalry between several Shinto priestly families.

The Manyoshu. Translated by the Japan Society for the Promotion of Scientific Research. Tokyo: Iwanami Shoten, 1940. Reprint ed., New York: Columbia University Press, 1965. Compiled in the eighth century, it is an invaluable source of ancient Japanese poetry and religion.

Matsumoto, Shigeru. *Motoori Norinaga, 1730–1801.* Cambridge, Mass.: Harvard University Press, 1970. A detailed study of the life and writings of the foremost scholar and proponent of Restoration Shinto.

Mizoguchi, Komazo. "Orientation in the Study of Shintoism." In *A Guide to Japanese Studies.* Tokyo: Kokusai Bunka Shinkokai (Society for International Cultural Relations), 1937, pp. 137–53. A prewar appeal for a historical-scientific study of Shinto. Other articles in this prewar volume and other works published by Kokusai Bunka Shinkokai (Society for International Cultural Relations) are valuable.

†Muraoka, Tsunetsugu. *Studies in Shinto Thought.* Translated by Delmer M. Brown and James T. Araki. Tokyo: Ministry of Educa-

tion, 1964. Scholarly articles on the nature of Shinto, with close attention to major proponents of Shinto thought systems.

Ono, Sokyo. *Shinto: The Kami Way.* Tokyo: Bridgeway Press, 1962. A systematic or "theological" interpretation of Shinto by a contemporary Shinto scholar.

Philippi, Donald L., trans. *Kojiki.* Tokyo: University of Tokyo Press, 1968. A recent translation emphasizing linguistic accuracy.

————, trans. *Norito: A New Translation of the Ancient Japanese Ritual Prayers.* Tokyo: Institute for Japanese Culture and Classics, Kokugakuin University, 1959. The most recent scholarly translation of the *norito,* with brief notes.

Ponsonby-Fane, R. A. B. *Studies in Shinto and Shrines.* Rev. ed. Kamikamo, Kyoto: Ponsonby Memorial Society, 1953. Collected articles of a technical nature by a lifelong student of Shinto. This is the first volume of the six-volume series of Ponsonby-Fane's works, all of which contain valuable detailed articles.

Sadler, A. L., trans. *The Ise Daijingu or Diary of a Pilgrim to Ise.* Introduction by Genchi Kato. Tokyo: Meiji Japan Society, 1940. This fourteenth-century pilgrim's diary provides an inside view of sincerity and piety in a Shinto context.

Satow, Sir Ernest, and Florenz, Karl. "Ancient Japanese Rituals." *Transactions of the Asiatic Society, Reprints,* Vol. 2 (1927), 5–164. An older translation of *norito* (ritual prayers) with illustrations and commentary on their religious significance.

*Saunders, E. Dale. "Japanese Mythology." In *Mythologies of the Ancient World.* Edited by S. N. Kramer. New York: Doubleday Anchor Books, 1961, pp. 409–40. A brief overview of the central myth and regional tales in Japanese mythology.

Schneider, Delwin B. *Konkokyo, a Japanese Religion: A Study in the Continuities of Native Faiths.* Tokyo: International Institute for the Study of Religions, 1962. An overview of the emergence of the new religion Konkokyo out of earlier Japanese religion, and its major practices.

Schwartz, M. L. "The Great Shrines of Idzumo: Some Notes on Shinto, Ancient and Modern." *Transactions of the Asiatic Society of Japan,* Vol. 61, Pt. 4 (1913), 493–681. An early description of a major Shinto shrine, with translations of shrine documents.

Starr, Frederick. "Ema." *Transactions of the Asiatic Society of Japan,* Vol. 48 (1920), 1–22. A general description (with many illustrations) of the *ema,* literally "horse-pictures," or votive offerings traditionally hung at Shinto shrines.

†Tange, Kenzo, and Kawazoe, Noboru. *Ise: Prototype of Japanese Architecture.* Cambridge, Mass.: M.I.T. Press, 1965. A large photo study of Ise, the most important Shinto shrine complex, with an introduction to its architecture and a closing essay on the religious and cultural features of the shrine.

†Ueda, Kenji. "Shinto." In *Japanese Religion.* Edited by Ichiro Hori. Translated by Yoshiya Abe and David Reid. Tokyo: Kodansha International, 1972, pp. 29–45. A concise overview of the aspects and dynamics of Shinto.

Watanabe, Yasutada. *Shinto Art: Ise and Izumo Shrines.* Translated by Robert Ricketts. Heibonsha Survey of Japanese Art, Vol. 3. New York: Weatherhill/Heibonsha, 1974. A lavish presentation (180 plates) and general introduction to the architectural form of two of the most important Shinto shrines, with brief comments on other shrine types.

BUDDHISM

For additional references, see Bando, Beautrix, Kitagawa, Reynolds, and Vessie in "Special Bibliographies on Japanese History and Religion."

Akamatsu, Toshihide, and Yampolksy, Philip. "Muromachi Zen and the Gozan System." In *Japan in the Muromachi Age.* Edited by John Whitney Hall and Takeshi Toyoda. Berkeley: University of California Press, 1977, pp. 313–29. A detailed analysis of the *gozan* (five temple) system and its political, cultural, and ecclesiastical significance.

Andrews, Allan. *The Teachings Essential for Rebirth: A Study of Genshin's Ojoyoshu.* Tokyo: Sophia University, 1973. A study of the Tendai priest Genshin's writing *Ojoyoshu*, which emphasized faith in Amida, influential in the development of Pure Land Buddhism.

Anesaki, Masaharu. *Nichiren the Buddhist Prophet.* Cambridge, Mass.: Harvard University Press, 1916. Still the standard work, a study from the viewpoint of religious psychology.

Bloom, Alfred. *Shinran's Gospel of Pure Grace.* Tucson: University of Arizona Press, 1965. A recent study of Shinran's thought.

*Ch'en, Kenneth. *Buddhism in China: A Historical Survey.* Princeton, N.J.: Princeton University Press, 1964. A scholarly, detailed survey of Chinese Buddhism, including descriptions of major Buddhist schools; useful as a background to the study of Japanese Buddhism.

Coates, Harper Havelock, and Ishizuka, Ryugaku. *Honen the Buddhist Saint: His Life and Teaching.* Kyoto: Chion-in, 1925; several later reprintings. A careful study of Honen; valuable for its wider treatment of Buddhism.

Collcutt, Martin. *Five Mountains: The Rinzai Monastic Institution in Medieval Japan.* Cambridge, Mass.: Harvard University Press, 1981. A detailed historical study of Rinzai Zen temples as social and economic institutions.

*Conze, Edward. *Buddhism: Its Essence and Development.* New York: Philosophical Library, 1951. Reprint ed., New York: Harper & Row, 1959. A general and concise introduction to Buddhism, valuable for its interpretation of the various schools and philosophies within Buddhism.

*†de Bary, William Theodore, et al. *The Buddhist Tradition in India, China, & Japan.* New York: Modern Library, 1969. A convenient anthology of translated texts (the materials on Japanese Buddhism are taken from de Bary's *Sources of Japanese Tradition*).

de Visser, Marinus Willem. *Ancient Buddhism in Japan: Sutras and Ceremonies in Use in the Seventh and Eighth Centuries A.D. and Their History in Later Times.* 2 vols. Leiden: E. J. Brill, 1935. Difficult reading, but the most authoritative Western reference.

————. *The Bodhisattva Ti-tsang (Jizo) in China and Japan.* Berlin: Oesterheld, 1914. A literary study of Jizo, one of the most important *bodhisattvas* in Japanese Buddhism.

*†Dumoulin, Heinrich. *A History of Zen Buddhism.* Translated by Paul Peachey. New York: Pantheon Books, 1963; several reprints. The best historical treatment of Zen, with a balanced consideration of the relationship between the history of Zen and the "essence" of Zen; contains a valuable bibliography.

Eliot, Sir Charles. *Japanese Buddhism.* London: Edward Arnold, 1935. Reprint ed., London: Routledge & Kegan Paul, 1959. An early handbook, it emphasizes continuity with Indian and Chinese Buddhism.

Foard, James H. "In Search of a Lost Reformation: A Reconsideration of Kamakura Buddhism." *Japanese Journal of Religious Studies,* Vol. 7, No. 4 (December 1980), 261–91. A reassessment of early Japanese Buddhist groups in sociological terms, reserving the label of "sect" for Jodo, Jodo Shinshu, and Nichiren groups.

Hakeda, Yoshito S., trans. *Kukai: Major Works.* New York: Columbia University Press, 1972. A scholarly introduction to the life and thought of the founder of Shingon Buddhism with translations of his works.

241
*Annotated
Bibliography
on Japanese
Religion:
Selected Works*

Hanayama, Shinsho, et al. "Buddhism in Japan." In *The Path of the Buddha*. Edited by Kenneth W. Morgan. New York: Ronald Press, 1956, pp. 307–63. A short treatment by leading Japanese scholars.

Hanayama, Shoyu, ed. *Understanding Japanese Buddhism*. Tokyo: The 12th WFB Confab Japan Committee, Japan Buddhist Federation, 1978. A volume of essays on the "history and thought," "life and culture," and "sources of information" concerning Japanese Buddhism by Japanese Buddhist scholars; some of the interpretive sections and especially the bibliography and reference sections are interesting and valuable.

Honpa Hongwanji Mission of Hawaii, comp. *The Shinshu Seiten: The Holy Scripture of Shinshu*. 2d ed. Translated by Kosho Yamamoto. Honolulu: Honpa Hongwanji Mission of Pure Land Buddhism, 1961.

Hurvitz, Leon Nahum. *Chih-i (538–597): An Introduction to the Life and Ideas of a Chinese Buddhist Monk*. Brussels: Institut belge des hautes études chinoises, 1962. A detailed account of the founder of T'ien-t'ai (Tendai) Buddhism.

Kamstra, J. H. *Encounter or Syncretism: The Initial Growth of Japanese Buddhism*. Leiden: E. J. Brill, 1967. A technical study of the introduction of Buddhism into Japan and its interrelationships with Chinese, Korean, and Japanese culture.

*Kapleau, Philip. *The Three Pillars of Zen: Teaching, Practice, and Enlightenment*. Boston: Beacon Press, 1967. Interprets the nature of Zen practice and its significance for modern men and women; includes autobiographical accounts by modern practitioners of Zen.

*Kern, H., trans. *Saddharma-Pundarika or The Lotus of the True Law*. Sacred Books of the East, Vol. 20. Reprint ed., New York: Dover Publications, 1963. A translation of one of the most important Buddhist texts in all of East Asia; it is central to some Japanese sects such as Tendai and Nichiren.

Kidder, J. Edward. *Early Buddhist Japan*. New York: Praeger Publishers, 1975. An archaeological study of the earliest traces of Buddhism in Japan (with a brief chapter on Shinto ritual sites).

Kim, Hee-Jin. *Dogen Kigen: Mystical Realist*. Association for Asian Studies, Monograph No. 29. Tucson: University of Arizona Press, 1975. The first major English-language work on the founding figure of Soto Zen, Dogen, considered by many Japanese to be the most creative Japanese thinker in the premodern era.

Kitagawa, Joseph M. "The Buddhist Transformation in Japan." *History of Religions*, Vol. 4, No. 2 (Winter 1965), 319–36. His division of Buddhism into national Buddhism and folk Buddhism is suggestive of the religious situation in Japanese history.

————. "Master and Saviour." In *Studies of Esoteric Buddhism and Tantrism: In Commemoration of the 1,150th Anniversary of the Founding of Koyasan*. Koyasan, Japan: Koyasan University, 1965, pp. 1–26. A valuable biography of Kobo Daishi, emphasizing his significance for popular religion.

†Kiyota, Minoru. "Buddhism in Postwar Japan: A Critical Survey." *Monumenta Nipponica*, Vol. 24, Nos. 1–2 (1969), 113–36. Analyzes the shortcomings of postwar Buddhism by reference to the success of New Religions such as Soka Gakkai.

————. "Presuppositions to the Understanding of Japanese Buddhist Thought." *Monumenta Nipponica*, Vol. 22, Nos. 3–4 (1967), 251–59. A technical treatment of Japanese Buddhist thought in relation to Mahayana philosophy.

————. *Shingon Buddhism: Theory and Practice*. Los Angeles: Buddhist Books International, 1978. The only comprehensive treatment of Shingon doctrine in English, this technical analysis focuses on the basic sutras, *mandala*, and practice that lead to the Shingon goal of "instant Buddhahood"; features a helpful glossary of Buddhist terms.

Masunaga, Reiho. *The Soto Approach to Zen*. Tokyo: Layman Buddhist Society Press, 1958. A popular treatment by a leading scholar.

Masutani, Fumio, and Undo, Yoshimichi. "Buddhism." In *Japanese Religion in the Meiji Era*. Edited by Hideo Kishimoto. Translated by John F. Howes. Tokyo: Obunsha, 1956, pp. 99–169. A balanced treatment of Buddhism in the Meiji period.

Matsunaga, Alicia. *The Buddhist Philosophy of Assimilation: The Historical Development of the Honji-Suijaku Theory*. Tokyo and Rutland, Vt.: Sophia University and Charles E. Tuttle Company, 1969. Interprets the interaction between aspects of Buddhism and aspects of Japanese culture.

†Matsunaga, Daigan, and Matsunaga, Alicia. *Foundation of Japanese Buddhism*. 2 vols. Los Angeles: Buddhist Books International, 1974. The most complete survey of Buddhist sects in English, from the appearance of Buddhism in Japan through the medieval period.

Nakamura, Kyoko Motomochi, trans. *Miraculous Stories from the Japanese Buddhist Tradition: The Nihon Ryoiki of the Monk Kyokai*. Cambridge, Mass.: Harvard University Press, 1973. Translation of a ninth-century document, "the earliest collection of Buddhist legends in Japan," which was important for the spread of Buddhism; a valuable overview of the ninth-century world-view is also provided.

Annotated Bibliography on Japanese Religion: Selected Works

*†Niwa, Fumio. *The Buddha Tree*. Translated by Kenneth Strong. London: Peter Owen, 1966; Rutland, Vt.: Charles E. Tuttle Company, 1971. A novel that spins a complicated web of human emotions within the setting of a Pure Land Buddhist temple; valuable for one Buddhist interpretation of the problem of desire and human failing.

Reischauer, Edwin O., trans. *Ennin's Diary: The Record of a Pilgrimage to China in Search of the Law*. New York: Ronald Press, 1953. The Japanese monk Ennin (792–862), who spent the years 838 to 847 in China studying Buddhism, has recorded in his diary a rare Japanese perception of Chinese Buddhism.

———. *Ennin's Travels in T'ang China*. New York: Ronald Press, 1955. Commentary and interpretation based on the translation of Ennin's diary.

*†Robinson, Richard H., and Johnson, Willard L. *The Buddhist Religion: A Historical Introduction*. 2d ed. Belmont, Calif.: Wadsworth, 1977. A brief survey of Buddhism, its philosophical and religious developments, and geographical expansion; includes a bibliography.

Saunders, E. Dale. *Mudra: A Study of Symbolic Gestures in Japanese Buddhist Sculpture*. New York: Pantheon Books, 1960. A detailed study of the artistic expression of esoteric Buddhism (and Buddhist sculpture in general), with profuse illustrations.

Sawa, Takaaki (or Ryuken). *Art in Japanese Esoteric Buddhism*. Translated by Richard L. Gage. Heibonsha Survey of Japanese Art, Vol. 8. New York: Weatherhill/Heibonsha, 1972. A good survey of esoteric Buddhist temples, *mandala*, and deities, with lavish illustrations.

*Suzuki, D. T. *Zen and Japanese Culture*. New York: Pantheon Books, 1959. Perceptive essays on the Zen penetration of Japanese culture by the foremost Zen spokesman. (Many of Suzuki's works are in paperback editions.)

†Tamaru, Noriyoshi. "Buddhism." In *Japanese Religion*. Edited by Ichiro Hori. Translated by Yoshiya Abe and David Reid. Tokyo: Kodansha International, 1972, pp. 47–69. A concise overview of the origin and historical development of Japanese Buddhism.

*Tsukamoto, Zenryu. "Japanese and Chinese Buddhism." In *Religions and the Promise of the Twentieth Century*. Edited by Guy S. Metraux and François Crouzet. New York: New American Library, 1965, pp. 229–44. A famous Buddhist scholar's critical analysis of the stagnation of "formalized Buddhism" in Tokugawa times and the resulting dilemma for contemporary Buddhism.

Ui, Hakuju. "A Study of Japanese Tendai Buddhism." In *Philosophical Studies of Japan*, Vol. 1, pp. 33–74. Compiled by Japanese National Commission for UNESCO. Tokyo: Japan Society for the Promotion of Science, 1959. A detailed analysis of Tendai doctrine, comparing its Chinese origins with its Japanese developments.

*Watanabe, Shoko. *Japanese Buddhism: A Critical Appraisal.* Translated by Alfred Bloom. Tokyo: Kokusai Bunka Shinkokai, 1964. A frank analysis of "the strong and weak points of Japanese Buddhism" by a Buddhist priest.

*Weinstein, Stanley. "Rennyo and the Shinshu Revival." In *Japan in the Muromachi Age.* Edited by John Whitney Hall and Takeshi Toyoda. Berkeley: University of California Press, 1977, pp. 331–58. A detailed analysis of Pure Land (Shinshu) developments from Shinran to Rennyo, when definitive doctrinal and ecclesiastical forms took shape.

Yampolsky, Philip B., trans. *The Zen Master Hakuin: Selected Writings.* New York: Columbia University Press, 1971. Translation of excerpts from works of an important Zen (Rinzai) master, preceded by a helpful introduction to Hakuin and Rinzai Zen.

CONFUCIANISM

For additional references, see Dobson, Fu and Chan, and Kitagawa in "Special Bibliographies on Japanese History and Religion."

Armstrong, Robert C. *Light from the East: Studies in Japanese Confucianism.* Toronto: University of Toronto, 1914. One of the first English-language surveys of Japanese Confucianism.

Bito, Masahide. "Ogyu Sorai and the Distinguishing Features of Japanese Confucianism." In *Japanese Thought in the Tokugawa Period, 1600–1868: Methods and Metaphors.* Edited by Tetsuo Najita and Irwin Scheiner. Chicago: University of Chicago Press, 1978, pp. 153–60. A brief but technical article that concludes that this particular Japanese thinker (Ogyu Sorai) did not simply ape Chinese Confucian thought but "reflects Japanese social consciousness."

*†Creel, H. G. *Confucius: The Man and the Myth*. New York: John Day Company, 1949. Reprinted as *Confucius and the Chinese Way*. New York: Harper & Row, 1960. A general introduction to the life and thought of Confucius and his influence on Chinese culture.

Fisher, Galen M. "Kumazawa Banzan, His Life and Ideas." *Transactions of the Asiatic Society of Japan*, Second Series, Vol. 16 (May 1938), 221–58. A brief study of the biography and thought of a Confucian thinker of the Oyomei school.

*†Hall, John Whitney. "The Confucian Teacher in Tokugawa Japan." In *Confucianism in Action*. Edited by David S. Nivison and Arthur F. Wright. Stanford, Calif.: Stanford University Press, 1959, pp. 268–301. Describes the Confucian contribution to Tokugawa Japan and its relationship to Shinto and Buddhism.

Ishida, Ichiro. "Tokugawa Feudal Society and Neo-Confucian Thought." In *Philosophical Studies of Japan*. Vol. 5. Edited by Japanese National Commission for UNESCO. Tokyo, 1964, pp. 1–37. A technical article analyzing Neo-Confucian thought and its significance in terms of "a secularized religion."

Kaibara, Ekken. *The Way of Contentment*. Translated by Ken Hoshino. London: John Murray, 1913; New York: Dutton, 1913. One of the few translations of the writings of this Neo-Confucian thinker.

*Shively, Donald H. "Motoda Eifu: Confucian Lecturer to the Meiji Emperor." In *Confucianism in Action*. Edited by David S. Nivison and Arthur F. Wright. Stanford, Calif.: Stanford University Press, 1959, pp. 302–33. An interpretation of the life and thought of Motoda Eifu (1818–91), who after the Meiji Restoration was "the man who more than any other was responsible for this resurgence of Confucianism."

Shryock, John K. *The Origin and Development of the State Cult of Confucius: An Introductory Study*. New York: Century, 1932. Reprint ed., New York: Paragon Book Reprint Corp., 1966. A scholarly overview of the formal cult of Confucius in China.

†Smith, Warren W., Jr. *Confucianism in Modern Japan: A Study of Conservatism in Japanese Intellectual History*. 2d ed. Tokyo: Hokuseido Press, 1973. A good treatment of Confucianism's (Neo-Confucianism's) cultural impact in Japan from 1600 through postwar times.

Spae, Joseph John. *Ito Jinsai: A Philosopher, Educator and Sinologist of the Tokugawa Period*. Monograph 12, *Monumenta Serica: Journal of Oriental Studies of the Catholic University of Peiping*, 1948. Reprint ed., New York: Paragon Book Reprint Corp., 1967. A detailed study of one Confucian thinker, especially valuable for the long first chapter, "Historical Notes on Confucianism in Japan."

Takaishi, Shingoro. *Women and Wisdom of Japan.* London: John Murray, 1905. Takaishi provides a "traditional" rationale for the role of women in Japan as an introduction to a translation of the "Greater Learning for Women" by Kaibara Ekken (1630–1714), a Neo-Confucianist who summarized and popularized Confucianism; the same translation can be found in Chamberlain, *Things Japanese,* "Woman (Status of)," listed in "Histories and Works on Japanese Culture."

†Tomikura, Mitsuo. "Confucianism." In *Japanese Religion.* Edited by Ichiro Hori. Translated by Yoshiya Abe and David Reid. Tokyo: Kodansha International, 1972, pp. 105–22. A concise overview of the role of Confucianism in Japanese thought and society.

*†Tsunoda, Ryusaku, et al. *Sources of Japanese Tradition.* New York: Columbia University Press, 1958. See Chapters 16–18 for translations and interpretations of Japanese Neo-Confucian thinkers.

*Waley, Arthur, trans. *The Analects of Confucius.* London: Allen & Unwin, 1938. Reprint ed., New York: Random House, 1966. A standard translation of the collected teachings of Confucius.

RELIGIOUS TAOISM

For additional references, see Dobson, Fu and Chan, and Yu in "Special Bibliographies on Japanese History and Religion."

Frank, Bernard. "Kata-imi et Kata-tagae: Étude sur les Interdits de direction a l'époque Heian." *Bulletin de la Maison Franco-Japonaise,* Nouvelle Série, Tome 5, Nos. 2–4 (1958), 1–246. The only lengthy treatment of the problem, but concerned mainly with the influence of religious Taoism upon medieval literature.

*Kaltenmark, Max. *Lao Tzu and Taoism.* Translated by Roger Greaves. Stanford, Calif.: Stanford University Press, 1969. A general treatment of the tradition of Taoism, its legendary founder (Lao Tzu), and its religious practices.

†Kubo, Noritada. "Introduction of Taoism to Japan." In *Religious Studies in Japan.* Tokyo: Maruzen, 1959, pp. 457–65. A good summary of an important Taoistic cult.

Miller, Alan L. "Ritsuryo Japan: The State as Liturgical Community." *History of Religions,* Vol. 11, No. 1 (August 1971), 98–124. Includes

247
*Annotated
Bibliography
on Japanese
Religion:
Selected Works*

descriptions of the bureau of *yin* and *yang* (Onmyoryo) in early Japan.

Saunders, E. Dale. "Koshin: An Example of Taoist Ideas in Japan." In *Proceedings of the IXth International Congress for the History of Religions*, pp. 423–32. Tokyo: Maruzen, 1960. Analyzes the history of Koshin and its dynamics as a Taoist cult.

†Seidel, Anna K. "Taoism." In *Encyclopaedia Britannica*. 15th ed. Vol. 17. Chicago: Encyclopaedia Britannica, 1978, pp. 1034–44. A succinct summary and interpretation of the various aspects of Taoism and its interaction with Confucianism.

*Waley, Arthur, trans. *The Way and Its Power: A Study of the Tao Te Ching and Its Place in Chinese Thought*. London: Allen & Unwin, 1934. Reprint ed., New York: Grove Press, 1958. A standard translation and helpful interpretation of a basic philosophical text of Taoism.

*Welch, Holmes. *Taoism: The Parting of the Way*. Boston: Beacon Press, 1957; rev. ed., 1965. A general introduction to the *Tao Te Ching* and a more detailed account of the history of Taoist movements.

FOLK RELIGION

For additional references, see Kitagawa in "Special Bibliographies on Japanese History and Religion."

Bernier, Bernard. *Breaking the Cosmic Circle: Religion in a Japanese Village*. Cornell East Asia Papers, 5. Ithaca, N.Y.: Cornell China-Japan Program, 1975. A description of the annual cycle and life cycle of religion in a fishing village of the late 1960s; comments on the role of two New Religions in this village.

†Blacker, Carmen. *The Catalpa Bow: A Study of Shamanistic Practices in Japan*. London: Allen & Unwin, 1975. The first comprehensive interpretation of shamanistic practices in Japan; rich with literary accounts of shamanism and observations of contemporary "shamans."

Bownas, Geoffrey. *Japanese Rainmaking and Other Folk Practices*. London: Allen & Unwin, 1963. Popular descriptions of folk religion and customs.

Casal, U. A. *The Five Sacred Festivals of Ancient Japan: Their Symbolism & Historical Development*. Tokyo and Rutland, Vt.: Sophia University and Charles E. Tuttle Company, 1967. A colorful description of the

major annual Japanese festivals showing the interpenetration of
Buddhism and Shinto in folk religion.

Czaja, Michael. *Gods of Myths and Stone: Phallicism in Japanese Folk
Religion.* New York: Weatherhill, 1974. A popular treatment, valuable especially for the hundred plates of the traditional stone
statues of Dosojin.

*†Dorson, Richard M. *Folk Legends of Japan.* Rutland, Vt.: Charles E.
Tuttle Company, 1962. A topical collection with brief introductions for each tale.

†———, ed. *Studies in Japanese Folklore.* Chief translator, Yasuyo Ishiwara. Bloomington: Indiana University Press, 1963. Translated
articles by leading Japanese folklorists, with a helpful introductory chapter on Japanese folklore by the editor.

Earhart, H. Byron. "The Celebration of *Haru-yama* (Spring Mountain):
An Example of Folk Religious Practices in Contemporary Japan."
Asian Folklore Studies, Vol. 27, No. 1 (1968), 1–18. Description of a
mountain pilgrimage celebrating the coming of spring.

———. "Four Ritual Periods of Haguro Shugendo in Northeastern
Japan." *History of Religions,* Vol. 5, No. 1 (Summer 1965), 93–113.
Description of the ritual year in an eclectic religious movement.

*Embree, John F. *Suye Mura.* Chicago: University of Chicago Press,
1939. The pioneer "village study" in Japan; Chapter 7, "Religions," demonstrates the interrelationships among the several
religious traditions. See the more recent Beardsley et al., *Village
Japan,* Chapter 14, listed in "Histories and Works on Japanese
Culture."

Holtom, Daniel C. "Some Notes on Japanese Tree Worship." *Transactions of the Asiatic Society of Japan,* Second Series, Vol. 8 (December
1931), 1–19. An interesting article on traditional folk (and Shinto)
beliefs and practices associated with trees.

†Hori, Ichiro. *Folk Religion in Japan: Continuity and Change.* Edited by
Joseph M. Kitagawa and Alan L. Miller. Chicago: University of
Chicago Press, 1968. Essays showing the complex makeup of folk
religion and its importance for understanding Japanese religion.

Ikeda, Hiroko. *A Type and Motif Index of Japanese Folk-Literature.* FF
Communications, No. 209. Helsinki: Soumalainen Tiedeakatemia, Academia Scientarum Fennica, 1971. The most complete
index of Japanese folk tales, with brief summaries of tales; sources
and distribution of the tales are given, with cross-references to
standard Western and other Japanese motif-indexes.

†Miyake, Hitoshi. "Folk Religion." In *Japanese Religion.* Edited by Ichiro
Hori. Translated by Yoshiya Abe and David Reid. Tokyo: Ko-

249
*Annotated
Bibliography
on Japanese
Religion:
Selected Works*

dansha International, 1972, pp. 121–43. A concise analysis of folk religion, describing its annual festivals, rites of passage, and social organization.

Norbeck, Edward. "Yakudoshi: A Japanese Complex of Supernatural Beliefs." *Southwestern Journal of Anthropology*, Vol. 8, No. 1 (Spring 1952), 269–85. Description of beliefs and practices of pollution and taboo as observed in a fishing community in 1950 and 1951.

Oto, Tokihiko. *Folklore in Japanese Life and Customs*. Tokyo: Kokusai Bunka Shinkokai (Society for International Cultural Relations), 1963. Although the section on religious activities is rather brief, the book is profusely illustrated with excellent drawings and photographs.

†Ouwehand, C. *Namazu-e and Their Themes: An Interpretative Approach to Some Aspects of Japanese Folk Religion*. Leiden: E. J. Brill, 1964. The most thorough and systematic treatment of Japanese folk religion in English, important for its holistic interpretation.

*Seki, Keigo, ed. *Folktales of Japan*. Translated by Robert J. Adams. Chicago: University of Chicago Press, 1963. A representative collection, featuring a scholarly foreword and comparative remarks on each tale.

†Smith, Robert J. *Ancestor Worship in Contemporary Japan*. Stanford, Calif.: Stanford University Press, 1974. The only full-length study of Japanese ancestor worship in English; it provides historical background and extensive reporting of actual practices and attitudes toward ancestor worship.

Yamamoto, Yoshiko. *The Namahage: A Festival in the Northeast of Japan*. Foreword by Robert J. Smith. Philadelphia: Institute for the Study of Human Issues, 1978. A field study of a New Year's festival of "masked visitors," with a survey of Japanese theories interpreting the religious significance of the festival.

CHRISTIANITY

For additional references, see Ikado and McGovern, and Kitagawa in "Special Bibliographies on Japanese History and Religion."

Boxer, C. R. *The Christian Century in Japan, 1549–1650*. Rev. ed. Berkeley: University of California Press, 1967. A scholarly survey of early Roman Catholicism in Japan, with translations of European documents.

*Caldarola, Carlo. *Christianity: The Japanese Way*. Leiden: E. J. Brill, 1979. An interpretation of Mukyokai (the nonchurch movement) and an offshoot Makuya as examples of an indigenous Japanese Christianity.

Cary, Otis. *A History of Christianity in Japan*. 2 vols. New York: Fleming H. Revell Company, 1909. Republished, St. Clair Shores, Mich.: Scholarly Press, 1970. Valuable especially for the detailed treatment of Protestantism up to 1909 in Volume 2.

*†Drummond, Richard H. *A History of Christianity in Japan*. Grand Rapids, Mich.: William B. Eerdmans Publishing Company, 1971. A convenient, one-volume history covering the entire span of Catholic, Protestant, and Orthodox developments.

Elison, George. *Deus Destroyed: The Image of Christianity in Early Modern Japan*. Cambridge, Mass.: Harvard University Press, 1973. A detailed, scholarly analysis of the "acceptance" and "rejection" of Christianity during the Christian century, with extensive translations of anti-Christian documents from this period.

Endo, Shusaku. *Silence*. Translated by William Johnston. Tokyo: Sophia University, 1969. A historical novel by a contemporary Japanese Roman Catholic about the trials of faith for both Japanese converts and European missionaries during the persecution of Christianity in the 1600s.

Germany, Charles H. *Protestant Theologies in Modern Japan*. Tokyo: HSR Press, 1965. A survey of the broad range of Protestant theology among Japanese theologians.

Iglehart, Charles W. *A Century of Protestant Christianity in Japan*. Rutland, Vt.: Charles E. Tuttle Company, 1959. A standard historical treatment of Protestantism in Japan.

Jennes, Joseph. *A History of the Catholic Church in Japan from Its Beginnings to the Early Meiji Era (1549–1873)*. Rev., enlarged ed. Tokyo: Oriens Institute for Religious Research, 1973. Intended as a handbook for missionaries, it surveys the Catholic mission to Japan and its interaction with political and cultural forces.

Kagawa, Toyohiko. *Christ and Japan*. Translated by William Axling. New York: Friendship Press, 1934. A famous Japanese (Protestant) Christian's praise and criticism of Japan, as viewed through his Christian faith.

Kitamori, Kazoh. *Theology of the Pain of God*. Richmond, Va.: John Knox Press, 1965. Kitamori, hailed as the first original theological writer in Japan, has here attempted a genuinely Japanese theology.

251
*Annotated
Bibliography
on Japanese
Religion:
Selected Works*

*Laures, Johannes. *The Catholic Church in Japan: A Short History.* Rutland, Vt.: Charles E. Tuttle Company, 1954; Notre Dame, Ind.: University of Notre Dame Press, 1962. A popular work by a church historian.

†Ohata, Kiyoshi, and Ikado, Fujio. "Christianity." In *Japanese Religion in the Meiji Era.* Edited by Hideo Kishimoto. Translated by John F. Howes. Tokyo: Obunsha, 1956, pp. 171–309. A historical treatment by two Japanese Christians, emphasizing the ideals of Christianity and the social realities of Japan.

Phillips, James M. *From the Rising of the Sun: Christians and Society in Contemporary Japan.* Mary Knoll, N.Y.: Orbis Books, 1981. A detailed treatment of Christianity in Japan since 1945, covering its relation to social, political, and educational issues as well as biblical and theological studies.

†Plath, David W. "The Japanese Popular Christmas: Coping with Modernity." *Journal of American Folklore,* Vol. 76 (1963), 309–17. An interesting description of the widespread celebration of Christmas in Japan.

†Scheiner, Irwin. *Christian Converts and Social Protest in Meiji Japan.* Berkeley: University of California Press, 1970. Examines the relationship between *samurai* ideals and Christian ethics in the lives of *samurai* converts to Christianity.

†Suzuki, Norihisa. "Christianity." In *Japanese Religion.* Edited by Ichiro Hori. Translated by Yoshiya Abe and David Reid. Tokyo: Kodansha International, 1972, pp. 71–87. A concise overview of the "foreignness" of Christianity in Japan and its major developments.

Takeda, Kiyoko. "Japanese Christianity: Between Orthodoxy and Heterodoxy." In *Authority and the Individual in Japan: Citizen Protest in Historical Perspective.* Edited by J. Victor Koschmann. Tokyo: University of Tokyo Press, 1978, pp. 82–107. A critical interpretation of the role of Christianity in modern Japan.

Uchimura, Kanzo. *How I Became a Christian: Out of My Diary.* Tokyo: Keiseisha, 1895. A fascinating account of the spiritual biography of a first-generation Japanese Christian, including his tribulations as a Christian in a "heathen" land as well as his disappointments while in "Christian" America.

Van Hecken, Joseph L. *The Catholic Church in Japan Since 1859.* Translated by John Van Hoydonck. Tokyo: Enderle Bookstore, 1963. Contains detailed facts and figures on the modern Catholic Church nationally and regionally.

252
*Japanese
Religion:
Unity and
Diversity*

NEW RELIGIONS

For additional references, see Earhart in "Special Bibliographies on Japanese History and Religion"; also, note the works on sect Shinto such as Hepner, Holtom *(The National Faith)*, and Schneider in the "Shinto" section, and Murakami in the "Histories and General Works" section.

†Arai, Ken. "New Religious Movements." In *Japanese Religion*. Edited by Ichiro Hori. Translated by Yoshiya Abe and David Reid. Tokyo: Kodansha International, 1972, pp. 89–104. A concise overview of the definition and major features of the New Religions.

Blacker, Carmen. "New Religious Cults in Japan." *Hibbert Journal*, Vol. 60 (July 1962), 305–13. A good first article to read, discussing the origins of the New Religions in folk religion and popular religion.

Caldarola, Carlo. "The Makuya Movement in Japan." *Japanese Religions*, Vol. 7, No. 4 (December 1972), 18–34. (Also included in Caldarola, *Christianity: The Japanese Way*, listed in the "Christianity" section.) Originally derived from the Japanese Christian movement known as Mukyokai ("Non-Church" movement), Makuya or Genshi Fukuin Undo is perhaps the most successful Christian movement among the lower classes and has incorporated so many Japanese features that it may be considered a Japanese New Religion.

*Dale, Kenneth J. *Circle of Harmony: A Case Study in Popular Japanese Buddhism with Implications for Christian Mission* (with a chapter by Susumu Akahoshi). South Pasadena, Calif.: William Carey Library, 1975. The most complete account in English of the *hoza* or group-counseling technique for which Rissho Kosei-kai is famous.

Davis, Winston Bradley. *Dojo: Exorcism and Miracles in Modern Japan*. Stanford, Calif.: Stanford University Press, 1980. A detailed sociological analysis of the beliefs and practices of members of the New Religion Sukyo Mahikari.

†Earhart, H. Byron. "Gedatsu-kai: One Life History and Its Significance for Interpreting Japanese New Religions." *Japanese Journal of Religious Studies*, Vol. 7, Nos. 2–3 (June–September 1980), 227–57. A lengthy interview ("life history") with one member of a New Religion, who tells about his religious life, how he hap-

pened to join a New Religion, and what it means to him to participate in a New Religion.

——. "The Significance of the 'New Religions' for Understanding Japanese Religion." *KBS Bulletin on Japanese Culture*, Vol. 101 (April–May 1970), 1–9. Reprinted in part in his *Religion in the Japanese Experience: Sources and Interpretations*. Belmont, Calif.: Wadsworth, 1974, pp. 250–54. A general discussion of the New Religions in terms of six persistent themes in Japanese religion.

†——. "Toward a Theory of the Formation of the Japanese New Religions: A Case Study of Gedatsu-kai." *History of Religions*, Vol. 20, Nos. 1–2 (August–November 1980), 175–97. A theoretical interpretation of the origin of New Religions in terms of a balance of social, historical, and innovative factors, as they relate to the New Religion Gedatsu-kai.

Ellwood, Robert S., Jr. *The Eagle and the Rising Sun: Americans and the New Religions of Japan*. Philadelphia: Westminster Press, 1974. General impressions of the activities of the five New Religions most widely accepted by Occidentals and Japanese-Americans in the United States.

Fujiwara, Hirotatsu. *I Denounce Soka Gakkai*. Translated by Worth C. Grant. Tokyo: Nishin Hodo Company, 1970. A polemical work; alleged suppression of the Japanese edition of this book was the cause of a public scandal investigation by the National Diet.

†Ikado, Fujio. "Trend and Problems of New Religions: Religion in Urban Society." In *The Sociology of Japanese Religion*. Edited by Kiyomi Morioka and William H. Newell. Leiden: E. J. Brill, 1968, pp. 101–17. Analysis of statistical and sociological information about the membership of the New Religions in the postwar urban setting.

*McFarland, H. Neill. *The Rush Hour of the Gods: A Study of the New Religious Movements in Japan*. New York: Macmillan, 1967. A general account of five New Religions.

Murakami, Shigeyoshi. "New Religions of Japan." In *The Symposium on Family and Religion in East Asian Countries*. Edited by Chie Nakane and Akira Goto. Tokyo: Center for East Asian Cultural Studies, 1972, pp. 17–27. Reprinted from *East Asian Cultural Studies*, Vol. 11, Nos. 1–4 (1972), 17–27. A concise historical and critical introduction to various New Religions and their characteristics.

Murata, Kiyoaki. *Japan's New Buddhism: An Objective Account of Soka Gakkai*. New York: Walker/Weatherhill, 1969. A general introduction based mainly on the publications of Soka Gakkai.

253
Annotated
Bibliography
on Japanese
Religion:
Selected Works

The Nichiren Shoshu Sokagakkai. Tokyo: Seikyo Press, 1966. An introduction to this New Religion by its staff, covering the history, doctrine, and distinctive features.

Offner, Clark B., and Straelen, Henry van. *Modern Japanese Religions: With Special Emphasis upon Their Doctrines of Healing.* Tokyo: Rupert Enderle, 1963. A brief treatment of Tenrikyo and seven other groups, focusing on healing techniques, by two Christian missionaries.

Plath, David W. "The Fate of Utopia: Adaptive Tactics in Four Japanese Groups." *American Anthropologist,* Vol. 68, No. 4 (August 1966), 1152–62. Analyzes the attempt of four communal groups to achieve utopian alternatives to the dilemmas of modernization.

Rissho Kosei-kai. Tokyo: Kosei Publishing Company, 1966. An introduction to this New Religion by its staff, covering such topics as the history, doctrine, and activities of the group.

†Shimazono, Susumu. "The Living Kami Idea in the New Religions of Japan." *Japanese Journal of Religious Studies,* Vol. 6, No. 3 (September 1979), 389–412. The best synthetic interpretation of the nature of founders as living *kami* in the rise and institutionalization of New Religions.

A Short History of Tenrikyo. Tenri, Japan: Tenrikyo Kyokai Honbu, 1956. Published by Tenrikyo headquarters, it includes chapters on the life of the founder, the history of the movement, and its activities.

Straelen, Henry van. *The Religion of Divine Wisdom: Japan's Most Powerful Movement.* Kyoto: Veritas Shoin, 1957 (and later editions). The most complete account of Tenrikyo by a Western scholar.

†Sugihara, Yoshie, and Plath, David W. *Sensei and His People: The Building of a Japanese Commune.* Berkeley: University of California Press, 1969. An interesting firsthand account of the development of a communal group, partly an offshoot of Tenrikyo, by the second wife of the founder.

†Tsuhima, Michihito; Nishiyama, Shigeru; Shimazono, Susumu; and Shiramizu, Hiroko. "The Vitalistic Conception of Salvation in Japanese New Religions: An Aspect of Modern Religious Consciousness." In *Proceedings of Tokyo Meeting of the International Conference on Sociology of Religion, 1978.* Reprinted in *Japanese Journal of Religious Studies,* Vol. 6, Nos. 1–2 (March–June 1979), 139–61. A valuable synthetic overview of "the common underlying structure to the teachings of the various New Religions."

Study Questions

To use the study questions most efficiently, read them before beginning to read each assignment. Keep the questions in mind and use them to identify the most important material. Then, after completing the reading, check your comprehension by answering the questions. Any of a number of techniques may be selected to answer the questions—making mental notes, underlining and writing in the book, keeping a journal. If you have trouble answering the questions, make a note to yourself to mention the troublesome points in class discussion.

These questions enable readers to use together the present book and the author's companion volume, *Religion in the Japanese Experience: Sources and Interpretations*. Those reading only the present book may disregard the questions referring to the latter work.

Introduction to Japanese Religion
Japanese Religion, pp. 1–17

Identify all the religious traditions and aspects of religious life found in Japanese history. How can this plurality of traditions and aspects form a unity in the religious life of the individual? How can the diversity of religious expression result in unity at different levels of life? Identify the six persistent themes in Japanese religious history, and try to weave together these six themes into a total picture of Japanese religion. (These notions of plurality, diversity, unity, and persistent themes will be helpful to you in unifying the material from both books.)

Religion in the Japanese Experience, pp. 1–5

Note the major differences between religion in America and Japanese religion. Try to describe, in your own words, the major characteristics of Japanese religion and the major outlines of Japanese religious history.

Japanese Religion, pp. 20–27

How did religion in Japan begin? What are the earliest forms of Japanese religion, and how are they related to economic, social, and political developments in early Japan? How do the religious significance of the dead, of fertility, and of divine descent all define a general pattern of religion in early Japan? (Use the "Table of Japanese Religious History" to view at a glance the social and religious history of Japan.)

Early Shinto

Japanese Religion, pp. 29–37

Religion in the Japanese Experience, pp. 7–9

How is Shinto related to the earliest Japanese religious tradition, and how did it develop into a tradition in its own right? What are the main themes in Japanese mythology, and how are these important for Shinto? What is the general outline of Shinto organization in terms of priests, rituals, and shrines?

Religion in the Japanese Experience, pp. 9–13

Compare and contrast the Judaeo-Christian notion of God with the Japanese notion of *kami*. Give at least three examples of *kami* to show how a wide variety of "things" can be divine beings or *kami*. What are the general features that define such *kami?*

Religion in the Japanese Experience, pp. 14–19

Compare and contrast the Judaeo-Christian story of creation with the Japanese story of creation. Analyze the Japanese creation story, noting the conditions at the beginning of creation, who the most important figures are, and the process by which creation occurred. One scholar has described Japanese religion in terms of "a sacred people in a sacred land." How does the creation story support such a description?

Religion in the Japanese Experience, pp. 19–24

Compare and contrast a Shinto shrine with a sacred place with which you are familiar, such as a church or synagogue. What is it that makes a Shinto shrine "sacred"? What is the relationship between nature and shrines? How do the *kami*, shrines, and Shinto worshipers relate to one another?

Early Japanese Buddhism

Japanese Religion, pp. 39–50

Religion in the Japanese Experience, pp. 35–36

How did the Indian religion of Buddhism happen to travel all the way to Japan, and how was it received in Japan? What was the role of the imperial court and the state in the acceptance of Buddhism in Japan?

Religion in the Japanese Experience, pp. 37–39

Note the particular circumstances surrounding Buddhism's arrival in Japan from Korea. How did the Korean envoys describe Buddhism, and how did the Japanese look upon this "foreign" religion?

Religion in the Japanese Experience, pp. 39–44

Describe the way in which Buddhist divinities and *kami* came to be very closely related—almost like two sides of the same coin. To what extent is this the influence of Buddhist divinities on Shinto *kami*, and to what extent is this the influence of Shinto *kami* on Buddhist divinities?

Confucianism and Taoism

Japanese Religion, pp. 52–58

How did Confucianism come to Japan; what are the major components of Confucianism; and what impact did it have on Japanese culture and religion? How did Taoism come to Japan; what are the major components of Taoism; and what impact did it have on Japanese culture and religion?

Religion in the Japanese Experience, pp. 75–80

Analyze the Taoist-influenced Koshin cult, explaining the religious theory behind the cult, and the practices the cult group *(ko)* engages in.

Religion in the Japanese Experience, pp. 80–84

In what way did religious Taoism influence Japanese popular beliefs? Give three examples of Japanese popular beliefs that show Taoist influence.

Folk Religion

Japanese Religion, pp. 60–66

Religion in the Japanese Experience, p. 89

How does folk religion differ from organized religion, and what are the major aspects of Japanese folk religion? How is folk religion delicately woven into family, village, occupational, and individual life?

Religion in the Japanese Experience, pp. 90–95

In the folk celebration of New Year's note the lack of control by organized religion. Who controls the celebration? Who participates in it? Where is the celebration held? What are the special practices, foods, etc? What are the "rules" for such observances?

Religion in the Japanese Experience, pp. 95–99

In the Japanese tradition what is a shaman; how does a person become a shaman; and what religious practices does a shaman perform?

Religion in the Japanese Experience, pp. 99–104

Try to sum up the story and message of each folk tale. How do folk tales constitute one aspect of folk religion?

Interaction in Japanese Religion

Japanese Religion, pp. 68–71

By about the ninth century, how have all the five formative traditions interacted to constitute Japanese religion? Try to describe the general picture of Japanese religion in the ninth century.

Tendai and Shingon Buddhism

Japanese Religion, pp. 74–88

Identify the major teachings and practices of Tendai and Shingon Buddhism. What changes are brought about by the founders of these two Buddhist sects? How do they attempt to restore or purify Japanese Buddhism, and what is the effect of their efforts upon Japanese Buddhism?

Religion in the Japanese Experience, pp. 45–47

Try to discover the religious "message" that the Buddha is preaching in the *Lotus Sutra.* What kind of practices should the people perform, and what will be the religious reward?

Religion in the Japanese Experience, pp. 47–52

What are some of the major symbols in Buddhist art? What religious message does Buddhist art contain?

Pure Land, Nichiren, and Zen Buddhism

Japanese Religion, pp. 92–104

Identify the major teachings and practices of Pure Land, Nichiren, and Zen Buddhism. What changes are brought about by the founders of these three Buddhist sects? How do they attempt to transform Japanese Buddhism into a more popular tradition, and what is the effect of their efforts upon Japanese Buddhism?

The novel *The Buddha Tree* describes devotion to Amida. Try to interpret in your own words what devotion to Amida means. What problem do people have that needs help from Amida? What is the frame of mind in which people approach Amida? What religious power does Amida represent, such that Amida can grant this request?

Medieval Shinto
Japanese Religion, pp. 106–13

How does medieval Shinto differ from early Shinto? How does thorough interaction of Shinto with Buddhism alter the character of Shinto? To what extent, and in what way, does medieval Shinto tend to assume its own organizational style?
Religion in the Japanese Experience, pp. 24–26

Carefully notice the attitude and emotions in this medieval pilgrim to one of the most important Shinto shrines. Compare and contrast this pilgrim's frame of mind with the frame of mind of the priest practicing devotion to Amida (pp. 52–61, *Religion in the Japanese Experience*).

The Christian Century
Japanese Religion, pp. 115–22

How did the European religion of Christianity happen to travel all the way to Japan, and how was it received in Japan? Compare and contrast the earlier arrival of another "foreign" religion, Buddhism. (How did Buddhism become a permanent part of the Japanese tradition, whereas Christianity had much greater difficulties?) Analyze political and economic factors related to the acceptance of Christianity, and interpret how Christianity was expelled from Japan.
Religion in the Japanese Experience, pp. 105–11

In what ways did the Jesuits attempt to become a part of Japanese culture? (To what extent do you think they were successful?) Note the distinction between religious relations with the West and economic relations with the West. Why do you think the Japanese were so strict in ruling out religious relations with the West?

Syncretism in Japanese Religion
Japanese Religion, pp. 125–27

By about the sixteenth century, how have all the formative traditions interacted and developed in such a way as to constitute Japanese religion? Try to describe the general picture of Japanese religion in the sixteenth century?

Religion in the Japanese Experience, pp. 117–21.

Identify Buddhist, Taoist, Confucian, and Shinto elements in this medieval will, and show how they are interrelated in the personal code of conduct of a medieval man. Describe in your own words this man's philosophy of life.

Religion in the Japanese Experience, pp. 121–23

Identify Buddhist, Confucian, and Shinto elements in this formal government document, and show how they are interrelated in the policy of late medieval government. Describe in your own words this government's general philosophy of life.

Religion in the Japanese Experience, pp. 124–25

Identify Buddhist, Confucian, and Shinto elements in this late medieval teacher's statement. Describe in your own words this teacher's prescription for religious cooperation.

Closeness of Human Beings, Gods, and Nature

Religion in the Japanese Experience, pp. 127–30

Analyze the attitude toward nature and gods in these poems. What do they tell us about ancient Japanese poetry and about the blending of religious and aesthetic themes?

Religion in the Japanese Experience, pp. 131–34

Follow Suzuki's argument about the basic difference between the Western attitude toward nature and the view of nature in Zen Buddhism. According to Suzuki, what is the relationship between humans and nature in the two traditions? What does his argument tell us about the differences between Western and Japanese culture?

Religion in the Japanese Experience, pp. 134–40

Analyze the understanding and expression of nature in Japanese theories of art, and try to locate the same in the painting of Sesshu. How do religious and aesthetic values concerning nature blend in these verbal and graphic expressions?

Religion in the Japanese Experience, pp. 140–44

In what way do *haiku* convey both an artistic and a religious message? Analyze the religious significance in each of the *haiku* in this selection.

The Family, Living and Dead

Religion in the Japanese Experience, pp. 145–48

In what way is the *dozoku* both a social and a religious institution? What is the religious significance of the calendar of 	stivals for the *dozoku?*

Religion in the Japanese Experience, pp. 61–64

Note what is necessary in a traditional funeral ceremony; then try to interpret the Japanese attitude and behavior toward the dead.

Religion in the Japanese Experience, pp. 148–54

Pay careful attention to the distinction between the "three categories of souls" and to the kinds of worship practiced. What are the major features of "ancestor worship"?

Religion in the Japanese Experience, pp. 154–59

What is the role of the individual in Japanese religion as (1) an active member in religious practices and (2) an object of veneration? How does this relate to "weak awareness of religious values," and how would you compare this with contemporary American religion?

Purification, Rituals, and Charms

Religion in the Japanese Experience, pp. 161–66

What are the "sins" to be exorcised in the Great Exorcism, and what are the means of purification in this ritual? On the basis of this ritual, try to compare and contrast purification in Japanese religion with sin in Christianity.

Religion in the Japanese Experience, pp. 167–71

What is "possession"; how does one "become possessed"; and what is the religious significance of the process? Interpret possession in terms of the notion of *kami.*

Local Festivals and Individual Cults

Religion in the Japanese Experience, pp. 173–79

New Year's and *bon* are the two most important annual Japanese festivals. Compare and contrast these two festivals in order to make a general definition of Japanese festivals.

Religion in the Japanese Experience, pp. 180–83

Note the times, preparations, and activities for festivals. In spite of the many variations, what are some general features of festivals?

Religion and Everyday Life

Religion in the Japanese Experience, pp. 185–89

What are the archaeological remains that have religious significance, and how do they throw light on the penetration of religion in the daily life of prehistoric times?

Religion in the Japanese Experience, pp. 189–93

Trace the religious significance of marriage, birth, and death as an example of the interrelationship between religion and daily life.

Religion in the Japanese Experience, pp. 193–97

Use this selection to analyze the interrelationship between "social structure and folk religion." What is the difference between the "little tradition" and the "great tradition"?

Religion in the Japanese Experience, pp. 197–200

What is the religious significance of the "art of tea"? Relate this religious significance to the place, attitudes, and performance of the tea ceremony.

Religion and State

Religion in the Japanese Experience, pp. 201–03

What is the significance of Prince Shotoku's "constitution" as a precedent for the relationship between state and religion? Identify the religious traditions mentioned in the "constitution" and try to state the principle by which they are interrelated (in Shotoku's conception).

Religion in the Tokugawa Period and Restoration Shinto

Japanese Religion, pp. 130–47

What does "formalism and renewal" mean? How does this set of terms describe the condition of Buddhism, Neo-Confucianism, and Shinto in the Tokugawa period? Identify the major teachings of Neo-Confucianism and Restoration Shinto.

Religion in the Japanese Experience, pp. 65–69

If "the role of Confucianism as a religion was limited," in what way was Confucianism a crucial influence upon the *samurai* of the Tokugawa period?

The Meiji Restoration and Nationalistic Shinto

Japanese Religion, pp. 150–59

What were the key political events of the Meiji Restoration, and how was religion interwoven with these political events? Trace the changes within Shinto during this period, showing how it emerged as "nationalistic Shinto."

Religion in the Japanese Experience, pp. 203–04

Analyze the Imperial Rescript on Education in terms of its religious motivation, its political motivation, and its educational objectives. Compare this document with Shotoku's "Constitution" (pp. 202–03) to show how it represents a continuity with ancient themes. In what ways does it also constitute a remarkable change?

Religious Currents from 1868–1945

Japanese Religion, pp. 161–70

What was the condition of Buddhism and Christianity during this period, and how did the New Religions fare by comparison?

Religion in the Japanese Experience, pp. 112–14

What is the gist of Uchimura's criticism of Western missionary notions, and what does he mean when he proposes a "Japanese Christianity"?

Religion in the Japanese Experience, pp. 69–74

What does "the nationalisation of Confucianism in Japan" mean, and how did this kind of Confucianism happen to support Japanese nationalism and militarism?

Religion in the Japanese Experience, pp. 205–10

What are the religious principles at the foundation of the *Kokutai no Hongi,* and how were these principles used to support the *Kokutai no Hongi?* What are the general objectives of this document?

New Religions

Religion in the Japanese Experience, pp. 84–87

Under what circumstances did Konkokyo arise, and how did the revelation of the founder result in a transformation of folk religious tradition into a New Religion?

Japanese Religion, pp. 172–82

Trace the emergence, organization, and activities of Tenrikyo and Soka Gakkai. How do these two movements compare and contrast with one another, and how do they compare and contrast with traditional Shinto and Buddhism?

Religion in the Japanese Experience, pp. 237–44

Analyze the revelation experience of the founder of Tenrikyo. First identify in this revelation experience the religious elements from the earlier tradition. Then show how this revelation has new features that lead to a New Religion.

Religion in the Japanese Experience, pp. 244–49

Analyze the "message" of Soka Gakkai, first identifying the religious goal and then showing how people can reach this goal. What is the relationship between the individual's daily worship, missionary work *(shakubuku),* and the discussion meetings?

Religion in Postwar Japan

Japanese Religion, pp. 184–89

What was the general condition of Shinto, Buddhism, Christianity, and the New Religions in the postwar period?

Religion in the Japanese Experience, pp. 27–34

What was the status of Shinto in 1945; why was the Allied occupation opposed to the continuation of this status; and how did the occupation eliminate this status without interfering with freedom of religion? How did this directive affect Shinto? In his Imperial Edict, how does the emperor appeal to the past; how does he change the religious-mythical heritage; and what does he see for the future?

Religion in the Japanese Experience, pp. 211–17

What is the religious ideal of Buddhism; how was this ideal compromised in the twentieth century; and how can the ideal be restored?

Religion in the Japanese Experience, pp. 218–22

What is the religious ideal of Shinto; how was this ideal compromised in the twentieth century; and how can the ideal be restored?

Religion in the Japanese Experience, pp. 222–31

In what way have changing conditions in Tokyo affected the religious life of the people generally? What is the impact of these changed circumstances on traditional Shinto and on traditional Buddhism?

Religion in the Japanese Experience, pp. 231–35

The pornographers are secularists; nothing is sacred. Interpret this secularism in terms of the contrast between filming a pornographic movie at a shrine and the sincere piety of the old lady at the shrine. (Why do these "secularist" pornographers still have to resort to their own kind of ritual at the wake? Try to interpret the religious significance of replacing a Buddhist sutra with a pornographic film.)

Religious Life in Contemporary Japan

Japanese Religion, pp. 192–207

"Are the Japanese religious?" How would you compare and contrast "being religious" in Japan and in Western countries? Over the centuries, how has Japanese religion remained the same, and how has it changed in the past century or so? Recently how has Japanese religion declined, and how has it "increased" or expanded?

The History and Future of Japanese Religion

Japanese Religion, pp. 209–11

Now that you have studied twenty-five hundred years of the history of Japanese religion, how do you view its future? How do you see the chances for Japanese religion as (1) dying out, (2) remaining the same, (3) changing? How would you compare and contrast the future of religion in Japan with the future of religion in Western countries?

Religion in the Japanese Experience, pp. 257–61

Anesaki, writing fifty years ago, laid out a criticism of modernism, a criticism of reactionary activities, and his own suggestion for more genuine "civilization." Try to carefully distinguish these three points. In what sense are these points still relevant today?

Religion in the Japanese Experience, pp. 262–64

In the search for identity after World War II, what are the alternatives for the Japanese people, and how is religion directly related to these alternatives? (What similarities and/or differences do you find in the search for identity in contemporary America?)

Religion in the Japanese Experience, pp. 265–69

How is Christmas practiced in Japan; what does Christian mean; and how is Japanese Christmas an attempt to "cope with modernity"?

Summary

At the end of this study of Japanese culture and religion, it may be useful to take stock of what you have learned and how your thinking has changed. Compare what you knew about Japan and Japanese religion before reading these materials with what you know now. What was the most interesting new information you learned about the Japanese tradition?

Compare your general attitudes or opinions toward Japanese culture you had before this course of study with those you have now. How has your thinking changed, and what persuaded you to change your thinking?

Most people outside Japan view the country in terms of its industrial achievements—cameras and automobiles. How would you balance this industrial and commercial image of Japan with what you have learned about its distinctive culture?

How would you compare Japanese culture and religion with Western (or American) culture and religion? In the past, some Americans have thought that Japan should adopt Western customs, such as Christianity and democracy; some Americans have claimed recently that Americans should adopt Japanese customs, such as greater cooperation between labor and management, and better coordination of business and government. Do you think it is possible for one society to borrow from another society, and if so, how would you select the features to be borrowed? Are there ethical or humanitarian principles that transcend individual cultures and should guide all cultures? How would you like to see the Japanese tradition develop in the future?

Index

Japanese names are cited in the text in Japanese fashion, with family name first, such as Tokugawa Ieyasu. The family name is Tokugawa, and will be found in the index under Tokugawa. In order to simplify use of the index, English equivalents are given for most Japanese and other foreign-language terms. Many religious terms have been grouped under the religion of which they are a part, such as Buddhism, Shinto, or Christianity. Dates or approximate century are provided for historical figures and historical periods. Where a term is illustrated in the text, the page number is followed by "(illus.)."

272
Index